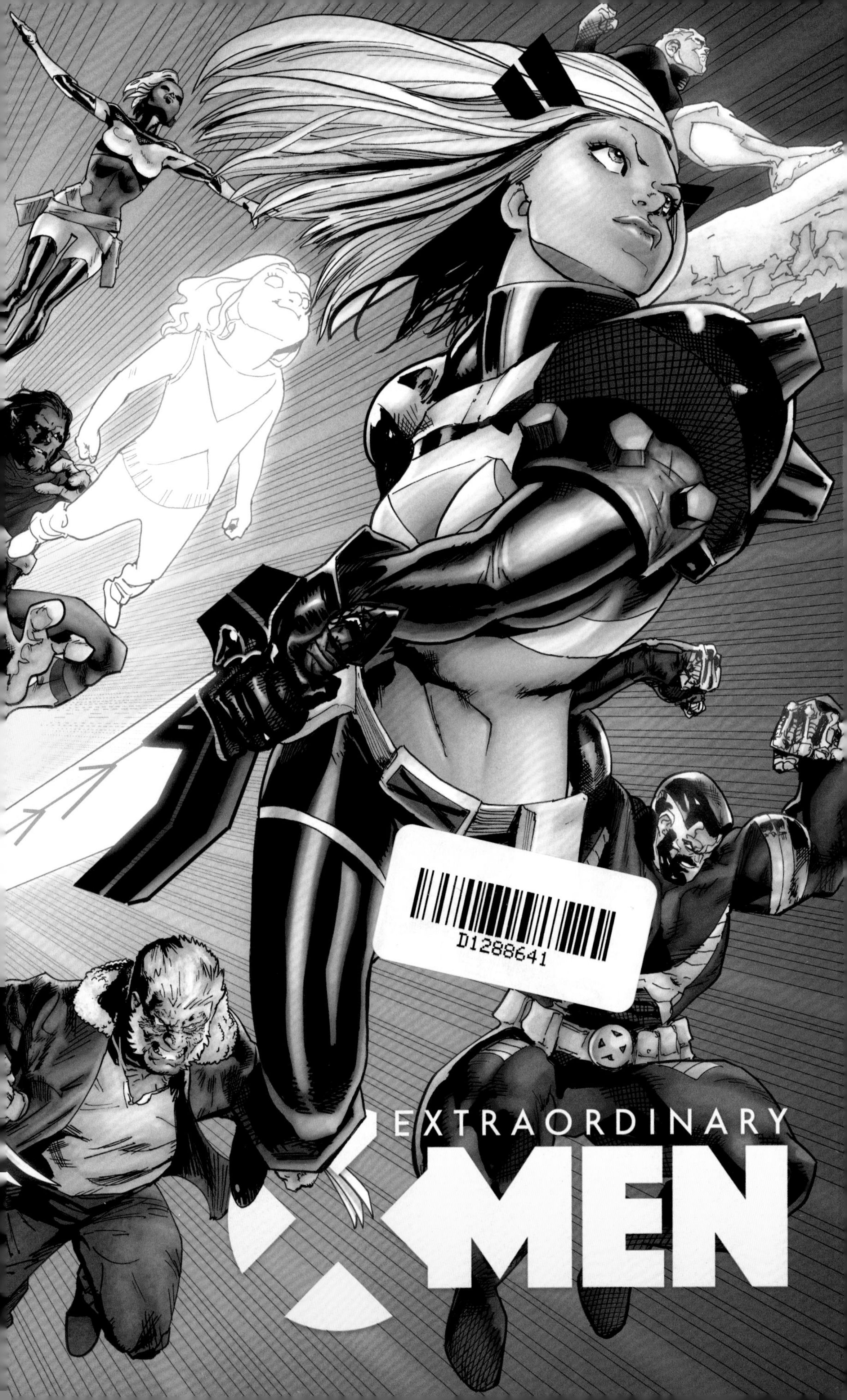
EXTRAORDINARY
X-MEN

PURPORTED TO BE THE NEXT STAGE IN HUMAN EVOLUTION, MUTANTS MANIFEST SUPERHUMAN POWERS AND ABILITIES UPON REACHING ADOLESCENCE. BUT RATHER THAN BEING CELEBRATED FOR THEIR GIFTS, MUTANTS ARE HATED AND FEARED. WITH THE FATE OF THEIR RACE HANGING IN THE BALANCE, MUTANTKIND NEEDS HEROES WHO WILL LEAD THEM INTO THE FUTURE. MUTANTKIND NEEDS...

EXTRAORDINARY X-MEN

REACTING TO THE DANGER OF THE TERRIGEN CLOUD — WHICH CREATES INHUMANS BUT KILLS MUTANTS — STORM, THE LEADER OF THE X-MEN, MOVED THE JEAN GREY SCHOOL TO LIMBO. X-HAVEN, AS IT HAS COME TO BE KNOWN, IS NOW A REFUGE FROM TERRIGEN FOR THE MUTANT POPULATION AND THEIR FAMILIES.

DISCOVERING THAT THE TERRIGEN CLOUD CIRCLING THE EARTH WAS ON THE VERGE OF DISSIPATING INTO THE ATMOSPHERE, RENDERING EARTH UNINHABITABLE FOR MUTANTS, THE X-MEN HAVE DECIDED TO TAKE DECISIVE ACTION AGAINST THE INHUMANS. BUT NOT EVERYONE IS COMPLETELY CONFIDENT IN THAT DECISION...

COLLECTION EDITOR: JENNIFER GRÜNWALD
ASSISTANT EDITOR: CAITLIN O'CONNELL
ASSOCIATE MANAGING EDITOR: KATERI WOODY
EDITOR, SPECIAL PROJECTS: MARK D. BEAZLEY

VP PRODUCTION & SPECIAL PROJECTS: JEFF YOUNGQUIST
SVP PRINT, SALES & MARKETING: DAVID GABRIEL
BOOK DESIGNERS: JAY BOWEN & ADAM DEL RE

EDITOR IN CHIEF: AXEL ALONSO
CHIEF CREATIVE OFFICER: JOE QUESADA
PRESIDENT: DAN BUCKLEY
EXECUTIVE PRODUCER: ALAN FINE

EXTRAORDINARY X-MEN VOL. 4: IVX. Contains material originally published in magazine form as EXTRAORDINARY X-MEN #17-20 and X-MEN PRIME #1. First printing 2017. ISBN# 978-0-7851-9937-3. Published by MARVEL WORLDWIDE, INC., a subsidiary of MARVEL ENTERTAINMENT, LLC. OFFICE OF PUBLICATION: 135 West 50th Street, New York, NY 10020. Copyright © 2017 MARVEL No similarity between any of the names, characters, persons, and/or institutions in this magazine with those of any living or dead person or institution is intended, and any such similarity which may exist is purely coincidental. **Printed in Canada.** DAN BUCKLEY, President, Marvel Entertainment; JOE QUESADA, Chief Creative Officer; TOM BREVOORT, SVP of Publishing; DAVID BOGART, SVP of Business Affairs & Operations, Publishing & Partnership; C.B. CEBULSKI, VP of Brand Management & Development, Asia; DAVID GABRIEL, SVP of Sales & Marketing, Publishing; JEFF YOUNGQUIST, VP of Production & Special Projects; DAN CARR, Executive Director of Publishing Technology; ALEX MORALES, Director of Publishing Operations; SUSAN CRESPI, Production Manager; STAN LEE, Chairman Emeritus. For information regarding advertising in Marvel Comics or on Marvel.com, please contact Vit DeBellis, Integrated Sales Manager, at vdebellis@marvel.com. For Marvel subscription inquiries, please call 888-511-5480. **Manufactured between 6/2/2017 and 7/4/2017 by SOLISCO PRINTERS, SCOTT, QC, CANADA.**

10 9 8 7 6 5 4 3 2 1

IVX

JEFF LEMIRE
WRITER

#17 & #19

ERIC KODA
PENCILER

TOM PALMER (#17) & **ERIC KODA** (#19)
INKERS

MORRY HOLLOWELL WITH
ANDREW CROSSLY (#19)
COLOR ARTISTS

DAVID YARDIN
COVER ART

#18 & #20

VICTOR IBAÑEZ WITH
ANDREA SORRENTINO (#18)
ARTISTS

JAY DAVID RAMOS WITH
MARCELO MAIOLO (#18)
COLOR ARTISTS

DAVID YARDIN
COVER ART

X-MEN PRIME #1

MARC GUGGENHEIM, GREG PAK & **CULLEN BUNN**
WRITERS

KEN LASHELY, IBRAIM ROBERSON & **LEONARD KIRK** WITH GUILLERMO ORTEGO
ARTISTS

MORRY HOLLOWELL, FRANK D'ARMATA & **MICHAEL GARLAND**
COLOR ARTISTS

ARDIAN SYAF, JAY LEISTEN & **LAURA MARTIN**
COVER ART

VC's JOE CARAMAGNA
LETTERER

CHRIS ROBINSON & CHRISTINA HARRINGTON
ASSISTANT EDITORS

DANIEL KETCHUM
EDITOR

MARK PANICCIA
X-MEN GROUP EDITOR

X-MEN CREATED BY STAN LEE & JACK KIRBY

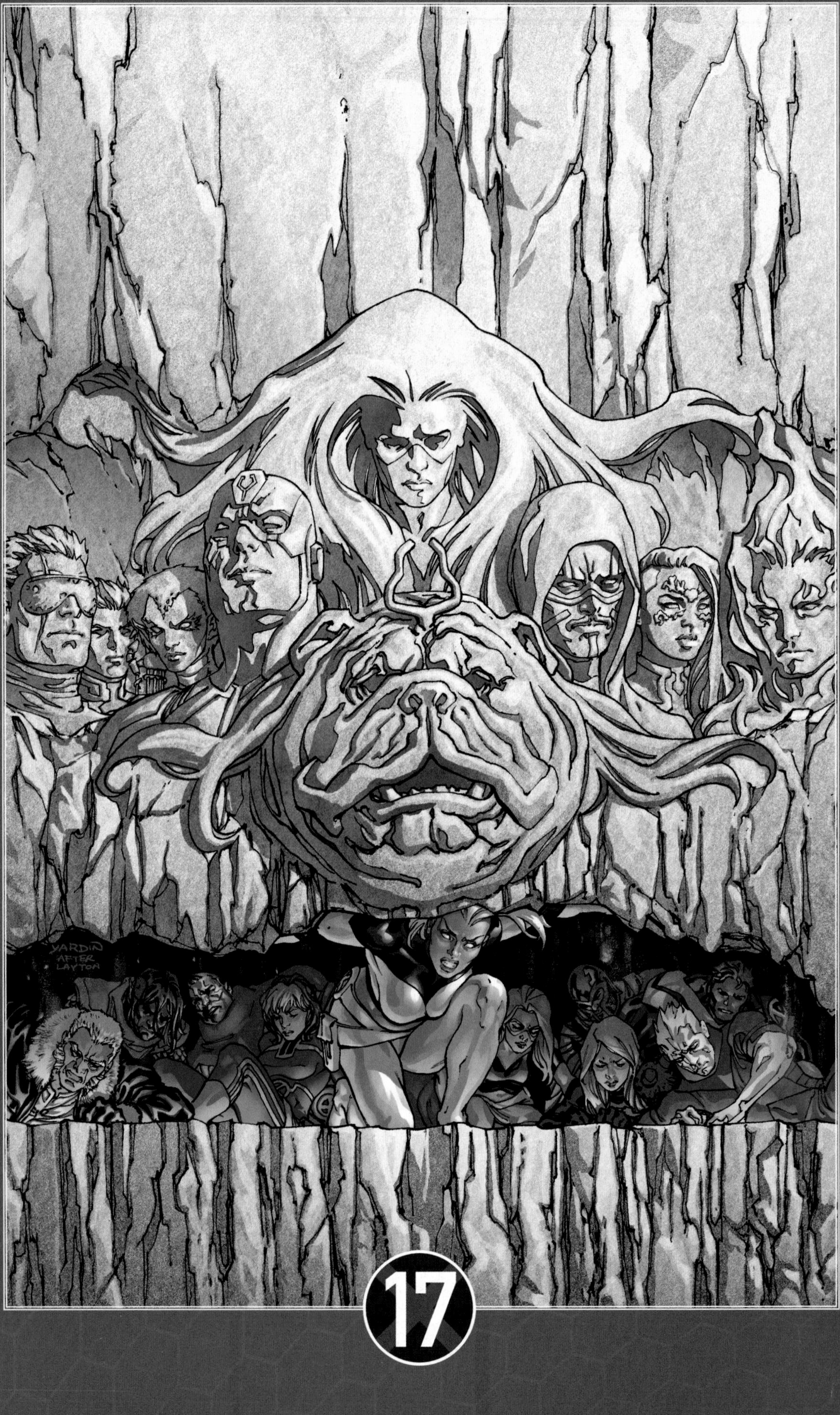
YARDIN AFTER LAYTON

17

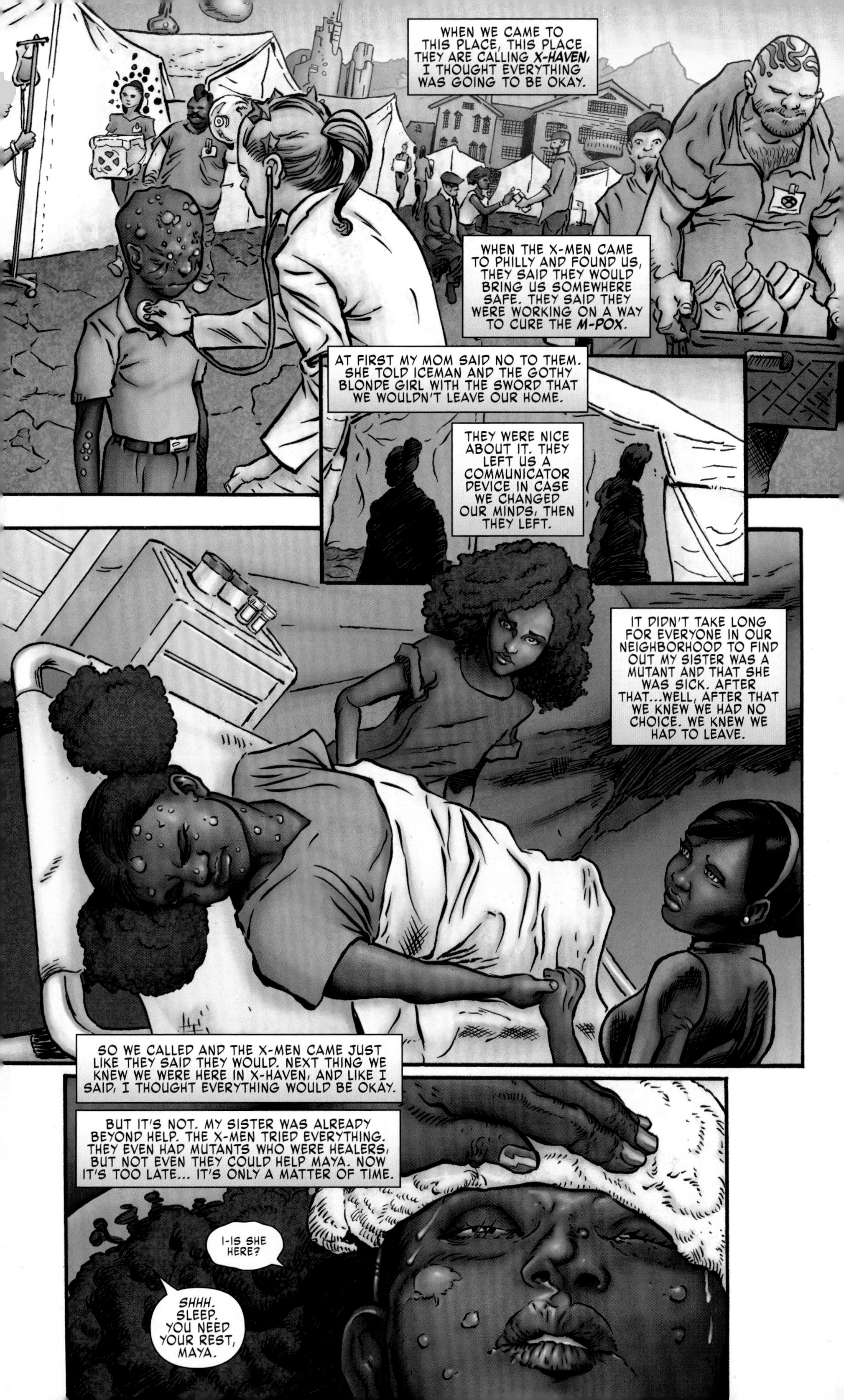
WHEN WE CAME TO THIS PLACE, THIS PLACE THEY ARE CALLING X-HAVEN, I THOUGHT EVERYTHING WAS GOING TO BE OKAY.
WHEN THE X-MEN CAME TO PHILLY AND FOUND US, THEY SAID THEY WOULD BRING US SOMEWHERE SAFE. THEY SAID THEY WERE WORKING ON A WAY TO CURE THE M-POX.
AT FIRST MY MOM SAID NO TO THEM. SHE TOLD ICEMAN AND THE GOTHY BLONDE GIRL WITH THE SWORD THAT WE WOULDN'T LEAVE OUR HOME.
THEY WERE NICE ABOUT IT. THEY LEFT US A COMMUNICATOR DEVICE IN CASE WE CHANGED OUR MINDS, THEN THEY LEFT.
IT DIDN'T TAKE LONG FOR EVERYONE IN OUR NEIGHBORHOOD TO FIND OUT MY SISTER WAS A MUTANT AND THAT SHE WAS SICK. AFTER THAT...WELL, AFTER THAT WE KNEW WE HAD NO CHOICE. WE KNEW WE HAD TO LEAVE.
SO WE CALLED AND THE X-MEN CAME JUST LIKE THEY SAID THEY WOULD. NEXT THING WE KNEW WE WERE HERE IN X-HAVEN, AND LIKE I SAID, I THOUGHT EVERYTHING WOULD BE OKAY.
BUT IT'S NOT. MY SISTER WAS ALREADY BEYOND HELP. THE X-MEN TRIED EVERYTHING. THEY EVEN HAD MUTANTS WHO WERE HEALERS, BUT NOT EVEN THEY COULD HELP MAYA. NOW IT'S TOO LATE... IT'S ONLY A MATTER OF TIME.
I-IS SHE HERE?
SHHH. SLEEP. YOU NEED YOUR REST, MAYA.

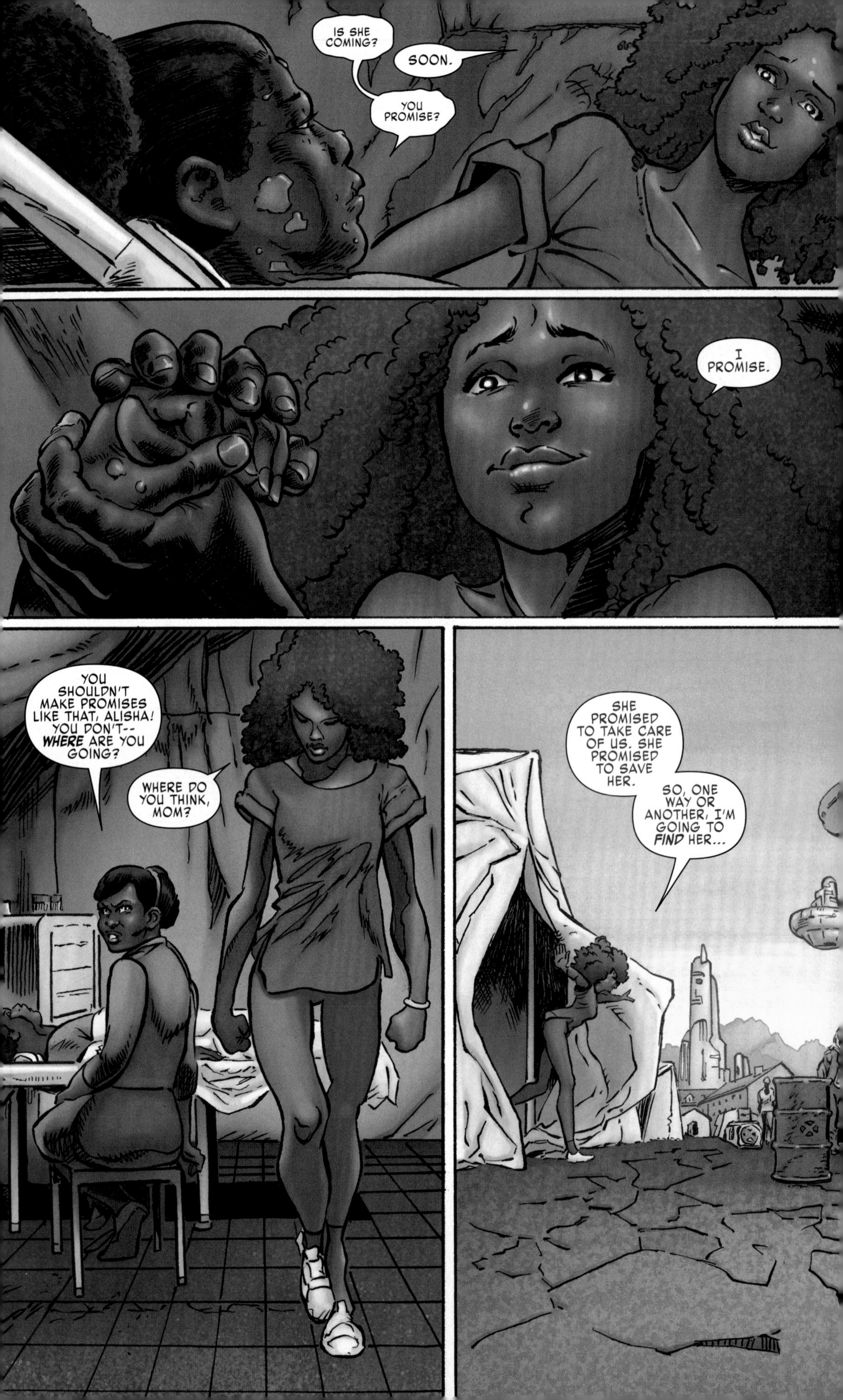

IS SHE COMING?
SOON.
YOU PROMISE?
I PROMISE.
YOU SHOULDN'T MAKE PROMISES LIKE THAT, ALISHA! YOU DON'T-- WHERE ARE YOU GOING?
WHERE DO YOU THINK, MOM?
SHE PROMISED TO TAKE CARE OF US. SHE PROMISED TO SAVE HER.
SO, ONE WAY OR ANOTHER, I'M GOING TO FIND HER...

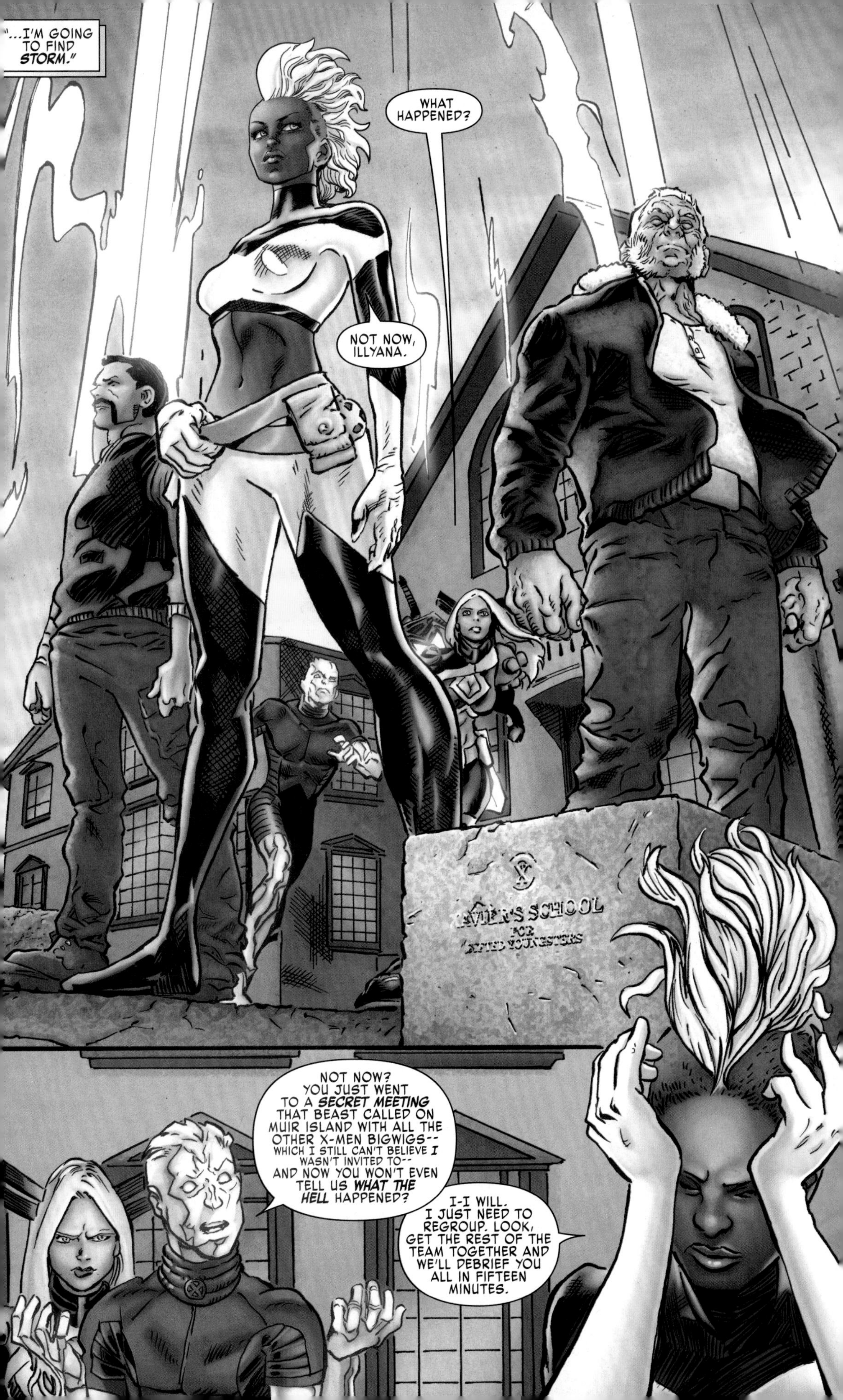

"...I'M GOING TO FIND STORM."
WHAT HAPPENED?
NOT NOW, ILLYANA.
NOT NOW? YOU JUST WENT TO A SECRET MEETING THAT BEAST CALLED ON MUIR ISLAND WITH ALL THE OTHER X-MEN BIGWIGS-- WHICH I STILL CAN'T BELIEVE I WASN'T INVITED TO-- AND NOW YOU WON'T EVEN TELL US WHAT THE HELL HAPPENED?
I-I WILL. I JUST NEED TO REGROUP. LOOK, GET THE REST OF THE TEAM TOGETHER AND WE'LL DEBRIEF YOU ALL IN FIFTEEN MINUTES.

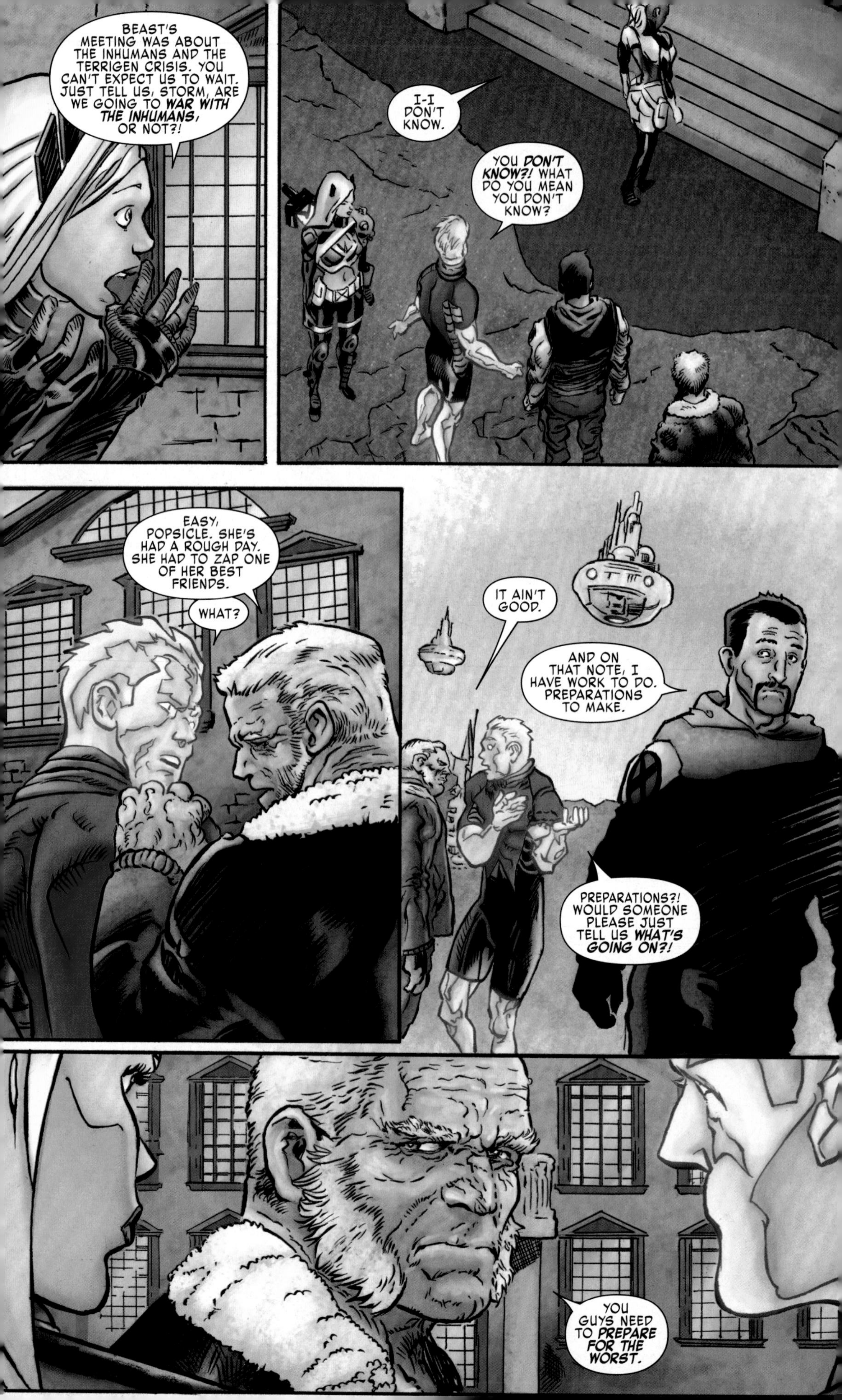

BEAST'S MEETING WAS ABOUT THE INHUMANS AND THE TERRIGEN CRISIS. YOU CAN'T EXPECT US TO WAIT. JUST TELL US, STORM, ARE WE GOING TO WAR WITH THE INHUMANS, OR NOT?!
I-I DON'T KNOW.
YOU DON'T KNOW?! WHAT DO YOU MEAN YOU DON'T KNOW?
EASY, POPSICLE. SHE'S HAD A ROUGH DAY. SHE HAD TO ZAP ONE OF HER BEST FRIENDS.
WHAT?
IT AIN'T GOOD.
AND ON THAT NOTE, I HAVE WORK TO DO. PREPARATIONS TO MAKE.
PREPARATIONS?! WOULD SOMEONE PLEASE JUST TELL US WHAT'S GOING ON?!
YOU GUYS NEED TO PREPARE FOR THE WORST.

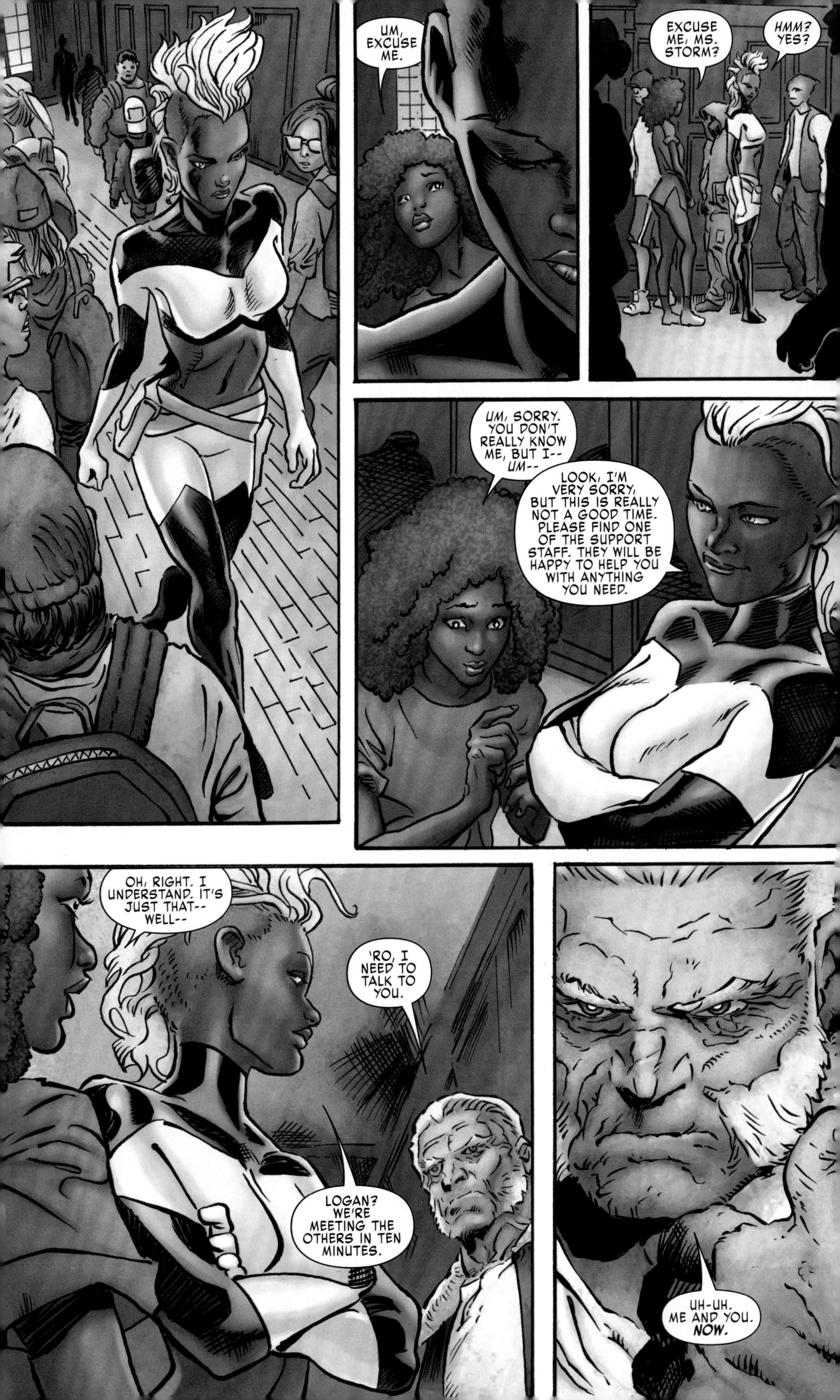

UM, EXCUSE ME.
EXCUSE ME, MS. STORM?
HMM? YES?
UM, SORRY. YOU DON'T REALLY KNOW ME, BUT I-- UM--
LOOK, I'M VERY SORRY, BUT THIS IS REALLY NOT A GOOD TIME. PLEASE FIND ONE OF THE SUPPORT STAFF. THEY WILL BE HAPPY TO HELP YOU WITH ANYTHING YOU NEED.
OH, RIGHT. I UNDERSTAND. IT'S JUST THAT-- WELL--
'RO, I NEED TO TALK TO YOU.
LOGAN? WE'RE MEETING THE OTHERS IN TEN MINUTES.
UH-UH. ME AND YOU. **NOW.**

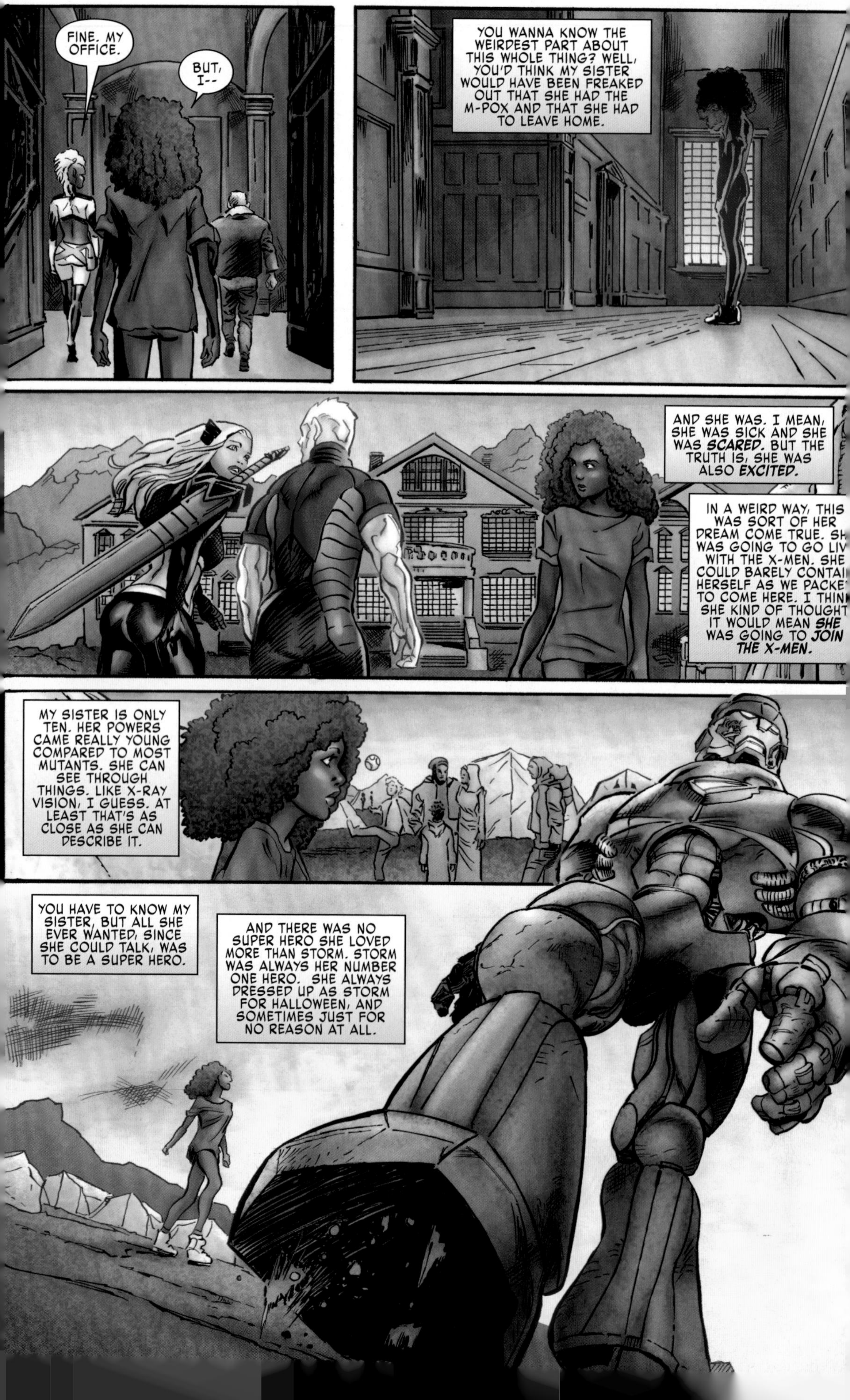

FINE. MY OFFICE.
BUT, I--
YOU WANNA KNOW THE WEIRDEST PART ABOUT THIS WHOLE THING? WELL, YOU'D THINK MY SISTER WOULD HAVE BEEN FREAKED OUT THAT SHE HAD THE M-POX AND THAT SHE HAD TO LEAVE HOME.
AND SHE WAS. I MEAN, SHE WAS SICK AND SHE WAS SCARED. BUT THE TRUTH IS, SHE WAS ALSO EXCITED.
IN A WEIRD WAY, THIS WAS SORT OF HER DREAM COME TRUE. SH WAS GOING TO GO LIV WITH THE X-MEN. SHE COULD BARELY CONTAI HERSELF AS WE PACKE TO COME HERE. I THIN SHE KIND OF THOUGHT IT WOULD MEAN SHE WAS GOING TO JOIN THE X-MEN.
MY SISTER IS ONLY TEN. HER POWERS CAME REALLY YOUNG COMPARED TO MOST MUTANTS. SHE CAN SEE THROUGH THINGS. LIKE X-RAY VISION, I GUESS. AT LEAST THAT'S AS CLOSE AS SHE CAN DESCRIBE IT.
YOU HAVE TO KNOW MY SISTER, BUT ALL SHE EVER WANTED, SINCE SHE COULD TALK, WAS TO BE A SUPER HERO.
AND THERE WAS NO SUPER HERO SHE LOVED MORE THAN STORM. STORM WAS ALWAYS HER NUMBER ONE HERO. SHE ALWAYS DRESSED UP AS STORM FOR HALLOWEEN, AND SOMETIMES JUST FOR NO REASON AT ALL.

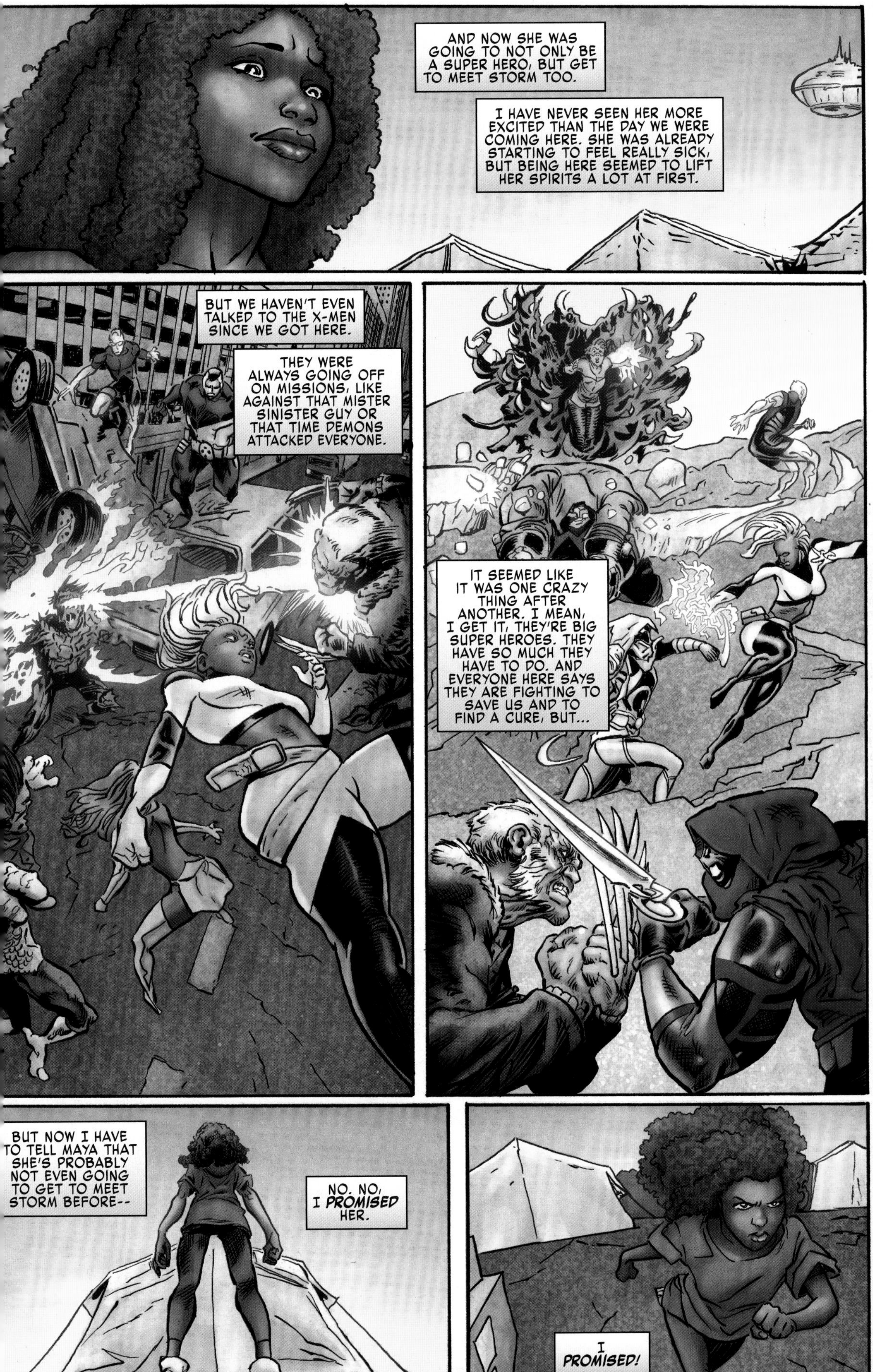
AND NOW SHE WAS GOING TO NOT ONLY BE A SUPER HERO, BUT GET TO MEET STORM TOO.
I HAVE NEVER SEEN HER MORE EXCITED THAN THE DAY WE WERE COMING HERE. SHE WAS ALREADY STARTING TO FEEL REALLY SICK, BUT BEING HERE SEEMED TO LIFT HER SPIRITS A LOT AT FIRST.
BUT WE HAVEN'T EVEN TALKED TO THE X-MEN SINCE WE GOT HERE.
THEY WERE ALWAYS GOING OFF ON MISSIONS, LIKE AGAINST THAT MISTER SINISTER GUY OR THAT TIME DEMONS ATTACKED EVERYONE.
IT SEEMED LIKE IT WAS ONE CRAZY THING AFTER ANOTHER. I MEAN, I GET IT, THEY'RE BIG SUPER HEROES. THEY HAVE SO MUCH THEY HAVE TO DO. AND EVERYONE HERE SAYS THEY ARE FIGHTING TO SAVE US AND TO FIND A CURE, BUT...
BUT NOW I HAVE TO TELL MAYA THAT SHE'S PROBABLY NOT EVEN GOING TO GET TO MEET STORM BEFORE--
NO. NO, I *PROMISED* HER.
I *PROMISED!*

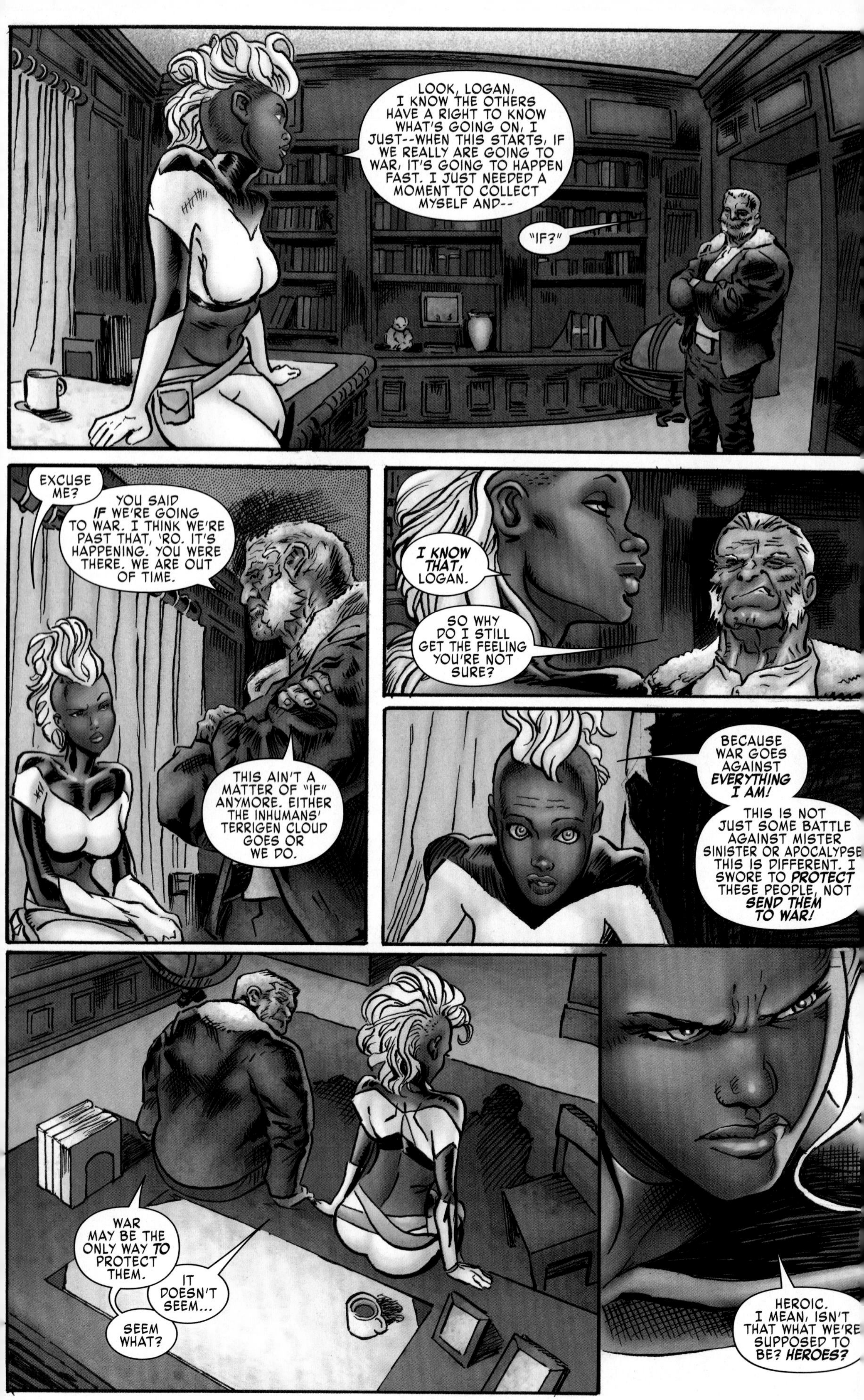
LOOK, LOGAN, I KNOW THE OTHERS HAVE A RIGHT TO KNOW WHAT'S GOING ON, I JUST--WHEN THIS STARTS, IF WE REALLY ARE GOING TO WAR, IT'S GOING TO HAPPEN FAST. I JUST NEEDED A MOMENT TO COLLECT MYSELF AND--
"IF?"
EXCUSE ME?
YOU SAID *IF* WE'RE GOING TO WAR. I THINK WE'RE PAST THAT, 'RO. IT'S HAPPENING. YOU WERE THERE. WE ARE OUT OF TIME.
THIS AIN'T A MATTER OF "IF" ANYMORE. EITHER THE INHUMANS' TERRIGEN CLOUD GOES OR WE DO.
I KNOW THAT, LOGAN.
SO WHY DO I STILL GET THE FEELING YOU'RE NOT SURE?
BECAUSE WAR GOES AGAINST *EVERYTHING I AM!*
THIS IS NOT JUST SOME BATTLE AGAINST MISTER SINISTER OR APOCALYPSE. THIS IS DIFFERENT. I SWORE TO *PROTECT* THESE PEOPLE, NOT *SEND THEM TO WAR!*
WAR MAY BE THE ONLY WAY TO PROTECT THEM.
IT DOESN'T SEEM...
SEEM WHAT?
HEROIC. I MEAN, ISN'T THAT WHAT WE'RE SUPPOSED TO BE? *HEROES?*

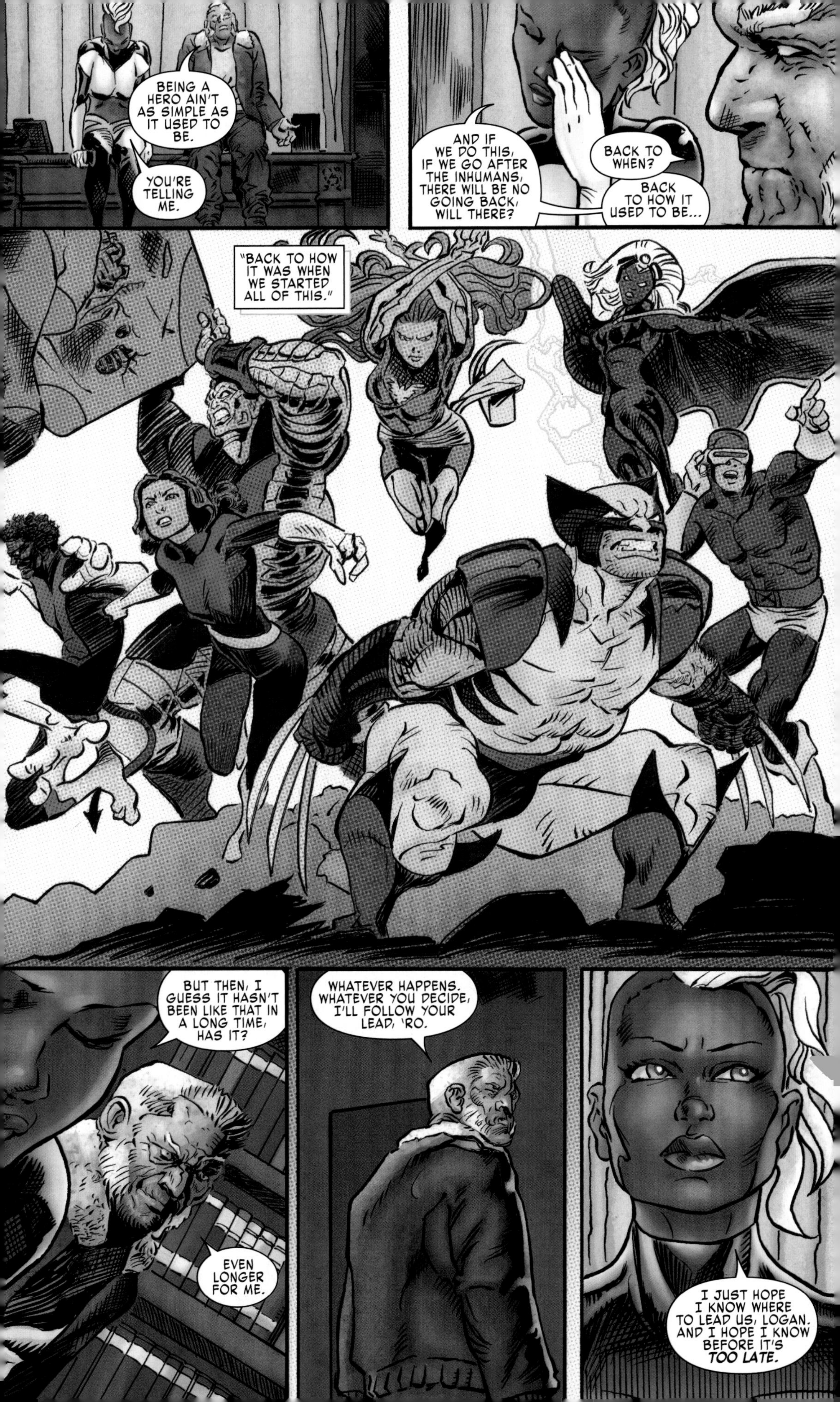
BEING A HERO AIN'T AS SIMPLE AS IT USED TO BE.
YOU'RE TELLING ME.
AND IF WE DO THIS, IF WE GO AFTER THE INHUMANS, THERE WILL BE NO GOING BACK, WILL THERE?
BACK TO WHEN?
BACK TO HOW IT USED TO BE...
"BACK TO HOW IT WAS WHEN WE STARTED ALL OF THIS."
BUT THEN, I GUESS IT HASN'T BEEN LIKE THAT IN A LONG TIME, HAS IT?
EVEN LONGER FOR ME.
WHATEVER HAPPENS. WHATEVER YOU DECIDE, I'LL FOLLOW YOUR LEAD, 'RO.
I JUST HOPE I KNOW WHERE TO LEAD US, LOGAN. AND I HOPE I KNOW BEFORE IT'S *TOO LATE.*

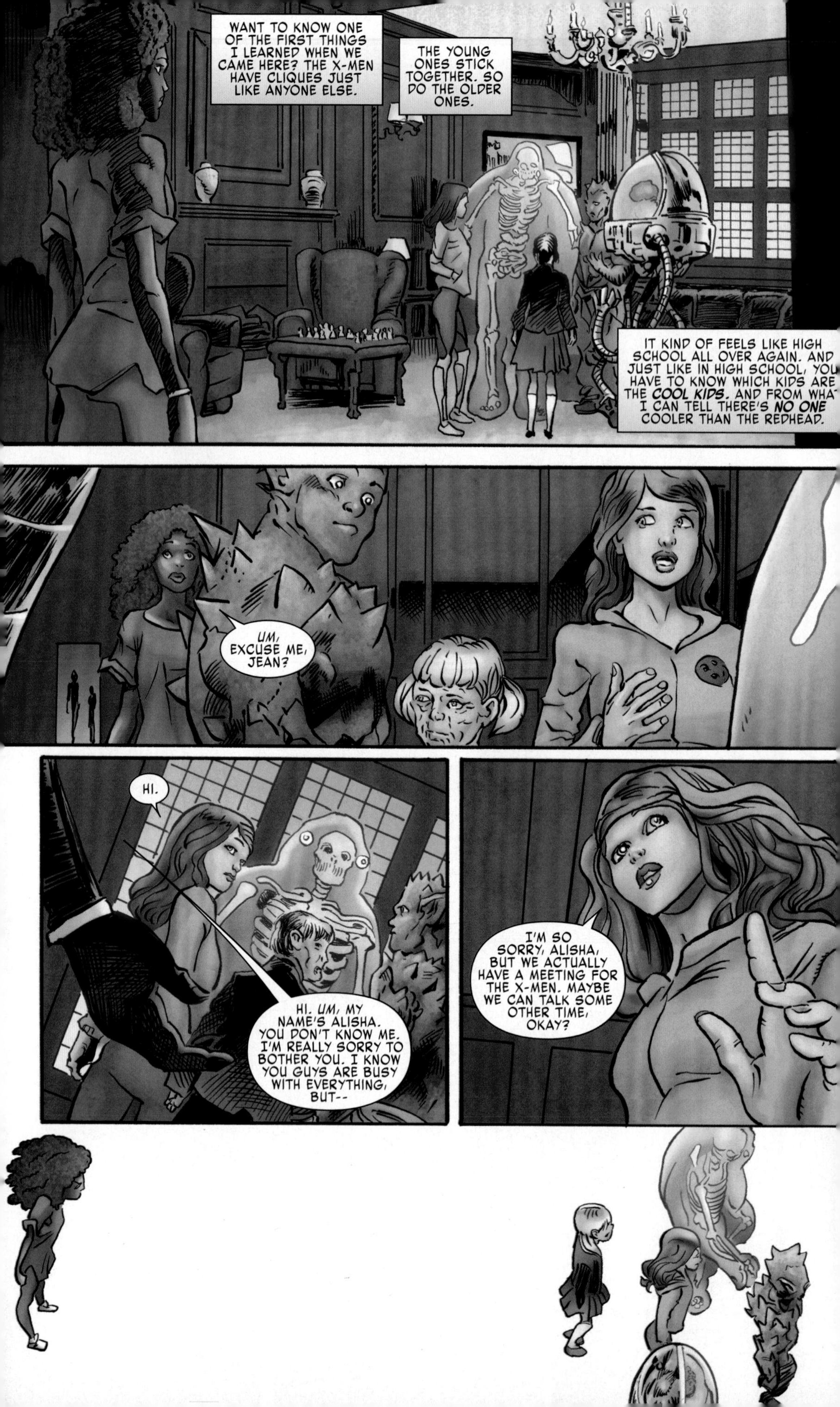

WANT TO KNOW ONE OF THE FIRST THINGS I LEARNED WHEN WE CAME HERE? THE X-MEN HAVE CLIQUES JUST LIKE ANYONE ELSE.
THE YOUNG ONES STICK TOGETHER. SO DO THE OLDER ONES.
IT KIND OF FEELS LIKE HIGH SCHOOL ALL OVER AGAIN. AND JUST LIKE IN HIGH SCHOOL, YOU HAVE TO KNOW WHICH KIDS ARE THE COOL KIDS. AND FROM WHAT I CAN TELL THERE'S NO ONE COOLER THAN THE REDHEAD.
UM, EXCUSE ME, JEAN?
HI.
HI. UM, MY NAME'S ALISHA. YOU DON'T KNOW ME. I'M REALLY SORRY TO BOTHER YOU. I KNOW YOU GUYS ARE BUSY WITH EVERYTHING, BUT--
I'M SO SORRY, ALISHA, BUT WE ACTUALLY HAVE A MEETING FOR THE X-MEN. MAYBE WE CAN TALK SOME OTHER TIME, OKAY?

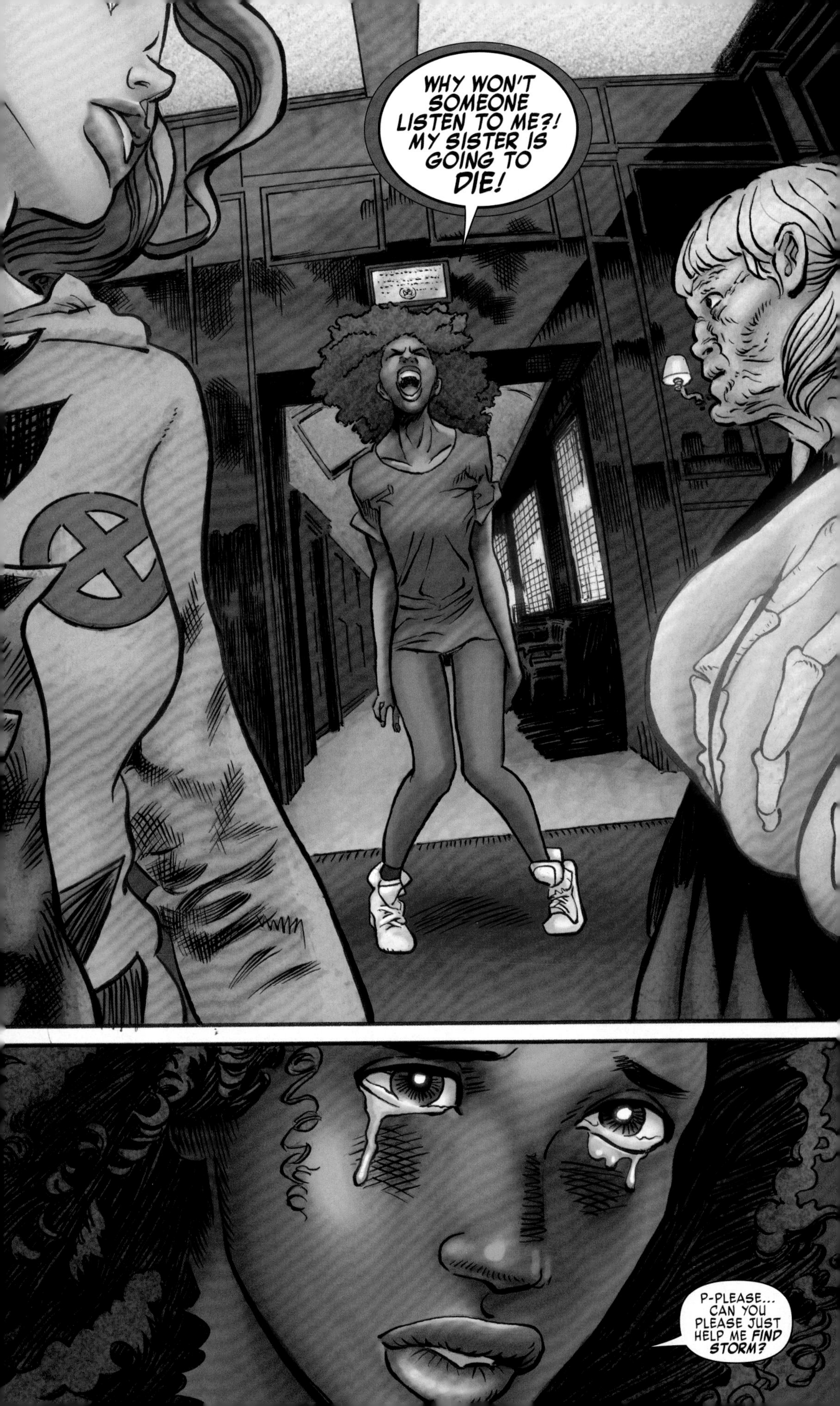
WHY WON'T SOMEONE LISTEN TO ME?! MY SISTER IS GOING TO DIE!
P-PLEASE... CAN YOU PLEASE JUST HELP ME FIND STORM?

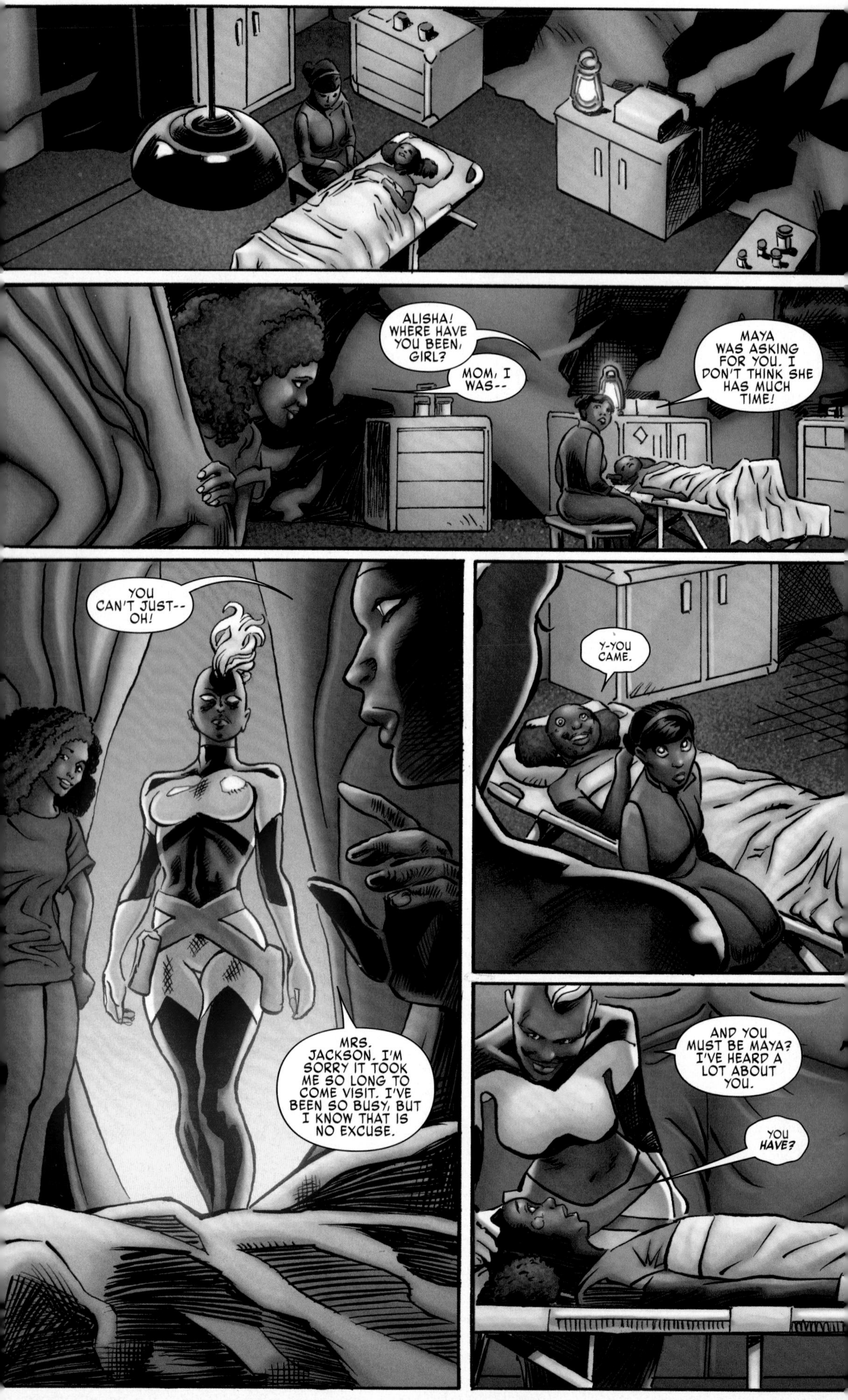

ALISHA! WHERE HAVE YOU BEEN, GIRL?
MOM, I WAS--
MAYA WAS ASKING FOR YOU. I DON'T THINK SHE HAS MUCH TIME!
YOU CAN'T JUST-- OH!
MRS. JACKSON. I'M SORRY IT TOOK ME SO LONG TO COME VISIT. I'VE BEEN SO BUSY, BUT I KNOW THAT IS NO EXCUSE.
Y-YOU CAME.
AND YOU MUST BE MAYA? I'VE HEARD A LOT ABOUT YOU.
YOU HAVE?

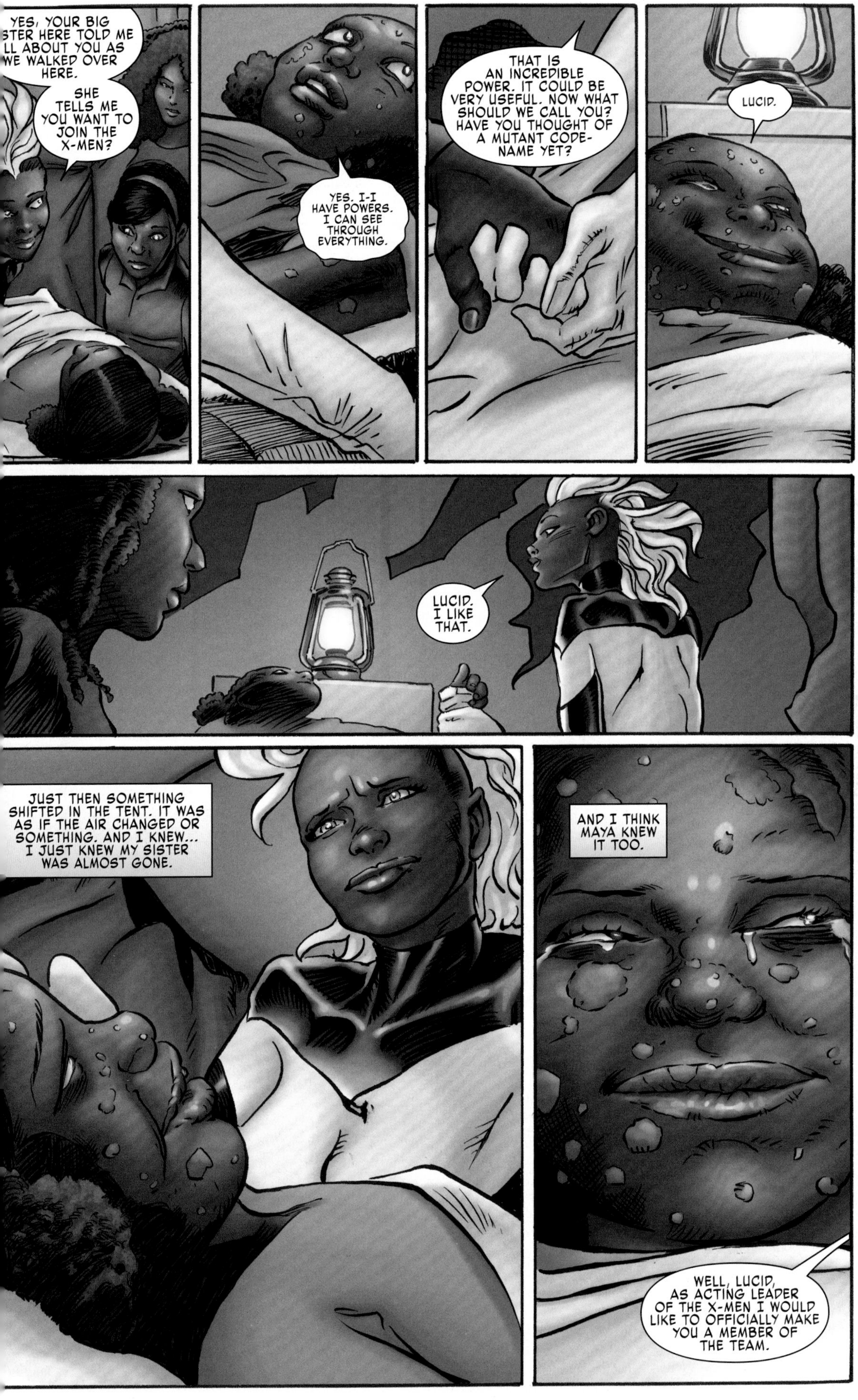

YES, YOUR BIG STER HERE TOLD ME LL ABOUT YOU AS WE WALKED OVER HERE.
SHE TELLS ME YOU WANT TO JOIN THE X-MEN?
YES. I-I HAVE POWERS. I CAN SEE THROUGH EVERYTHING.
THAT IS AN INCREDIBLE POWER. IT COULD BE VERY USEFUL. NOW WHAT SHOULD WE CALL YOU? HAVE YOU THOUGHT OF A MUTANT CODE-NAME YET?
LUCID.
LUCID. I LIKE THAT.
JUST THEN SOMETHING SHIFTED IN THE TENT. IT WAS AS IF THE AIR CHANGED OR SOMETHING. AND I KNEW... I JUST KNEW MY SISTER WAS ALMOST GONE.
AND I THINK MAYA KNEW IT TOO.
WELL, LUCID, AS ACTING LEADER OF THE X-MEN I WOULD LIKE TO OFFICIALLY MAKE YOU A MEMBER OF THE TEAM.

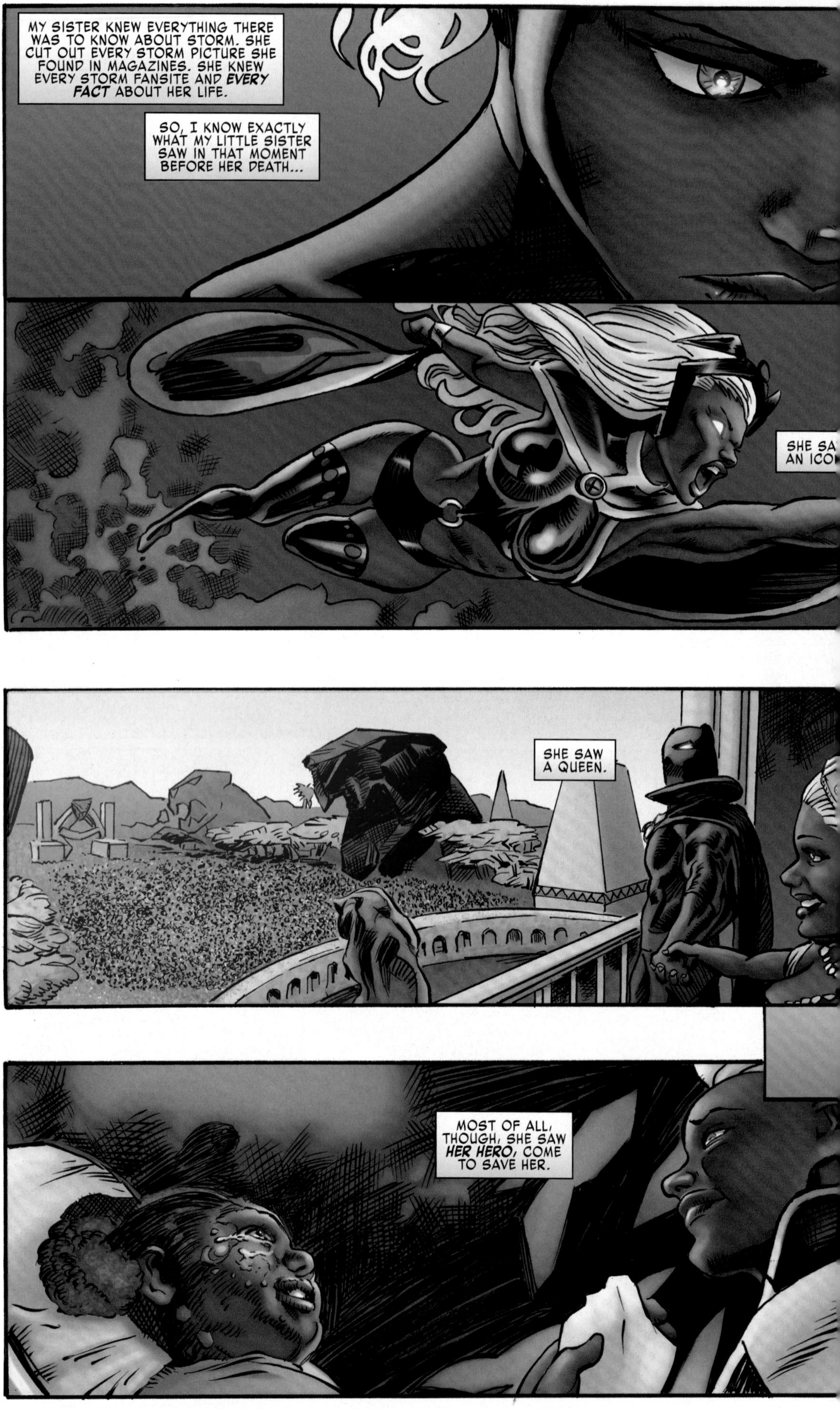
MY SISTER KNEW EVERYTHING THERE WAS TO KNOW ABOUT STORM. SHE CUT OUT EVERY STORM PICTURE SHE FOUND IN MAGAZINES. SHE KNEW EVERY STORM FANSITE AND EVERY FACT ABOUT HER LIFE.
SO, I KNOW EXACTLY WHAT MY LITTLE SISTER SAW IN THAT MOMENT BEFORE HER DEATH...
SHE SA AN ICO
SHE SAW A QUEEN.
MOST OF ALL, THOUGH, SHE SAW HER HERO, COME TO SAVE HER.

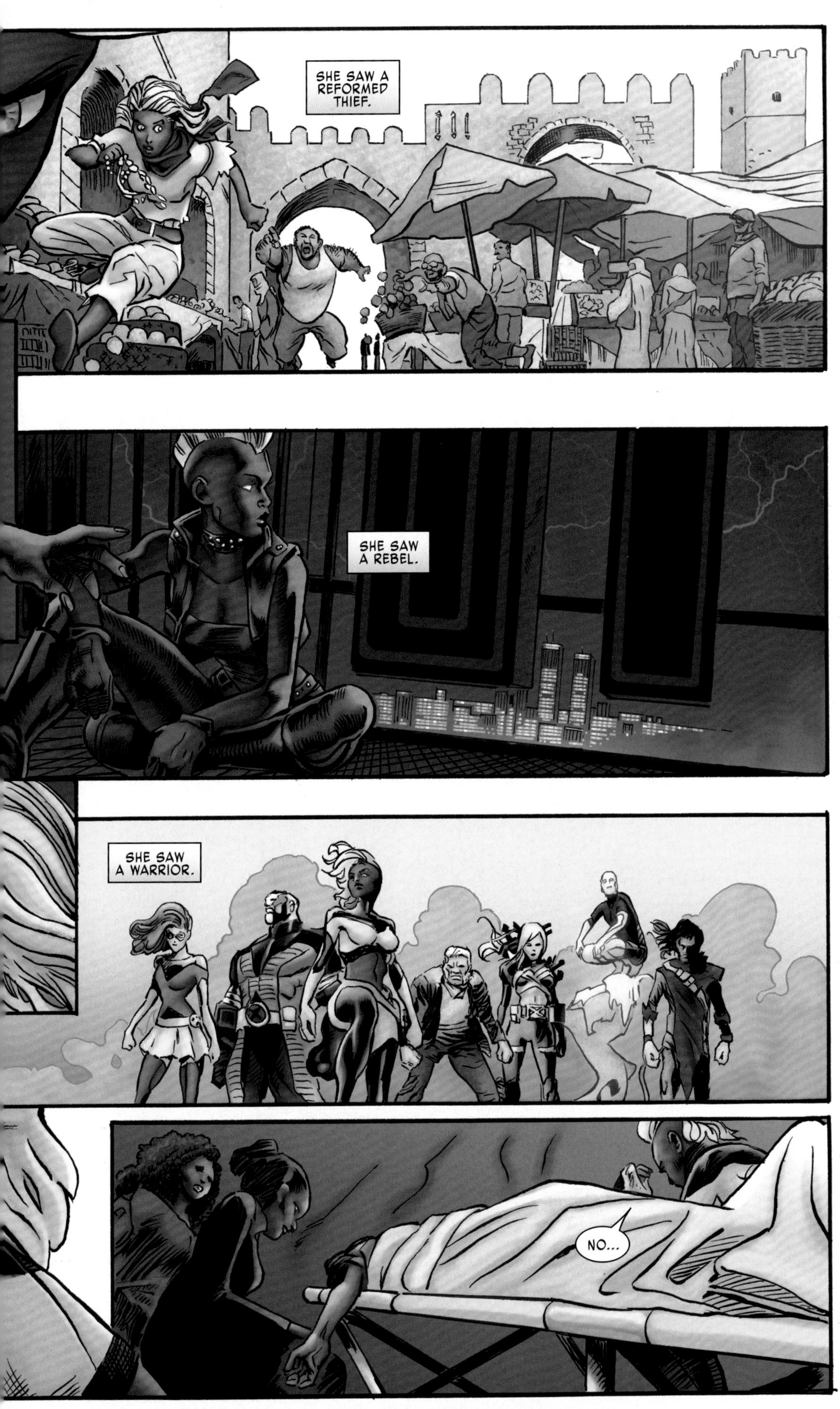
SHE SAW A REFORMED THIEF.
SHE SAW A REBEL.
SHE SAW A WARRIOR.
NO...

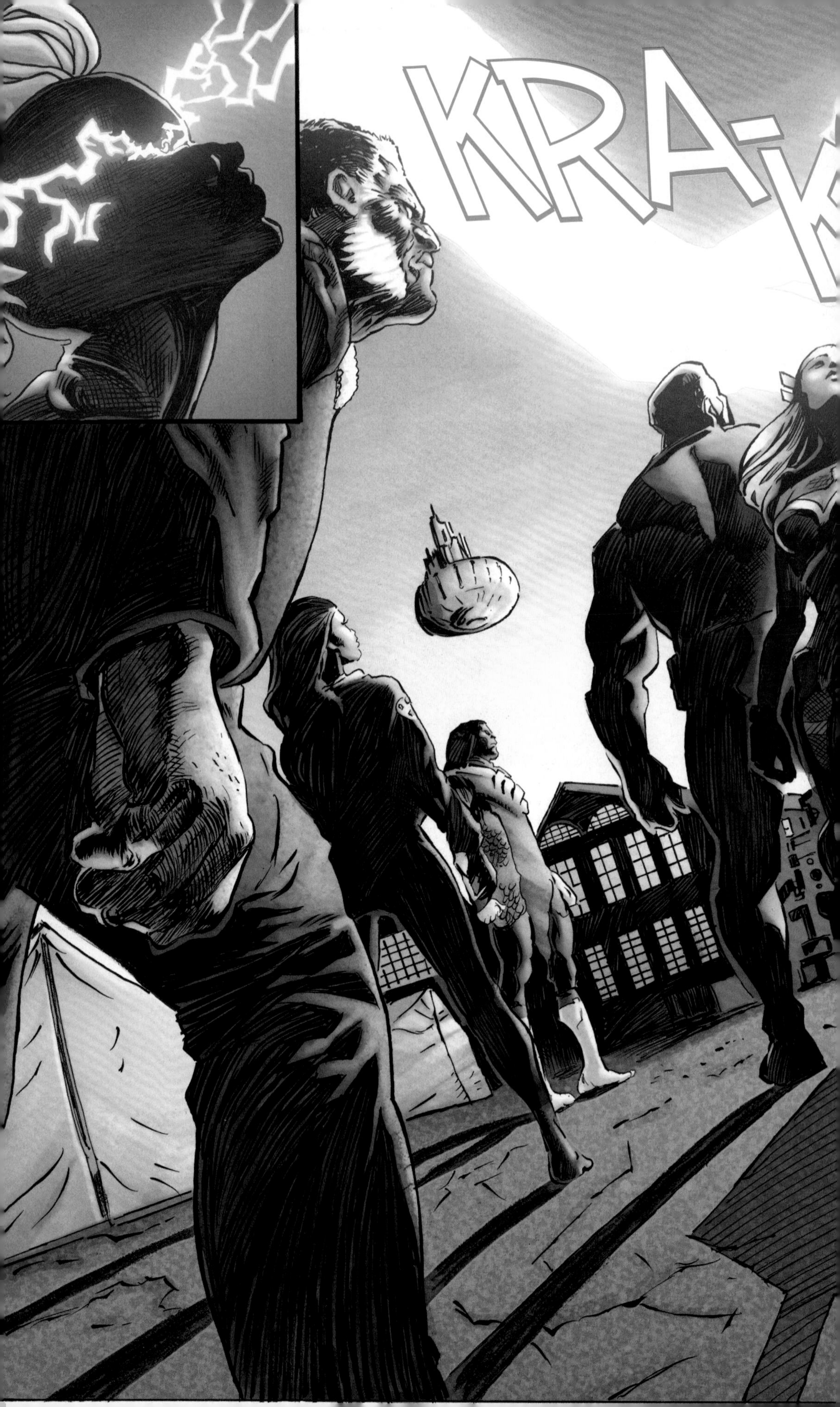
KRA-K

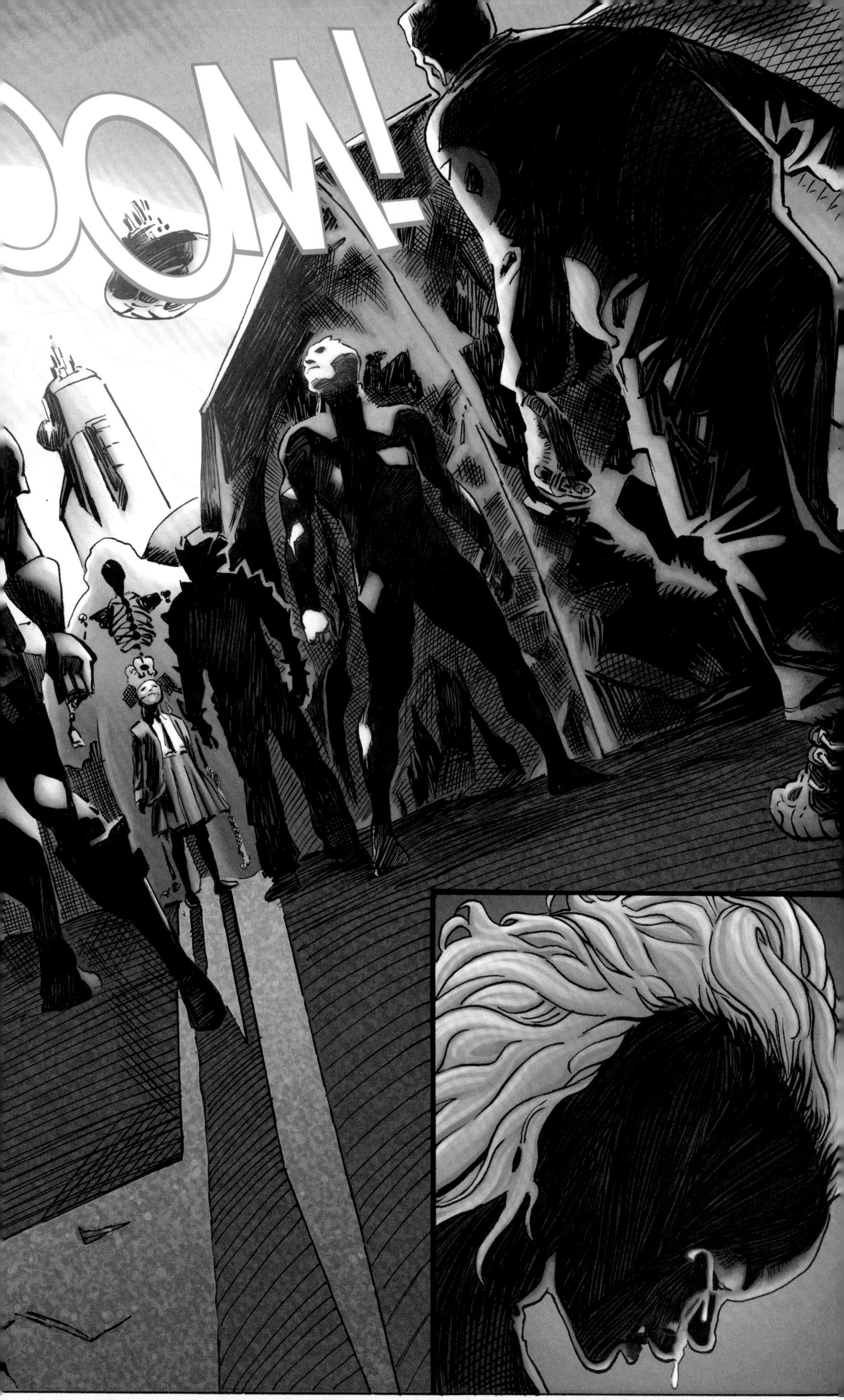
OOM!

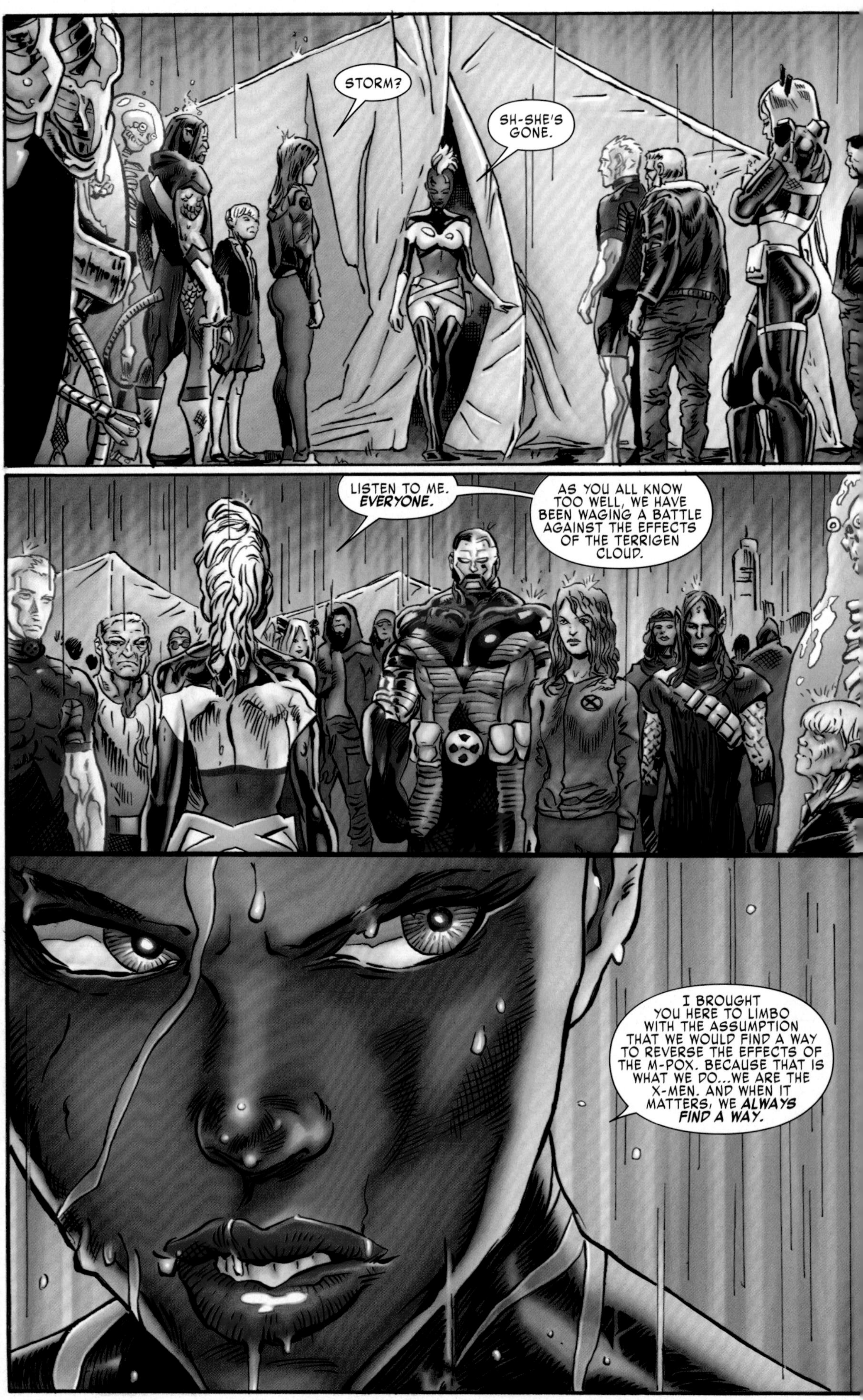

STORM?
SH-SHE'S GONE.
LISTEN TO ME. **EVERYONE.**
AS YOU ALL KNOW TOO WELL, WE HAVE BEEN WAGING A BATTLE AGAINST THE EFFECTS OF THE TERRIGEN CLOUD.
I BROUGHT YOU HERE TO LIMBO WITH THE ASSUMPTION THAT WE WOULD FIND A WAY TO REVERSE THE EFFECTS OF THE M-POX. BECAUSE THAT IS WHAT WE DO...WE ARE THE X-MEN. AND WHEN IT MATTERS, WE ***ALWAYS FIND A WAY.***

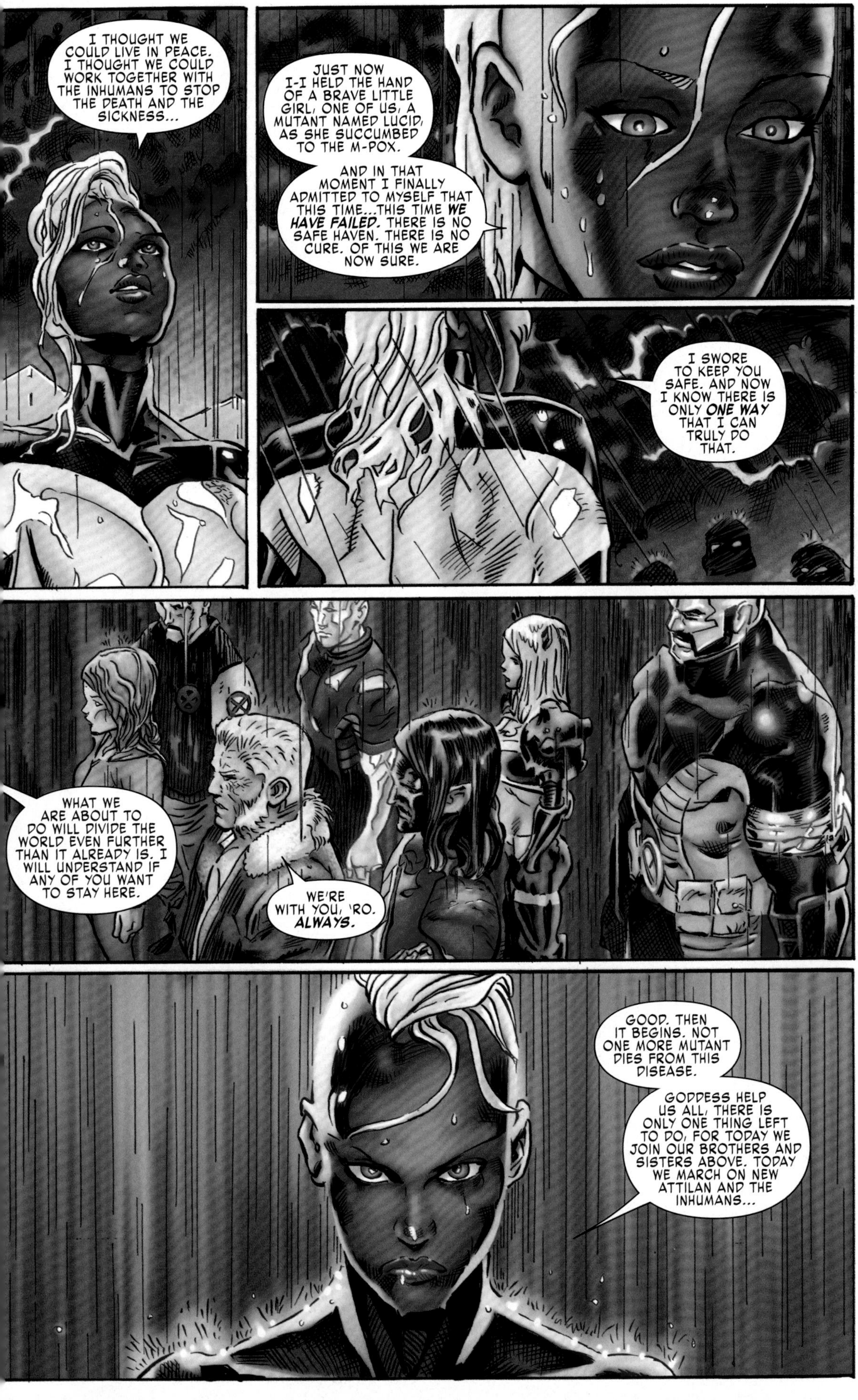

I THOUGHT WE COULD LIVE IN PEACE. I THOUGHT WE COULD WORK TOGETHER WITH THE INHUMANS TO STOP THE DEATH AND THE SICKNESS...
JUST NOW I-I HELD THE HAND OF A BRAVE LITTLE GIRL, ONE OF US, A MUTANT NAMED LUCID, AS SHE SUCCUMBED TO THE M-POX.
AND IN THAT MOMENT I FINALLY ADMITTED TO MYSELF THAT THIS TIME...THIS TIME WE HAVE FAILED. THERE IS NO SAFE HAVEN. THERE IS NO CURE. OF THIS WE ARE NOW SURE.
I SWORE TO KEEP YOU SAFE. AND NOW I KNOW THERE IS ONLY ONE WAY THAT I CAN TRULY DO THAT.
WHAT WE ARE ABOUT TO DO WILL DIVIDE THE WORLD EVEN FURTHER THAN IT ALREADY IS. I WILL UNDERSTAND IF ANY OF YOU WANT TO STAY HERE.
WE'RE WITH YOU, 'RO. ALWAYS.
GOOD. THEN IT BEGINS. NOT ONE MORE MUTANT DIES FROM THIS DISEASE.
GODDESS HELP US ALL, THERE IS ONLY ONE THING LEFT TO DO, FOR TODAY WE JOIN OUR BROTHERS AND SISTERS ABOVE. TODAY WE MARCH ON NEW ATTILAN AND THE INHUMANS...

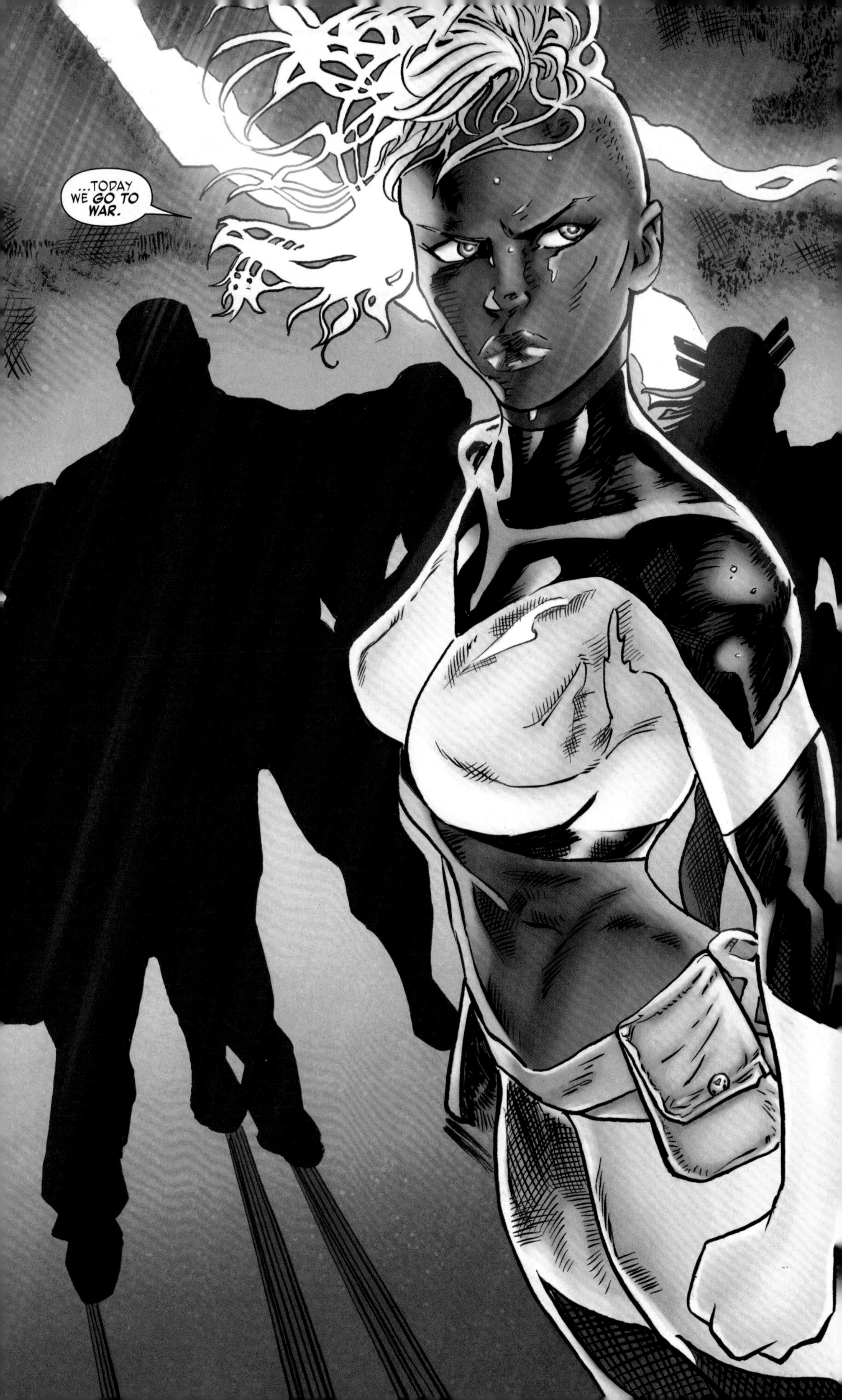
...TODAY WE GO TO WAR.

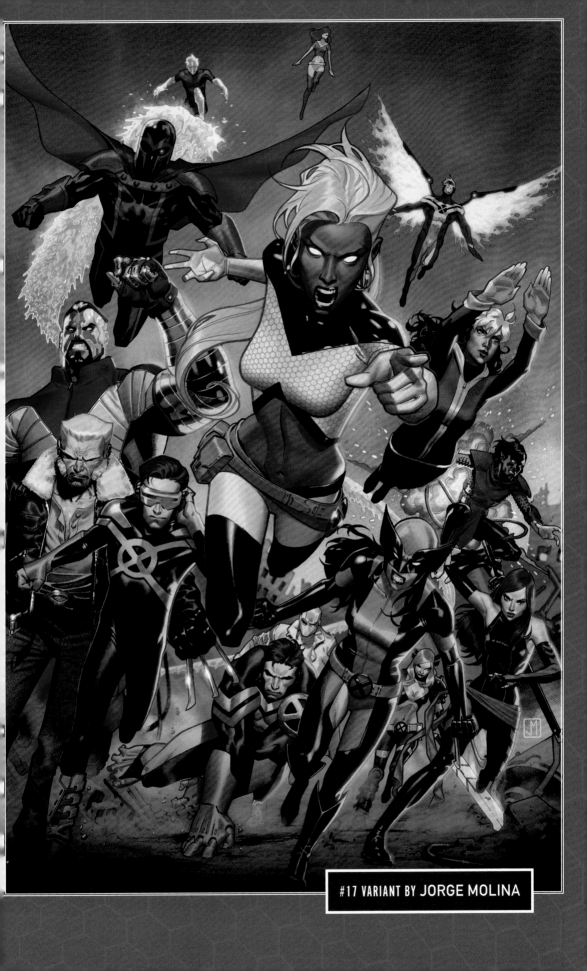

#17 VARIANT BY JORGE MOLINA

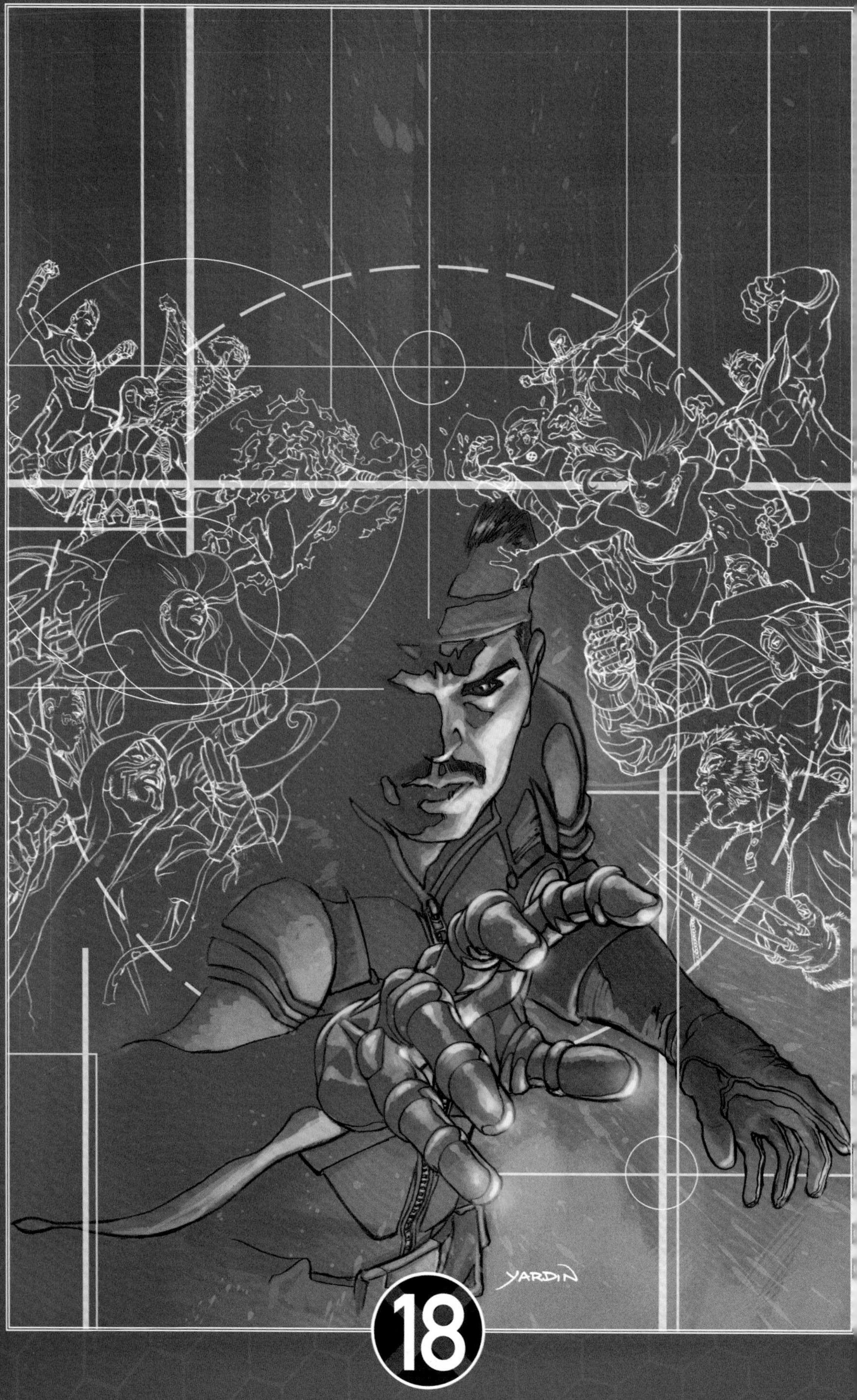
YARDIN
18

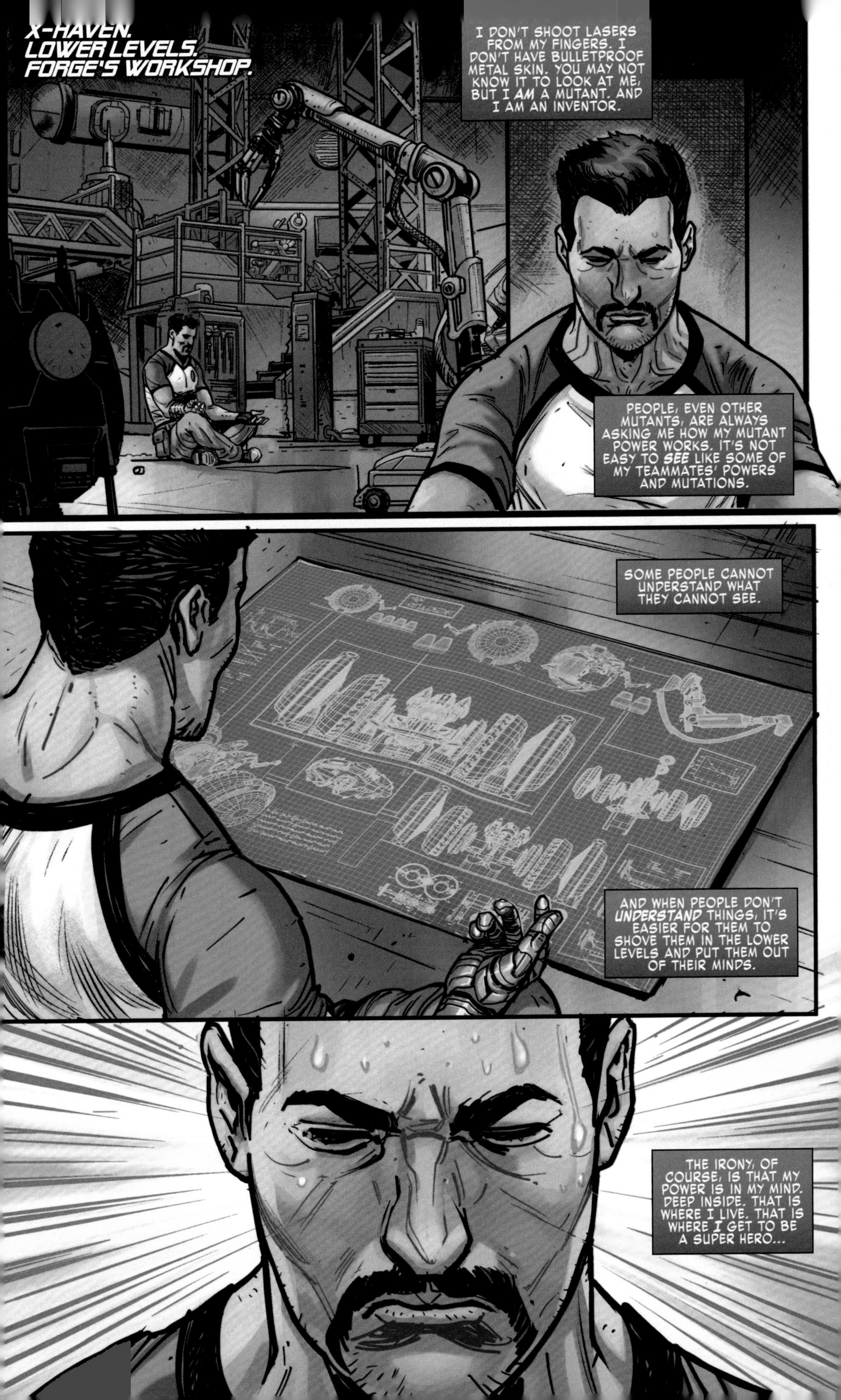
X-HAVEN. LOWER LEVELS. FORGE'S WORKSHOP.
I DON'T SHOOT LASERS FROM MY FINGERS. I DON'T HAVE BULLETPROOF METAL SKIN. YOU MAY NOT KNOW IT TO LOOK AT ME, BUT I AM A MUTANT. AND I AM AN INVENTOR.
PEOPLE, EVEN OTHER MUTANTS, ARE ALWAYS ASKING ME HOW MY MUTANT POWER WORKS. IT'S NOT EASY TO SEE LIKE SOME OF MY TEAMMATES' POWERS AND MUTATIONS.
SOME PEOPLE CANNOT UNDERSTAND WHAT THEY CANNOT SEE.
AND WHEN PEOPLE DON'T UNDERSTAND THINGS, IT'S EASIER FOR THEM TO SHOVE THEM IN THE LOWER LEVELS AND PUT THEM OUT OF THEIR MINDS.
THE IRONY, OF COURSE, IS THAT MY POWER IS IN MY MIND. DEEP INSIDE. THAT IS WHERE I LIVE. THAT IS WHERE I GET TO BE A SUPER HERO...

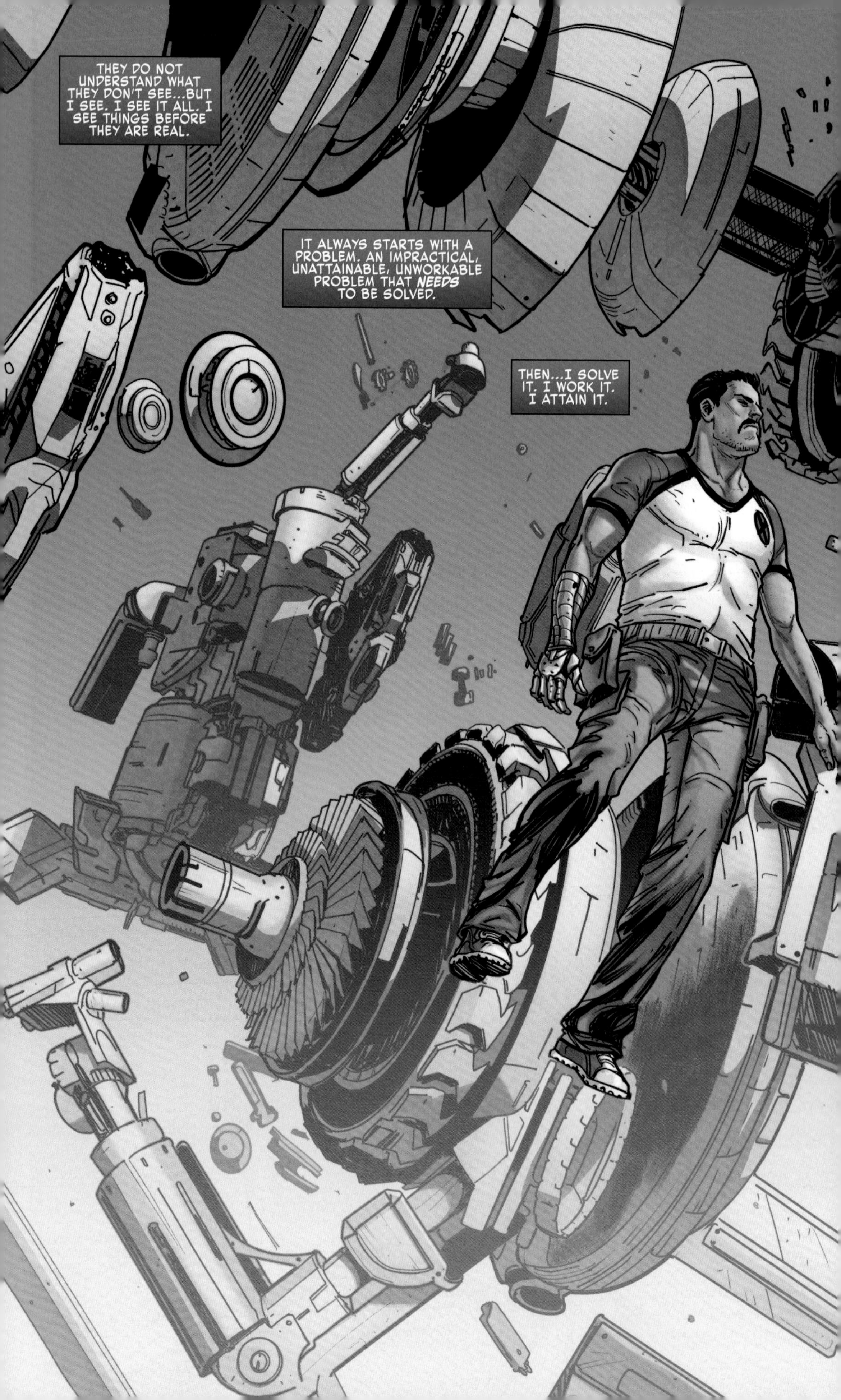
THEY DO NOT UNDERSTAND WHAT THEY DON'T SEE...BUT I SEE. I SEE IT ALL. I SEE THINGS BEFORE THEY ARE REAL.
IT ALWAYS STARTS WITH A PROBLEM. AN IMPRACTICAL, UNATTAINABLE, UNWORKABLE PROBLEM THAT *NEEDS* TO BE SOLVED.
THEN...I SOLVE IT. I WORK IT. I ATTAIN IT.

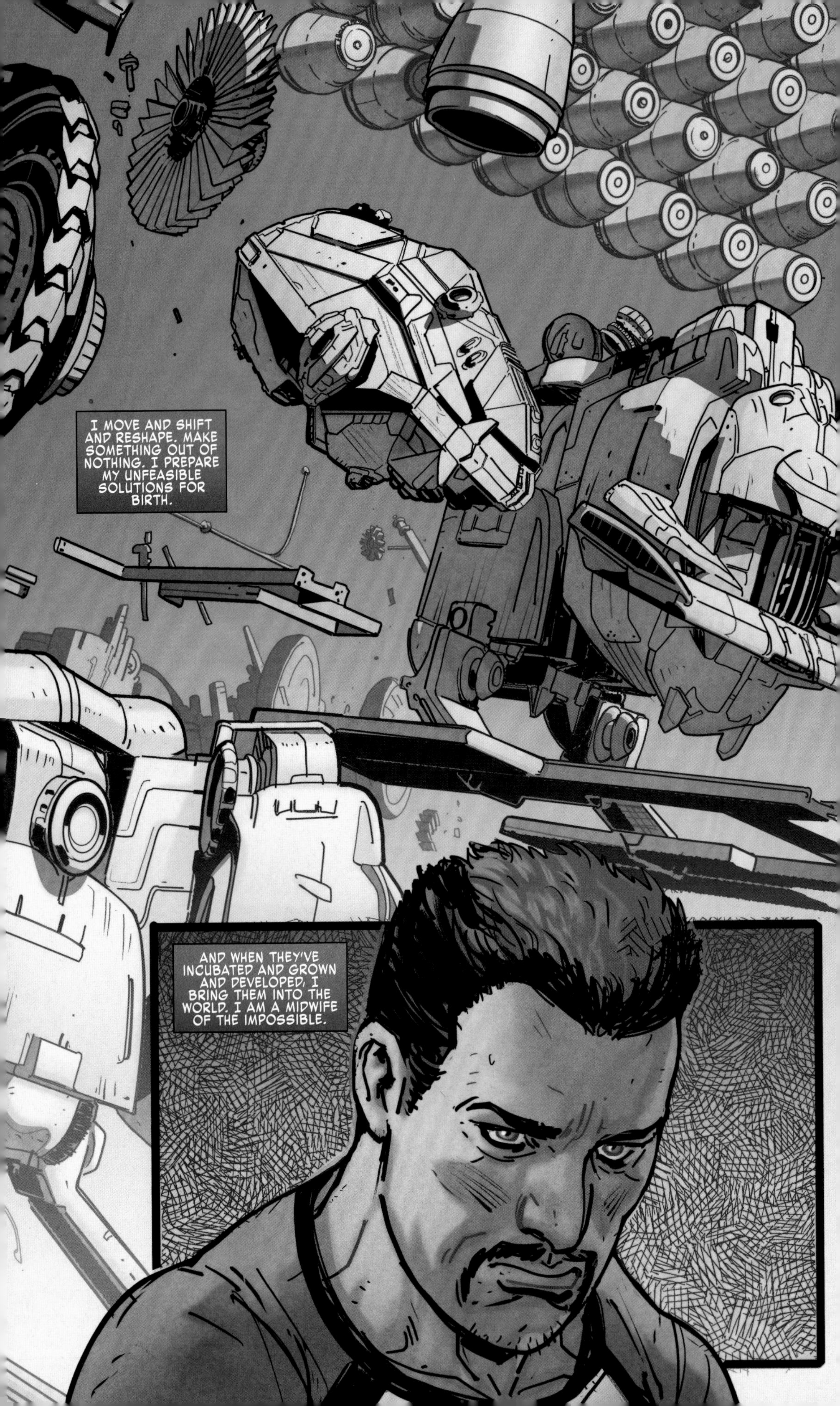
I MOVE AND SHIFT AND RESHAPE. MAKE SOMETHING OUT OF NOTHING. I PREPARE MY UNFEASIBLE SOLUTIONS FOR BIRTH.
AND WHEN THEY'VE INCUBATED AND GROWN AND DEVELOPED, I BRING THEM INTO THE WORLD. I AM A MIDWIFE OF THE IMPOSSIBLE.

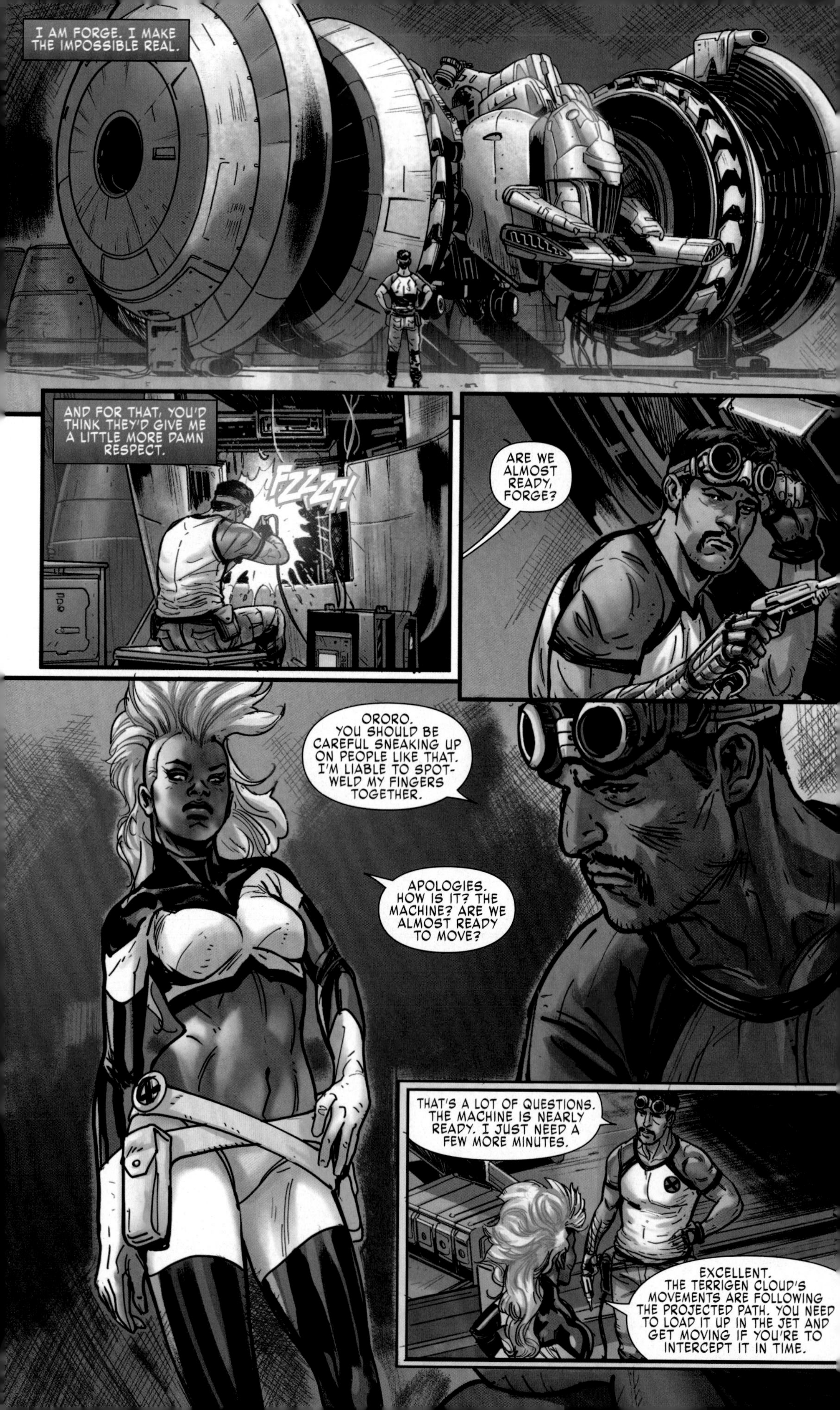

I AM FORGE. I MAKE THE IMPOSSIBLE REAL.
AND FOR THAT, YOU'D THINK THEY'D GIVE ME A LITTLE MORE DAMN RESPECT.
FZZZT!
ARE WE ALMOST READY, FORGE?
ORORO. YOU SHOULD BE CAREFUL SNEAKING UP ON PEOPLE LIKE THAT. I'M LIABLE TO SPOT-WELD MY FINGERS TOGETHER.
APOLOGIES. HOW IS IT? THE MACHINE? ARE WE ALMOST READY TO MOVE?
THAT'S A LOT OF QUESTIONS. THE MACHINE IS NEARLY READY. I JUST NEED A FEW MORE MINUTES.
EXCELLENT. THE TERRIGEN CLOUD'S MOVEMENTS ARE FOLLOWING THE PROJECTED PATH. YOU NEED TO LOAD IT UP IN THE JET AND GET MOVING IF YOU'RE TO INTERCEPT IT IN TIME.

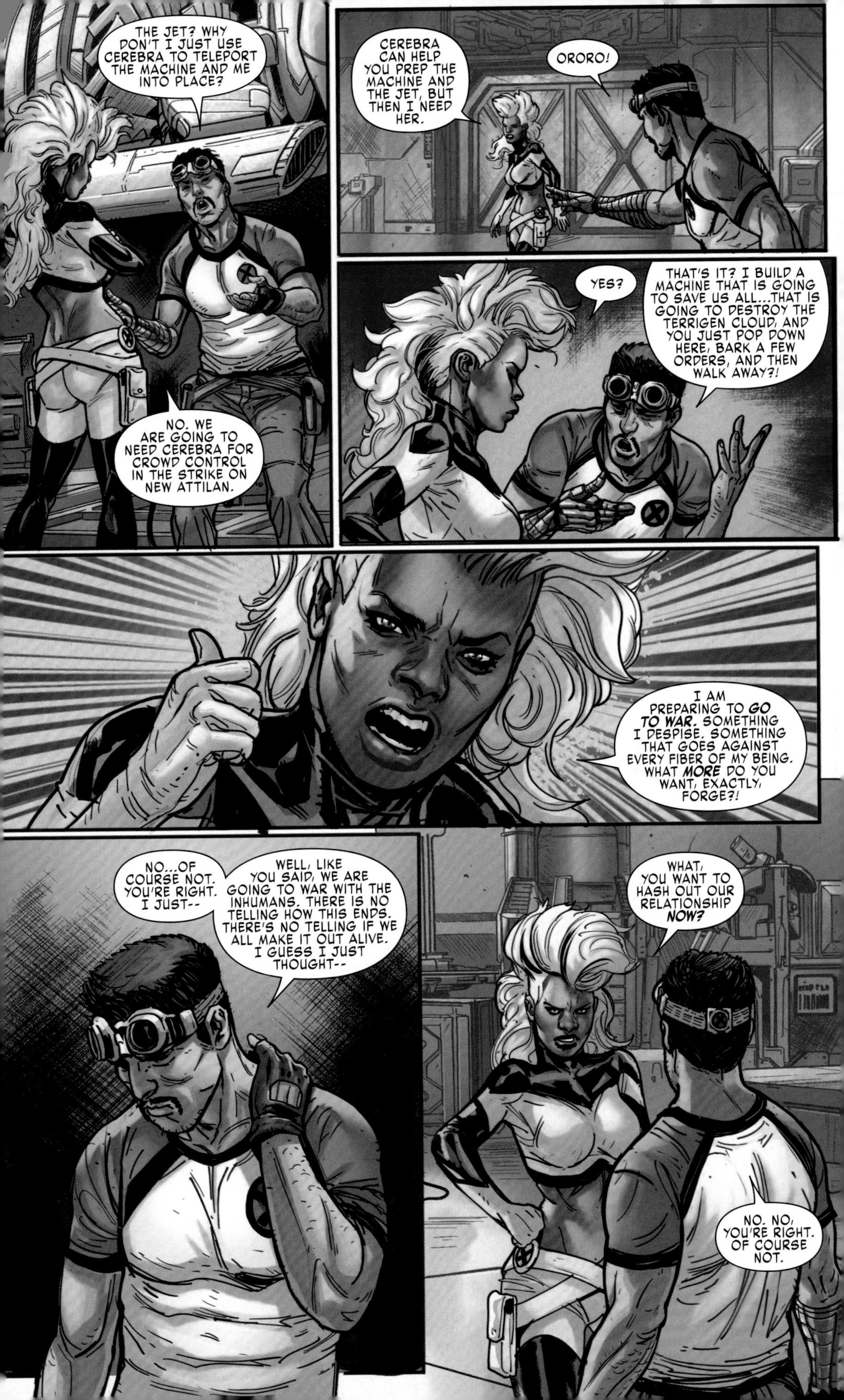
THE JET? WHY DON'T I JUST USE CEREBRA TO TELEPORT THE MACHINE AND ME INTO PLACE?
NO. WE ARE GOING TO NEED CEREBRA FOR CROWD CONTROL IN THE STRIKE ON NEW ATTILAN.
CEREBRA CAN HELP YOU PREP THE MACHINE AND THE JET, BUT THEN I NEED HER.
ORORO!
YES?
THAT'S IT? I BUILD A MACHINE THAT IS GOING TO SAVE US ALL...THAT IS GOING TO DESTROY THE TERRIGEN CLOUD, AND YOU JUST POP DOWN HERE, BARK A FEW ORDERS, AND THEN WALK AWAY?!
I AM PREPARING TO **GO TO WAR.** SOMETHING I DESPISE. SOMETHING THAT GOES AGAINST EVERY FIBER OF MY BEING. WHAT ***MORE*** DO YOU WANT, EXACTLY, FORGE?!
NO...OF COURSE NOT. YOU'RE RIGHT. I JUST--
WELL, LIKE YOU SAID, WE ARE GOING TO WAR WITH THE INHUMANS. THERE IS NO TELLING HOW THIS ENDS. THERE'S NO TELLING IF WE ALL MAKE IT OUT ALIVE. I GUESS I JUST THOUGHT--
WHAT, YOU WANT TO HASH OUT OUR RELATIONSHIP ***NOW?***
NO. NO, YOU'RE RIGHT. OF COURSE NOT.

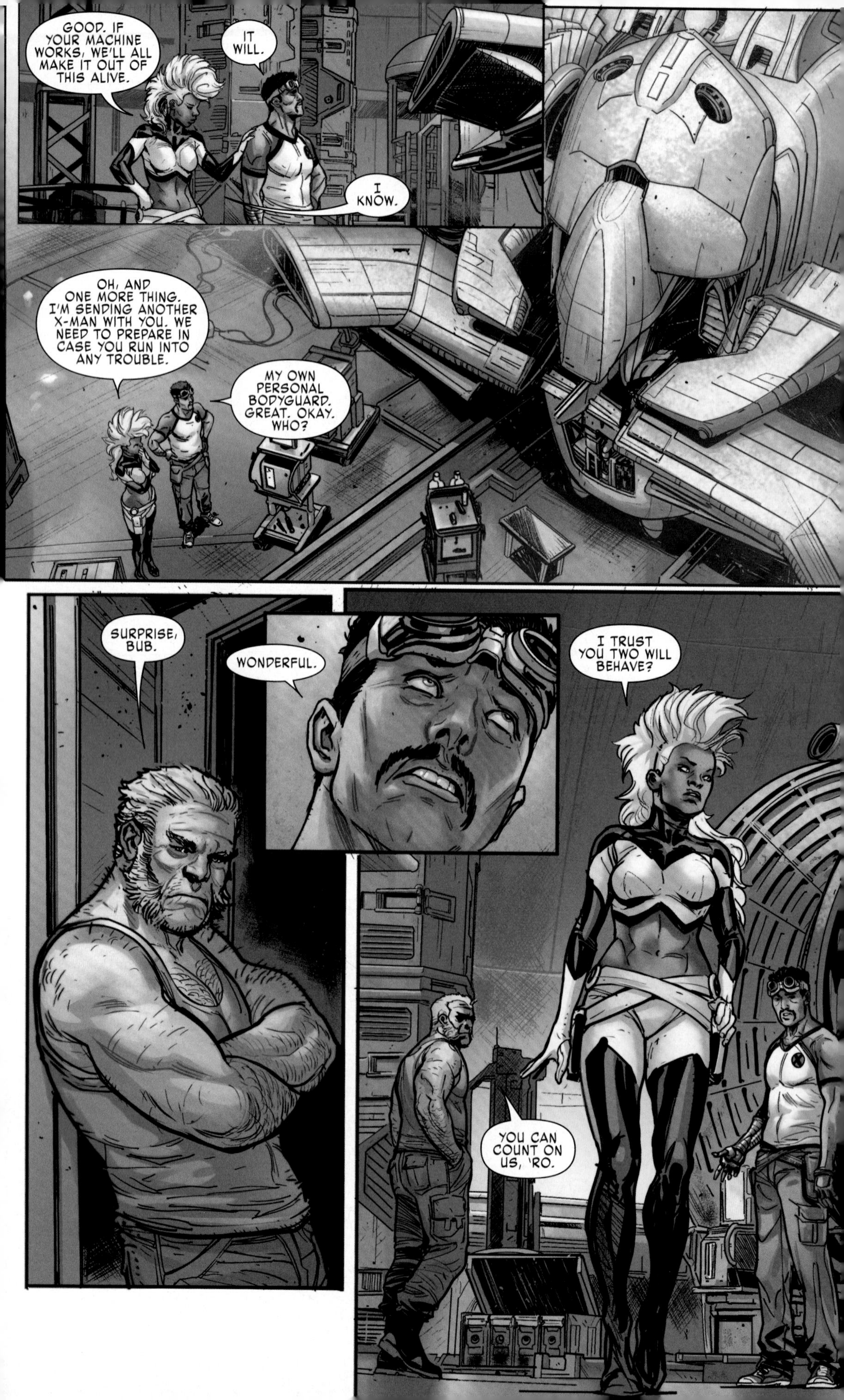
GOOD. IF YOUR MACHINE WORKS, WE'LL ALL MAKE IT OUT OF THIS ALIVE.
IT WILL.
I KNOW.
OH, AND ONE MORE THING. I'M SENDING ANOTHER X-MAN WITH YOU. WE NEED TO PREPARE IN CASE YOU RUN INTO ANY TROUBLE.
MY OWN PERSONAL BODYGUARD. GREAT. OKAY. WHO?
SURPRISE, BUB.
WONDERFUL.
I TRUST YOU TWO WILL BEHAVE?
YOU CAN COUNT ON US, 'RO.

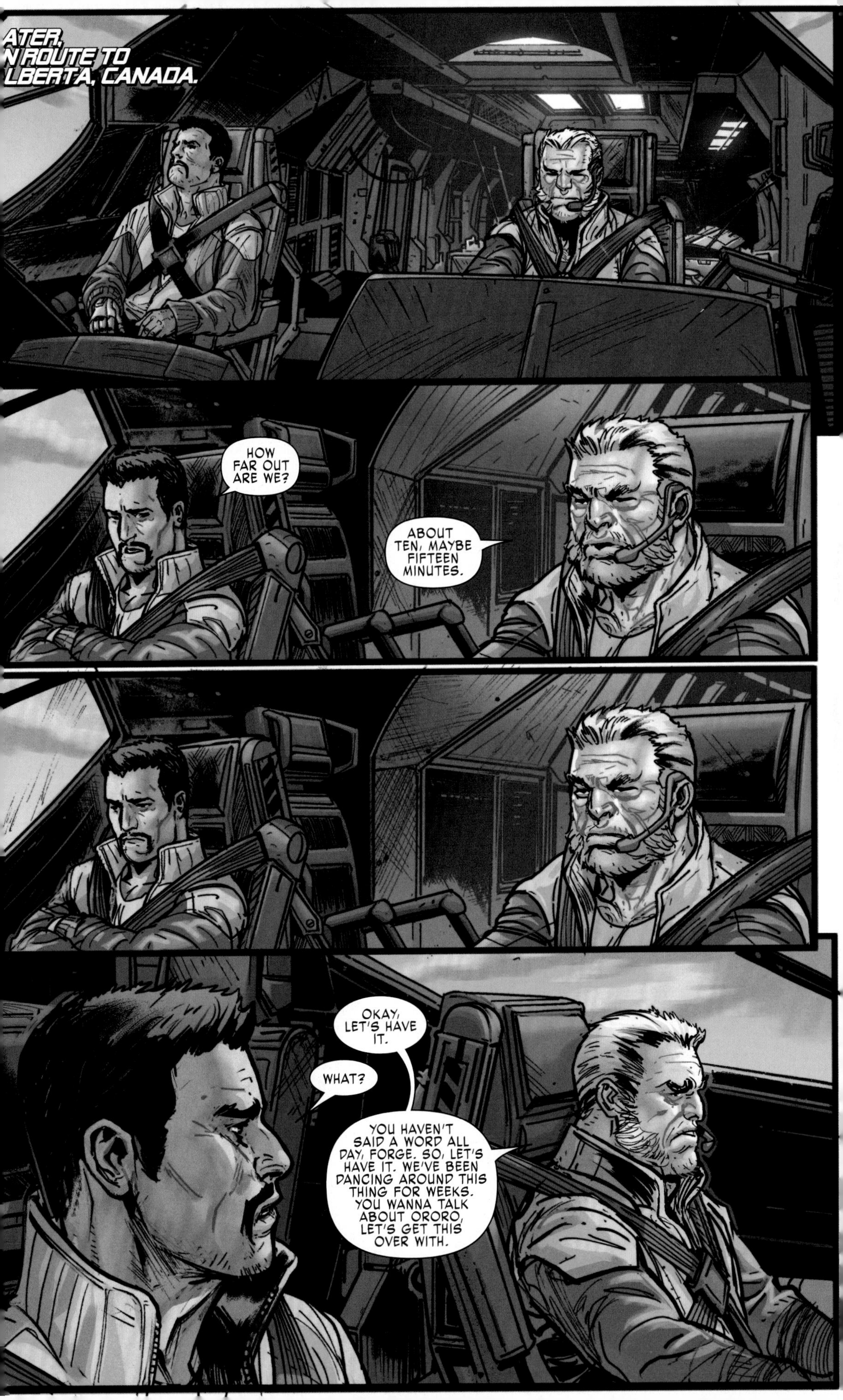
ATER, N ROUTE TO LBERTA, CANADA.
HOW FAR OUT ARE WE?
ABOUT TEN, MAYBE FIFTEEN MINUTES.
OKAY, LET'S HAVE IT.
WHAT?
YOU HAVEN'T SAID A WORD ALL DAY, FORGE. SO, LET'S HAVE IT. WE'VE BEEN DANCING AROUND THIS THING FOR WEEKS. YOU WANNA TALK ABOUT ORORO, LET'S GET THIS OVER WITH.

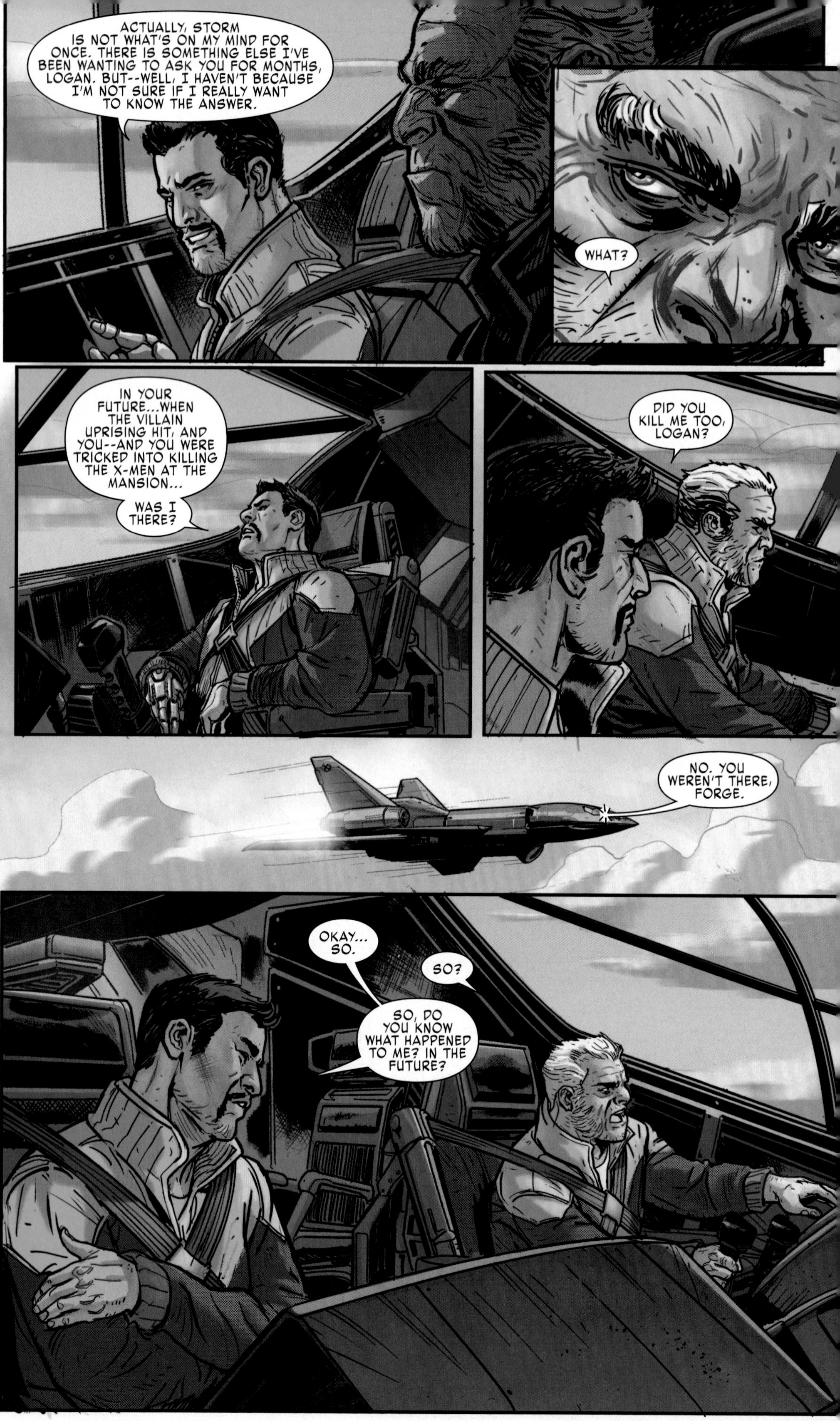
ACTUALLY, STORM IS NOT WHAT'S ON MY MIND FOR ONCE. THERE IS SOMETHING ELSE I'VE BEEN WANTING TO ASK YOU FOR MONTHS, LOGAN. BUT--WELL, I HAVEN'T BECAUSE I'M NOT SURE IF I REALLY WANT TO KNOW THE ANSWER.
WHAT?
IN YOUR FUTURE...WHEN THE VILLAIN UPRISING HIT, AND YOU--AND YOU WERE TRICKED INTO KILLING THE X-MEN AT THE MANSION...
WAS I THERE?
DID YOU KILL ME TOO, LOGAN?
NO. YOU WEREN'T THERE, FORGE.
OKAY... SO.
SO?
SO, DO YOU KNOW WHAT HAPPENED TO ME? IN THE FUTURE?

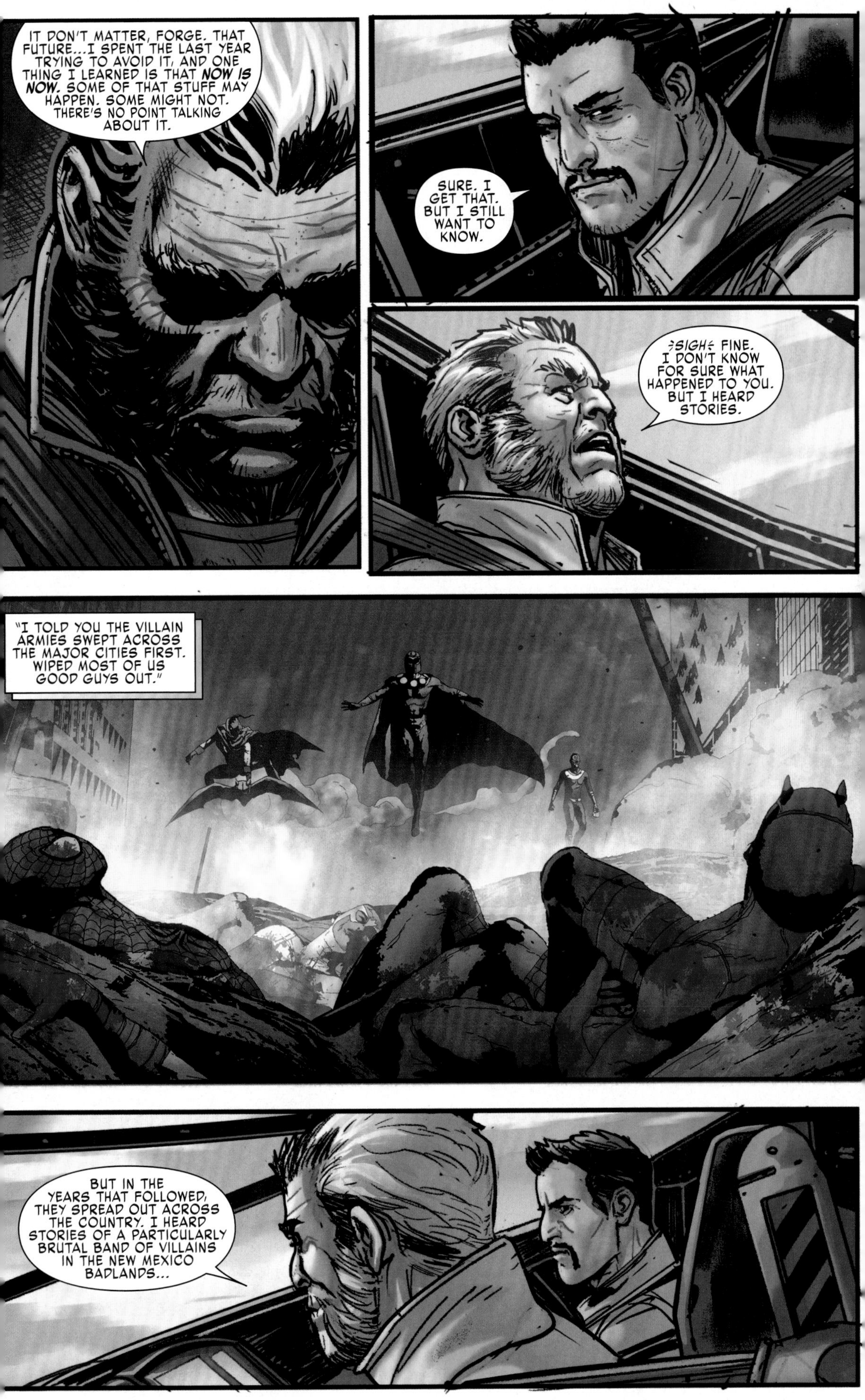
IT DON'T MATTER, FORGE. THAT FUTURE...I SPENT THE LAST YEAR TRYING TO AVOID IT, AND ONE THING I LEARNED IS THAT NOW IS NOW. SOME OF THAT STUFF MAY HAPPEN. SOME MIGHT NOT. THERE'S NO POINT TALKING ABOUT IT.
SURE. I GET THAT. BUT I STILL WANT TO KNOW.
SIGH FINE. I DON'T KNOW FOR SURE WHAT HAPPENED TO YOU. BUT I HEARD STORIES.
"I TOLD YOU THE VILLAIN ARMIES SWEPT ACROSS THE MAJOR CITIES FIRST. WIPED MOST OF US GOOD GUYS OUT."
BUT IN THE YEARS THAT FOLLOWED, THEY SPREAD OUT ACROSS THE COUNTRY. I HEARD STORIES OF A PARTICULARLY BRUTAL BAND OF VILLAINS IN THE NEW MEXICO BADLANDS...

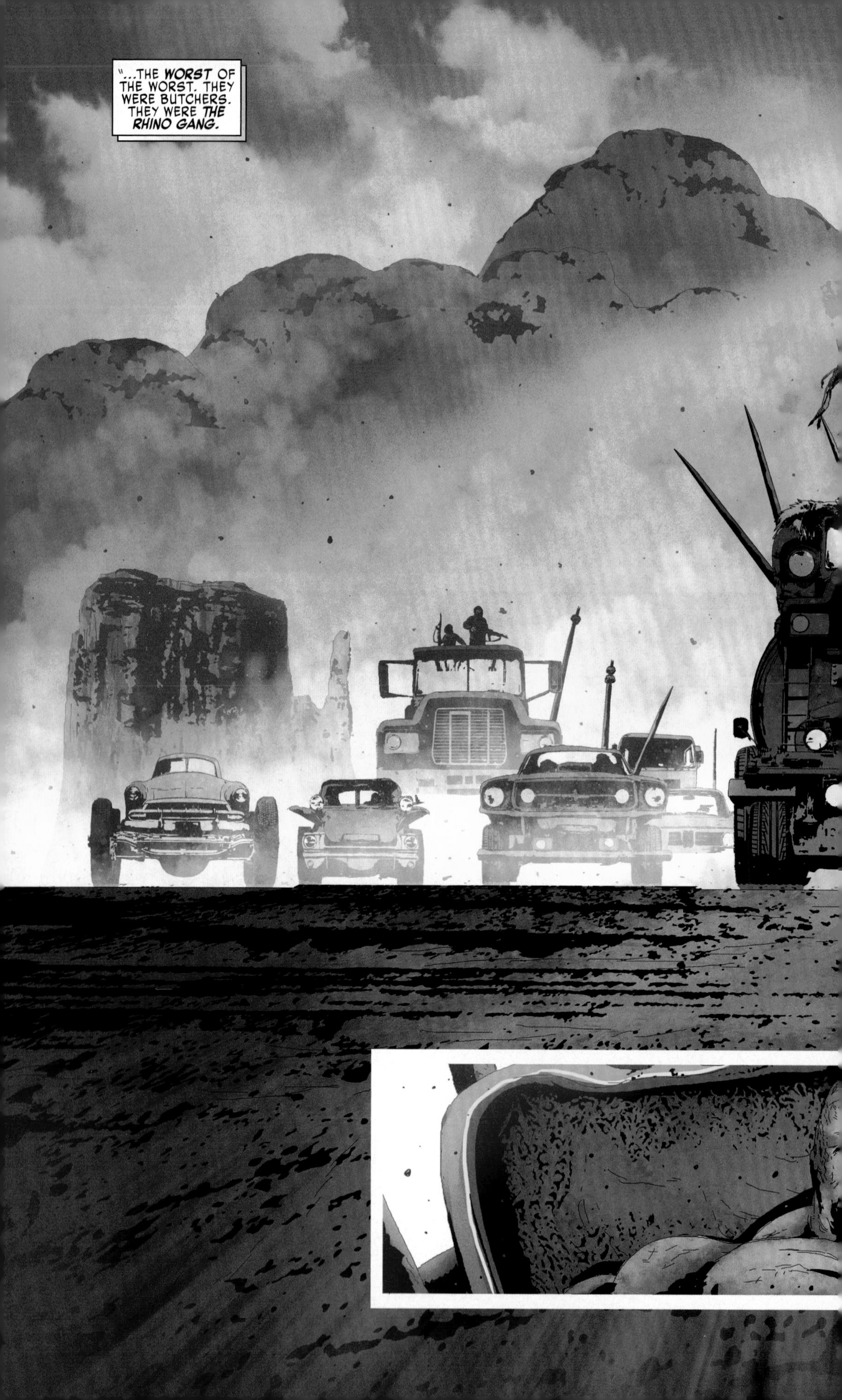
"...THE *WORST* OF THE WORST. THEY WERE BUTCHERS. THEY WERE *THE RHINO GANG*.

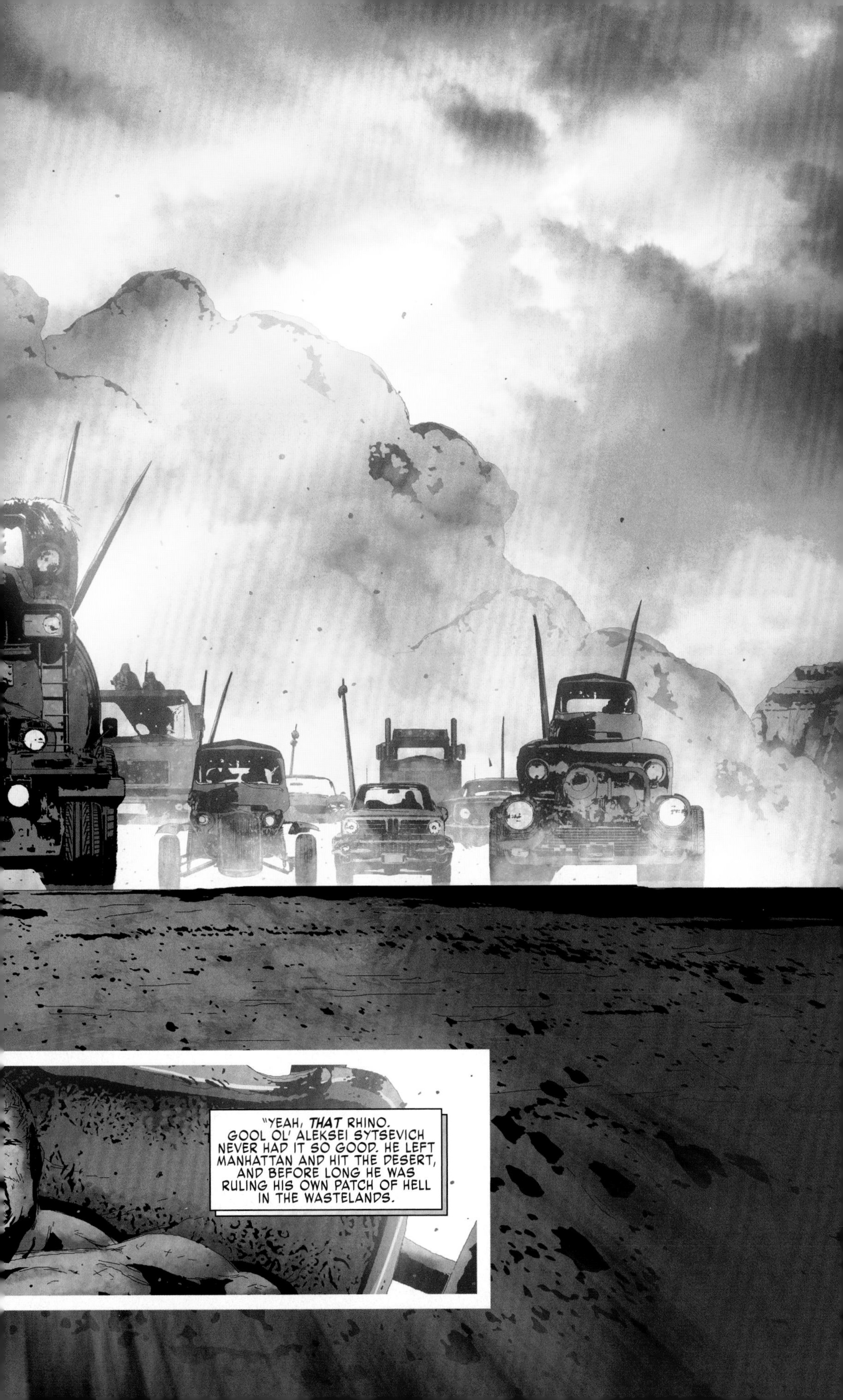
"YEAH, *THAT* RHINO. GOOL OL' ALEKSEI SYTSEVICH NEVER HAD IT SO GOOD. HE LEFT MANHATTAN AND HIT THE DESERT, AND BEFORE LONG HE WAS RULING HIS OWN PATCH OF HELL IN THE WASTELANDS.

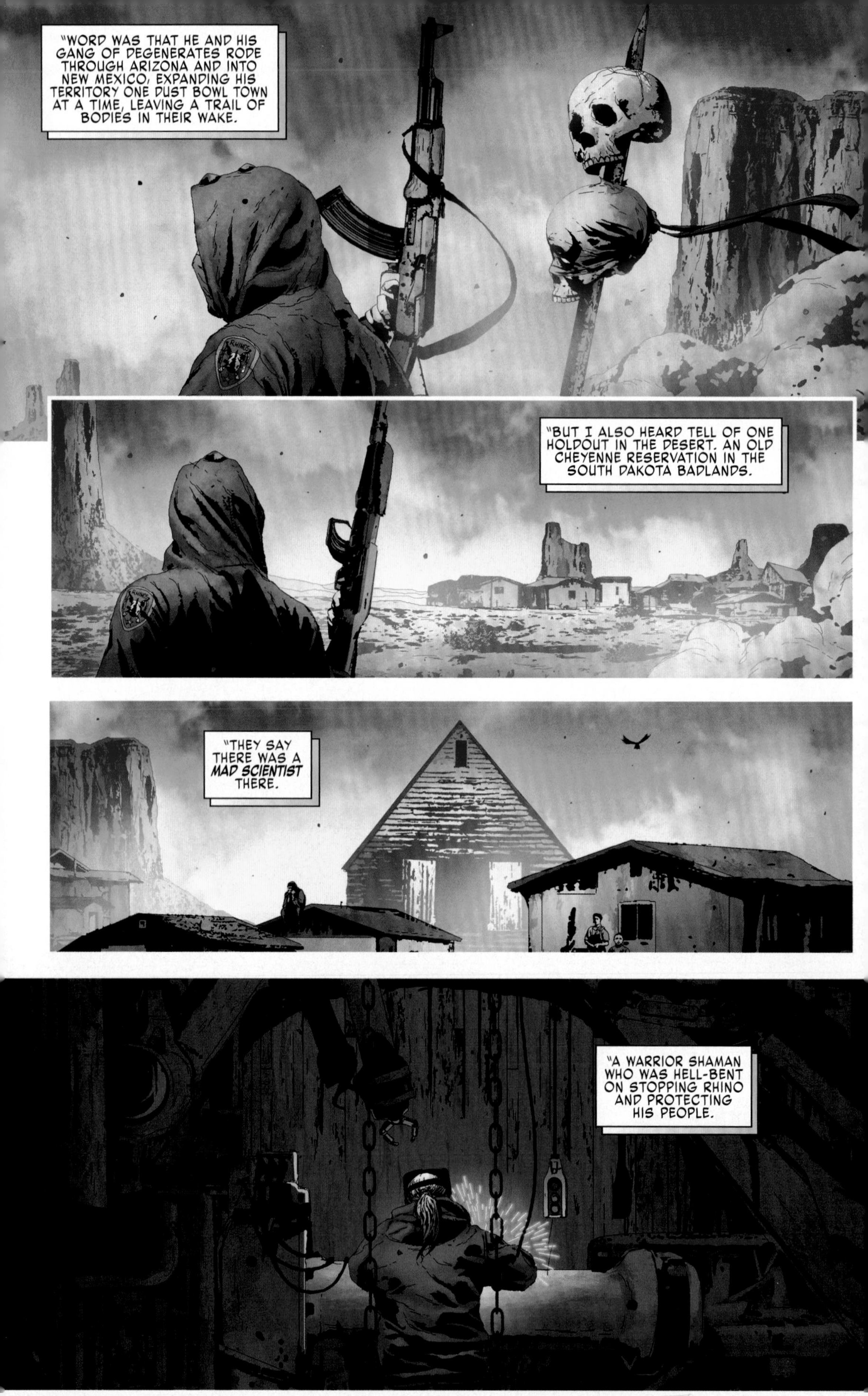
"WORD WAS THAT HE AND HIS GANG OF DEGENERATES RODE THROUGH ARIZONA AND INTO NEW MEXICO, EXPANDING HIS TERRITORY ONE DUST BOWL TOWN AT A TIME, LEAVING A TRAIL OF BODIES IN THEIR WAKE.
"BUT I ALSO HEARD TELL OF ONE HOLDOUT IN THE DESERT. AN OLD CHEYENNE RESERVATION IN THE SOUTH DAKOTA BADLANDS.
"THEY SAY THERE WAS A *MAD SCIENTIST* THERE.
"A WARRIOR SHAMAN WHO WAS HELL-BENT ON STOPPING RHINO AND PROTECTING HIS PEOPLE.

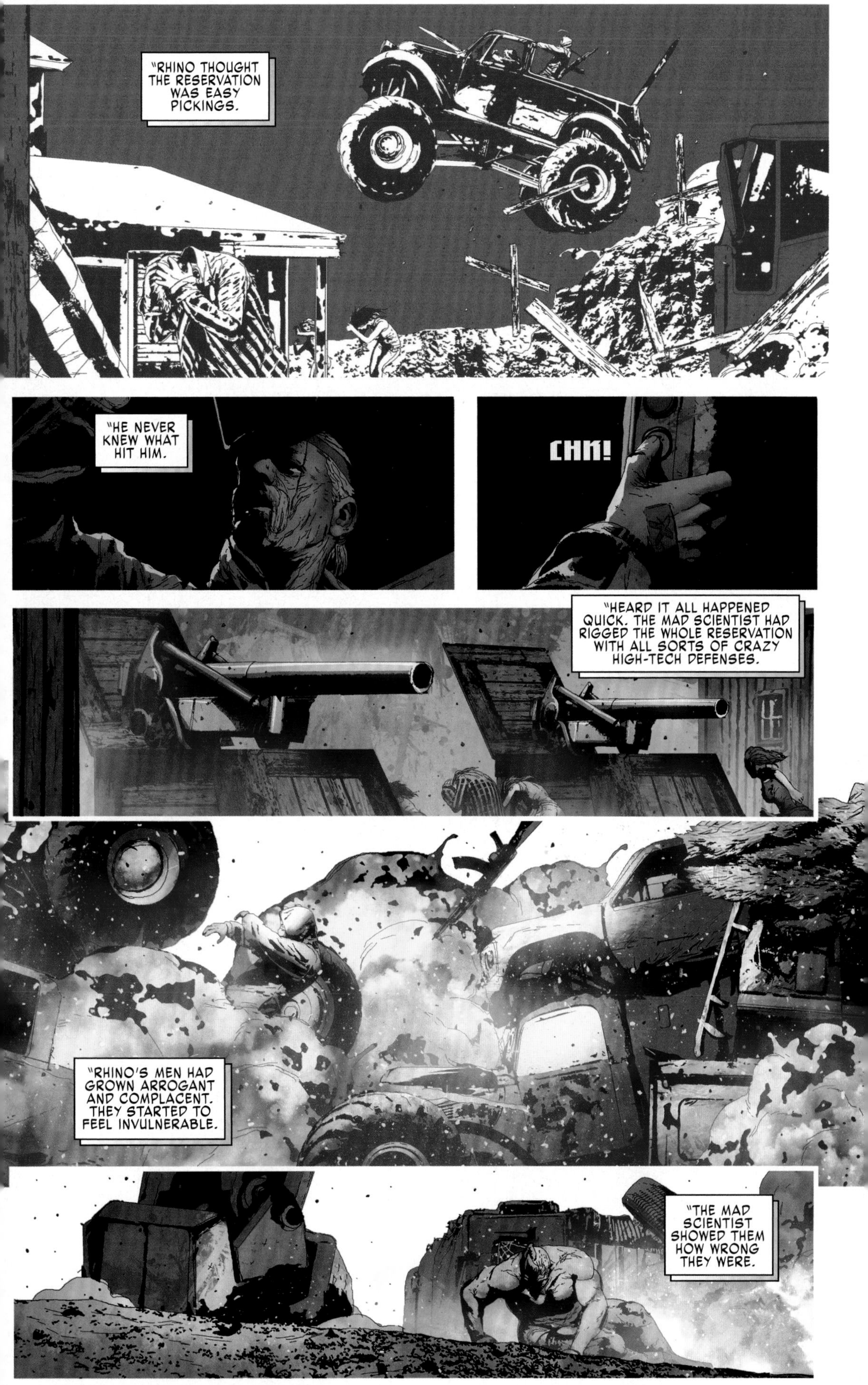
"RHINO THOUGHT THE RESERVATION WAS EASY PICKINGS.
"HE NEVER KNEW WHAT HIT HIM.
CHK!
"HEARD IT ALL HAPPENED QUICK. THE MAD SCIENTIST HAD RIGGED THE WHOLE RESERVATION WITH ALL SORTS OF CRAZY HIGH-TECH DEFENSES.
"RHINO'S MEN HAD GROWN ARROGANT AND COMPLACENT. THEY STARTED TO FEEL INVULNERABLE.
"THE MAD SCIENTIST SHOWED THEM HOW WRONG THEY WERE.

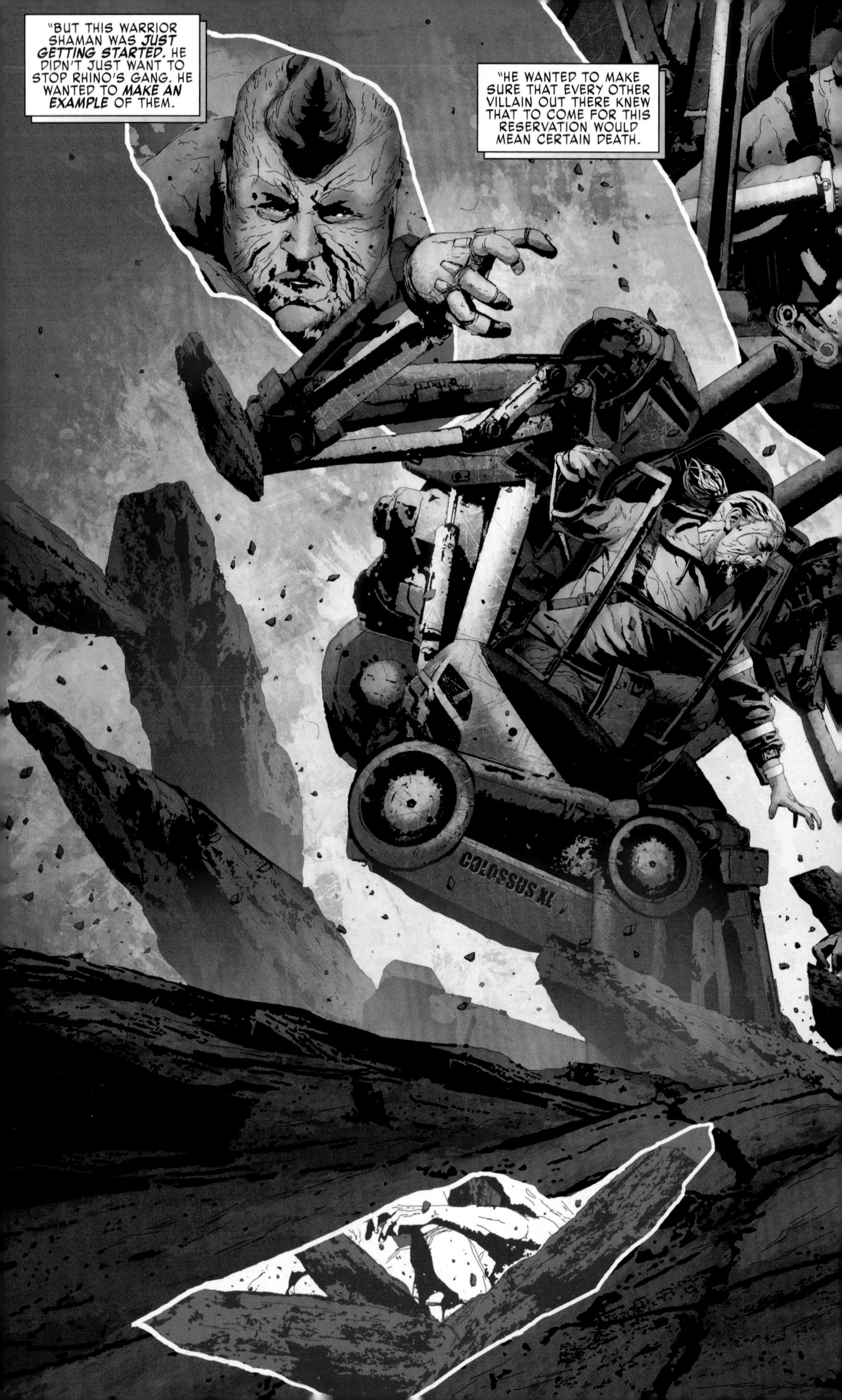
"BUT THIS WARRIOR SHAMAN WAS ***JUST GETTING STARTED.*** HE DIDN'T JUST WANT TO STOP RHINO'S GANG. HE WANTED TO ***MAKE AN EXAMPLE*** OF THEM.
"HE WANTED TO MAKE SURE THAT EVERY OTHER VILLAIN OUT THERE KNEW THAT TO COME FOR THIS RESERVATION WOULD MEAN CERTAIN DEATH.

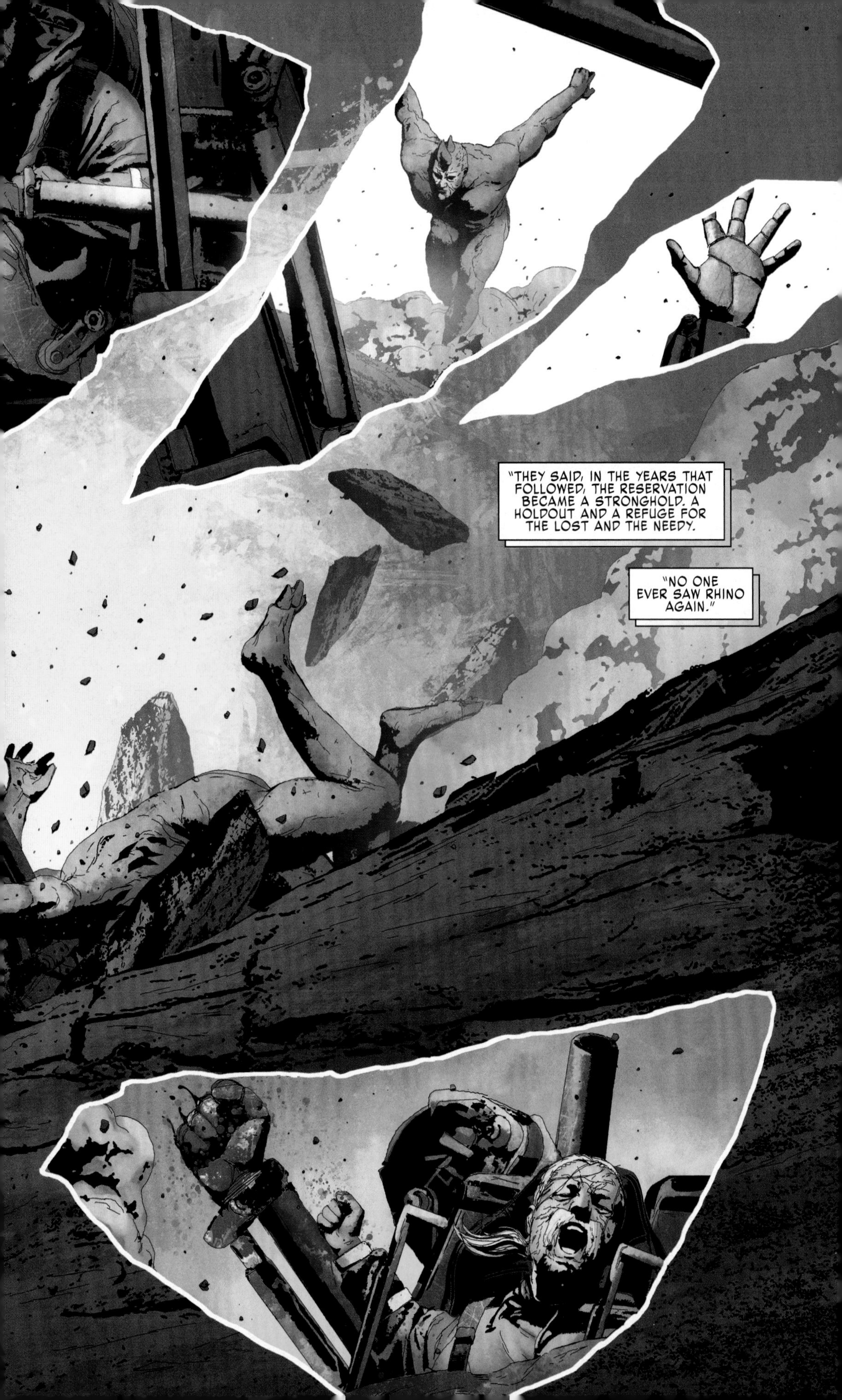
"THEY SAID, IN THE YEARS THAT FOLLOWED, THE RESERVATION BECAME A STRONGHOLD. A HOLDOUT AND A REFUGE FOR THE LOST AND THE NEEDY.
"NO ONE EVER SAW RHINO AGAIN."

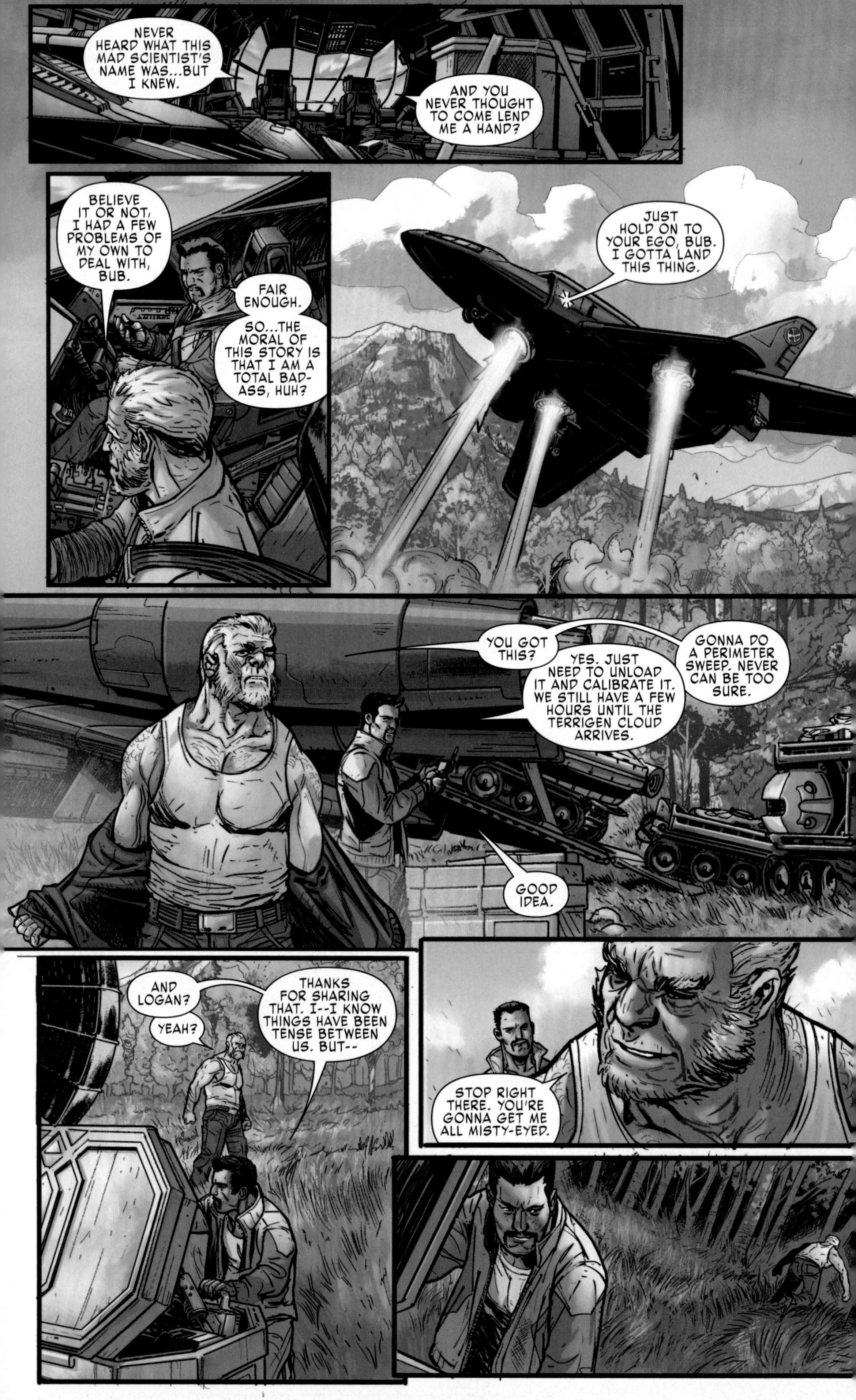
NEVER HEARD WHAT THIS MAD SCIENTIST'S NAME WAS...BUT I KNEW.
AND YOU NEVER THOUGHT TO COME LEND ME A HAND?
BELIEVE IT OR NOT, I HAD A FEW PROBLEMS OF MY OWN TO DEAL WITH, BUB.
FAIR ENOUGH.
SO...THE MORAL OF THIS STORY IS THAT I AM A TOTAL BAD-ASS, HUH?
JUST HOLD ON TO YOUR EGO, BUB. I GOTTA LAND THIS THING.
YOU GOT THIS?
YES. JUST NEED TO UNLOAD IT AND CALIBRATE IT. WE STILL HAVE A FEW HOURS UNTIL THE TERRIGEN CLOUD ARRIVES.
GONNA DO A PERIMETER SWEEP. NEVER CAN BE TOO SURE.
GOOD IDEA.
AND LOGAN?
YEAH?
THANKS FOR SHARING THAT. I--I KNOW THINGS HAVE BEEN TENSE BETWEEN US. BUT--
STOP RIGHT THERE. YOU'RE GONNA GET ME ALL MISTY-EYED.

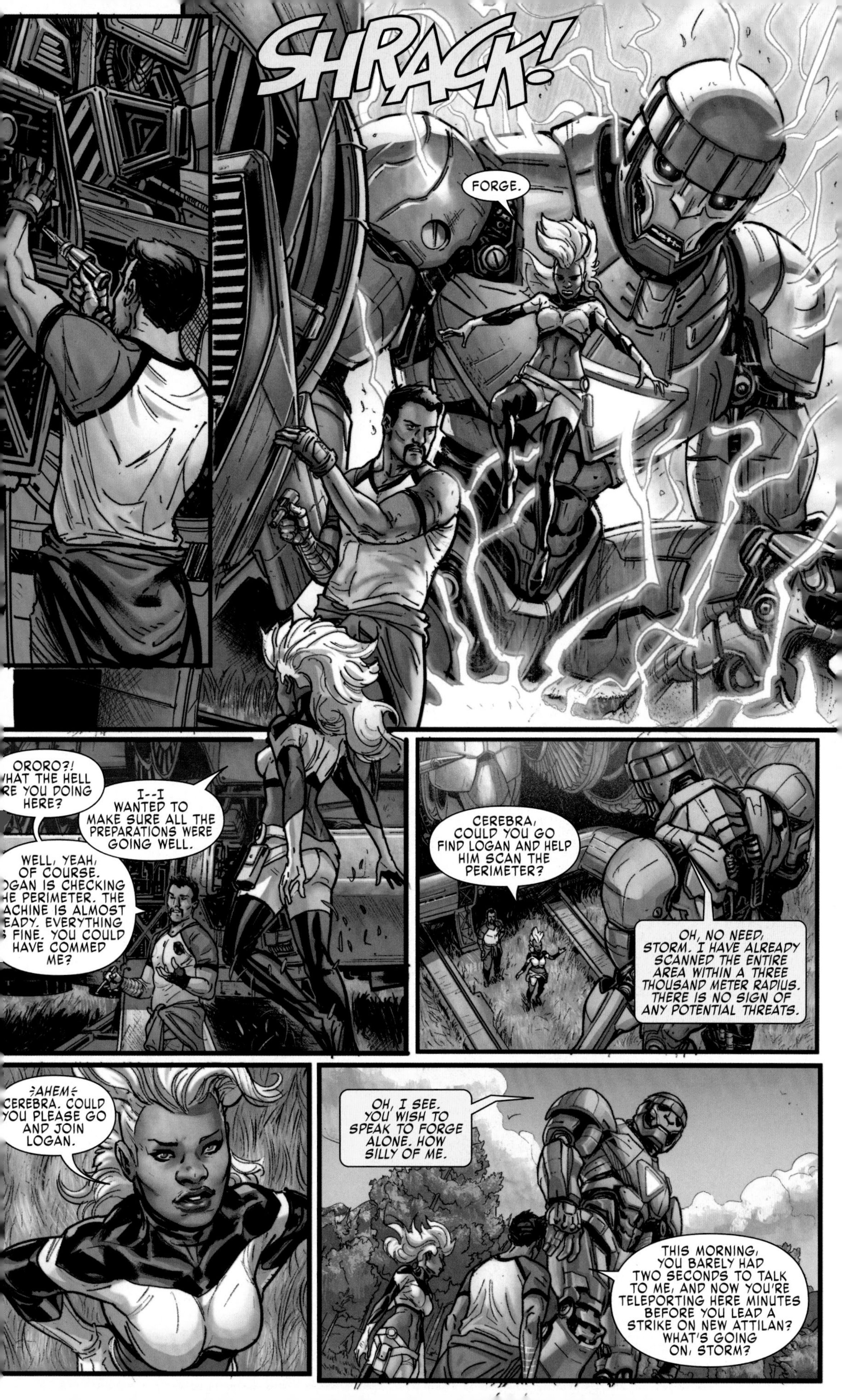
SHRACK!
FORGE.
ORORO?! WHAT THE HELL ARE YOU DOING HERE?
I--I WANTED TO MAKE SURE ALL THE PREPARATIONS WERE GOING WELL.
WELL, YEAH, OF COURSE. LOGAN IS CHECKING THE PERIMETER. THE MACHINE IS ALMOST READY. EVERYTHING IS FINE. YOU COULD HAVE COMMED ME?
CEREBRA, COULD YOU GO FIND LOGAN AND HELP HIM SCAN THE PERIMETER?
OH, NO NEED, STORM. I HAVE ALREADY SCANNED THE ENTIRE AREA WITHIN A THREE THOUSAND METER RADIUS. THERE IS NO SIGN OF ANY POTENTIAL THREATS.
AHEM CEREBRA. COULD YOU PLEASE GO AND JOIN LOGAN.
OH, I SEE. YOU WISH TO SPEAK TO FORGE ALONE. HOW SILLY OF ME.
THIS MORNING, YOU BARELY HAD TWO SECONDS TO TALK TO ME, AND NOW YOU'RE TELEPORTING HERE MINUTES BEFORE YOU LEAD A STRIKE ON NEW ATTILAN? WHAT'S GOING ON, STORM?

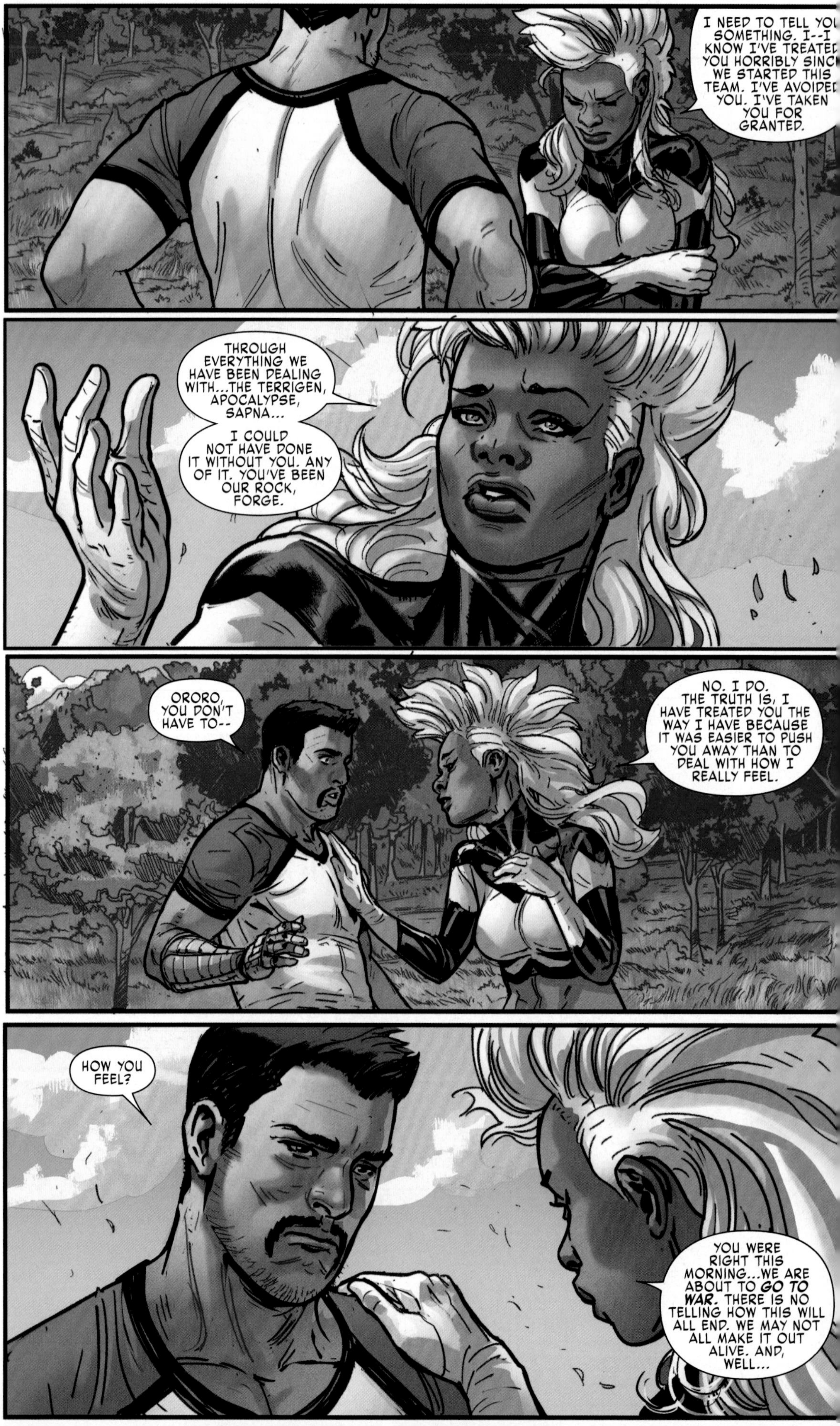
I NEED TO TELL YO SOMETHING. I--I KNOW I'VE TREATE YOU HORRIBLY SINC WE STARTED THIS TEAM. I'VE AVOIDE YOU. I'VE TAKEN YOU FOR GRANTED.
THROUGH EVERYTHING WE HAVE BEEN DEALING WITH...THE TERRIGEN, APOCALYPSE, SAPNA...
I COULD NOT HAVE DONE IT WITHOUT YOU. ANY OF IT. YOU'VE BEEN OUR ROCK, FORGE.
ORORO, YOU DON'T HAVE TO--
NO. I DO. THE TRUTH IS, I HAVE TREATED YOU THE WAY I HAVE BECAUSE IT WAS EASIER TO PUSH YOU AWAY THAN TO DEAL WITH HOW I REALLY FEEL.
HOW YOU FEEL?
YOU WERE RIGHT THIS MORNING...WE ARE ABOUT TO GO TO WAR. THERE IS NO TELLING HOW THIS WILL ALL END. WE MAY NOT ALL MAKE IT OUT ALIVE. AND, WELL...

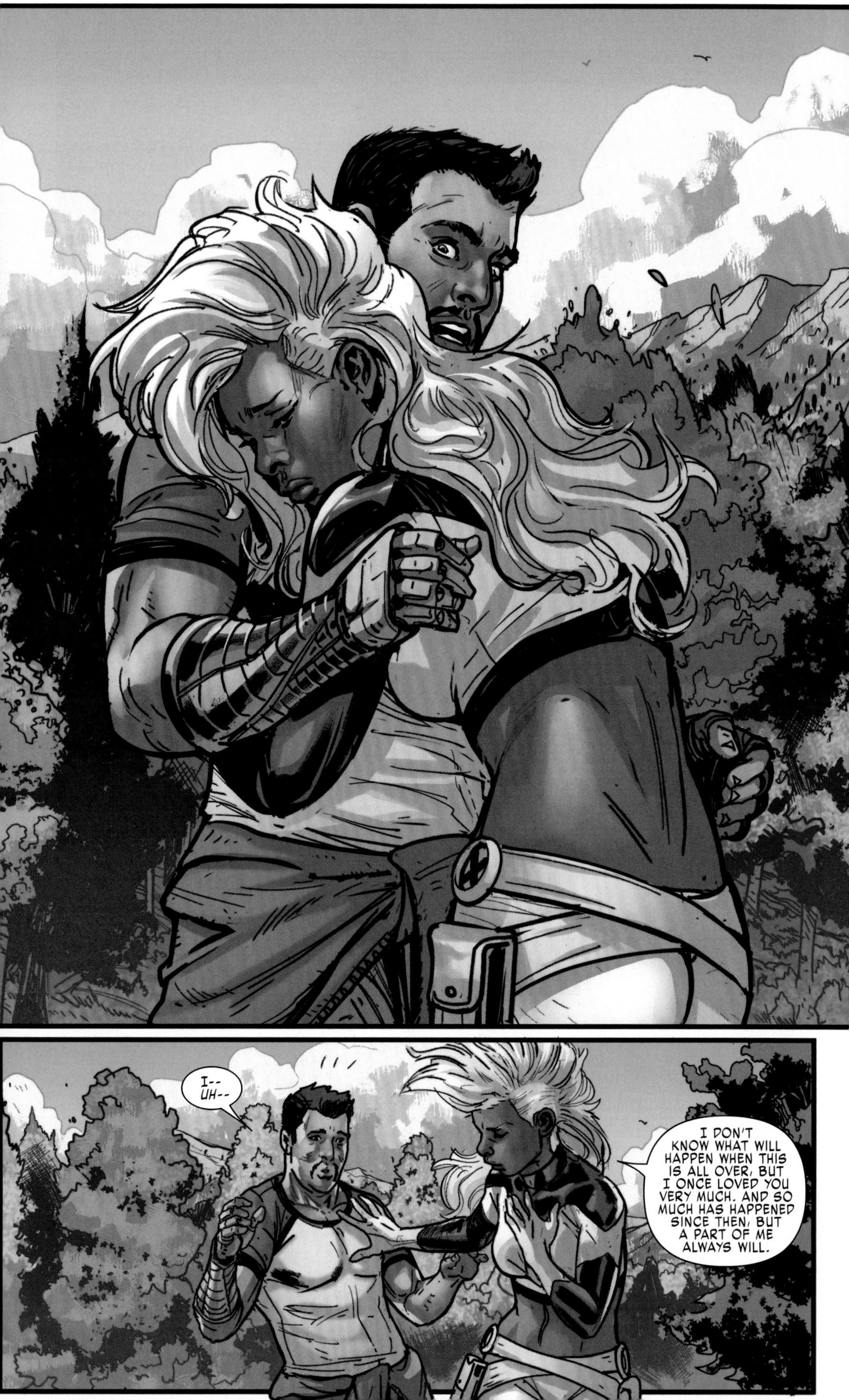
I-- UH--
I DON'T KNOW WHAT WILL HAPPEN WHEN THIS IS ALL OVER, BUT I ONCE LOVED YOU VERY MUCH. AND SO MUCH HAS HAPPENED SINCE THEN, BUT A PART OF ME ALWAYS WILL.

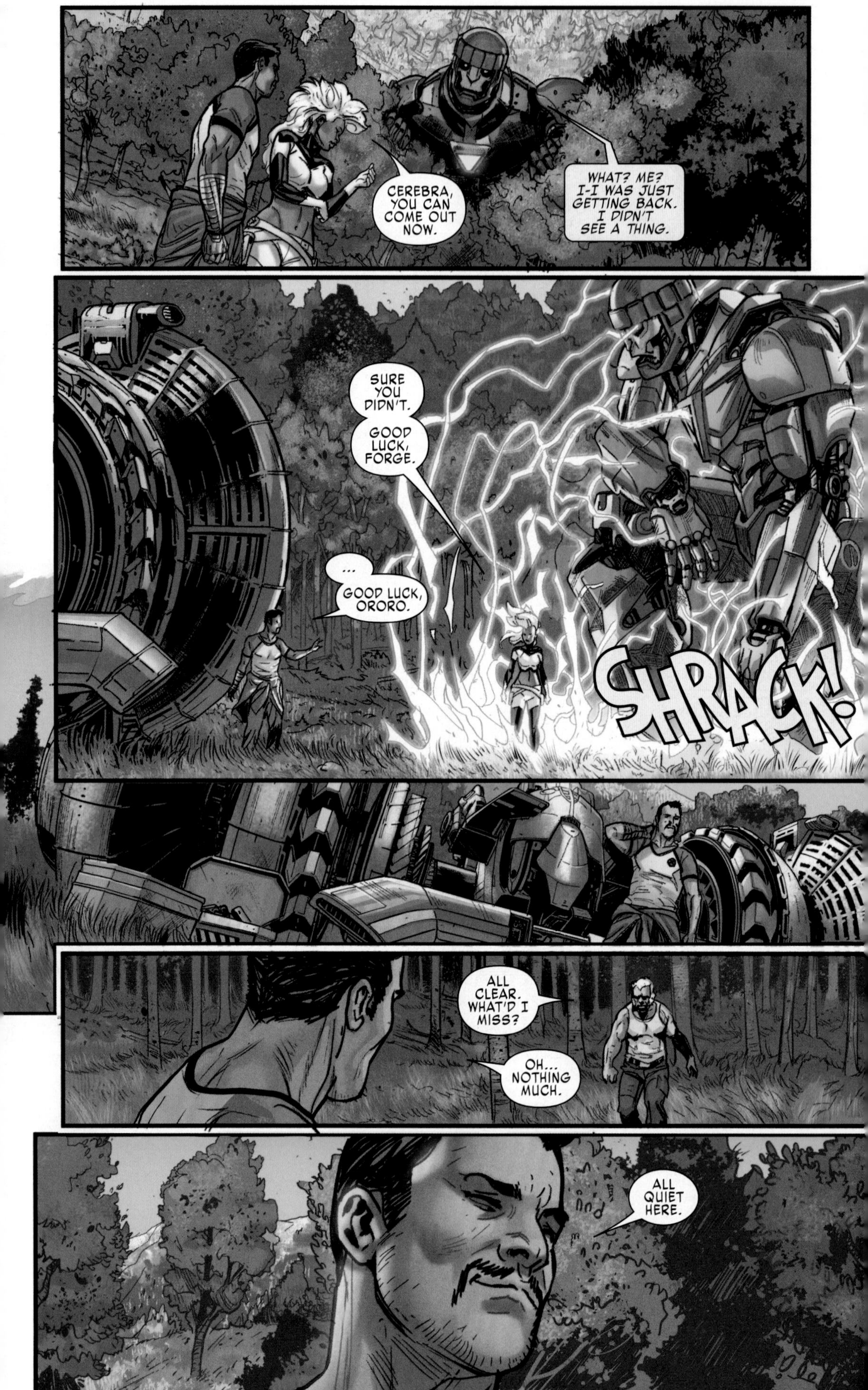
CEREBRA, YOU CAN COME OUT NOW.
WHAT? ME? I-I WAS JUST GETTING BACK. I DIDN'T SEE A THING.
SURE YOU DIDN'T.
GOOD LUCK, FORGE.
... GOOD LUCK, ORORO.
SHRACK!
ALL CLEAR. WHAT'D I MISS?
OH... NOTHING MUCH.
ALL QUIET HERE.

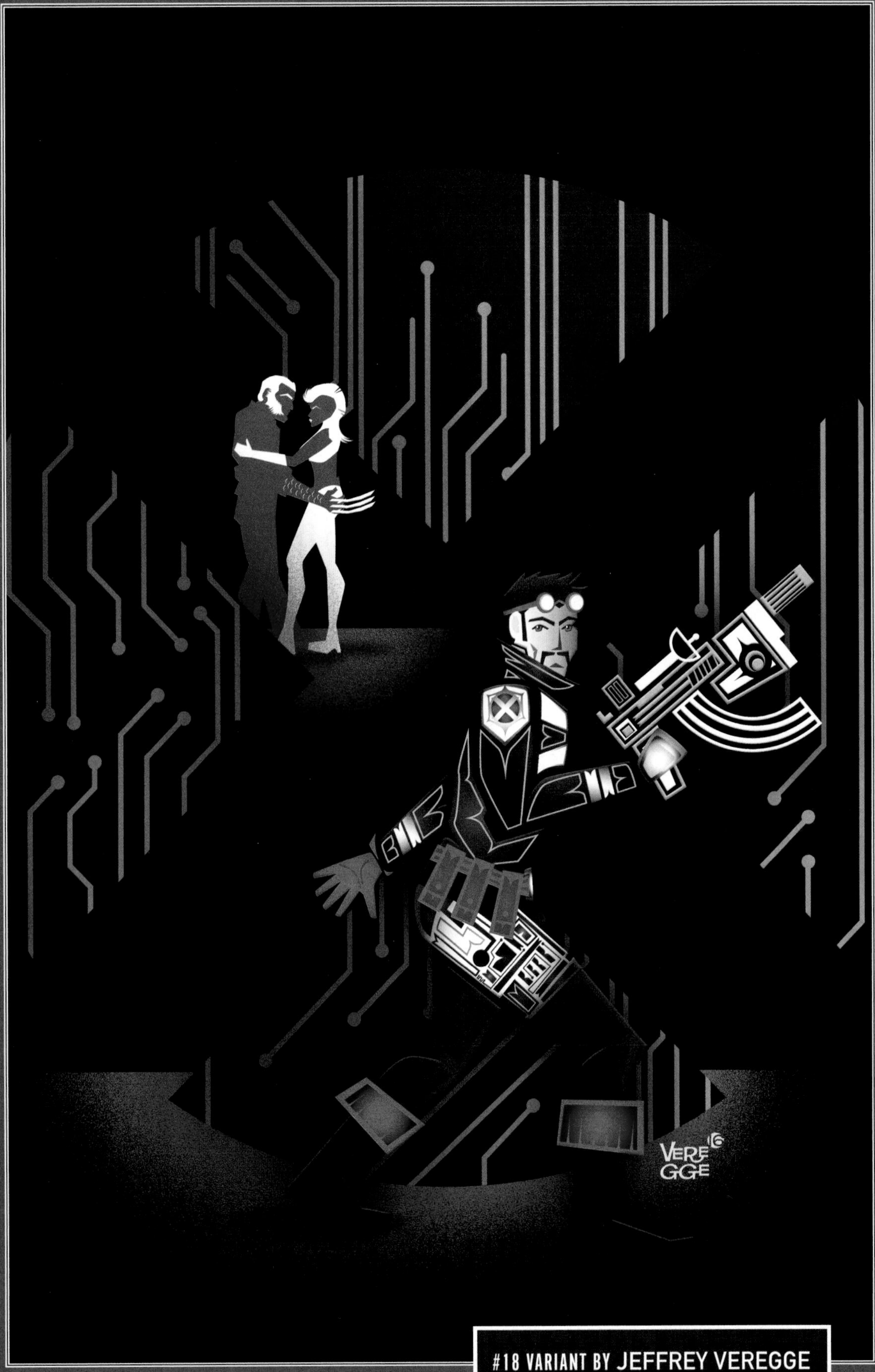
VEREGGE 16

#18 VARIANT BY JEFFREY VEREGGE

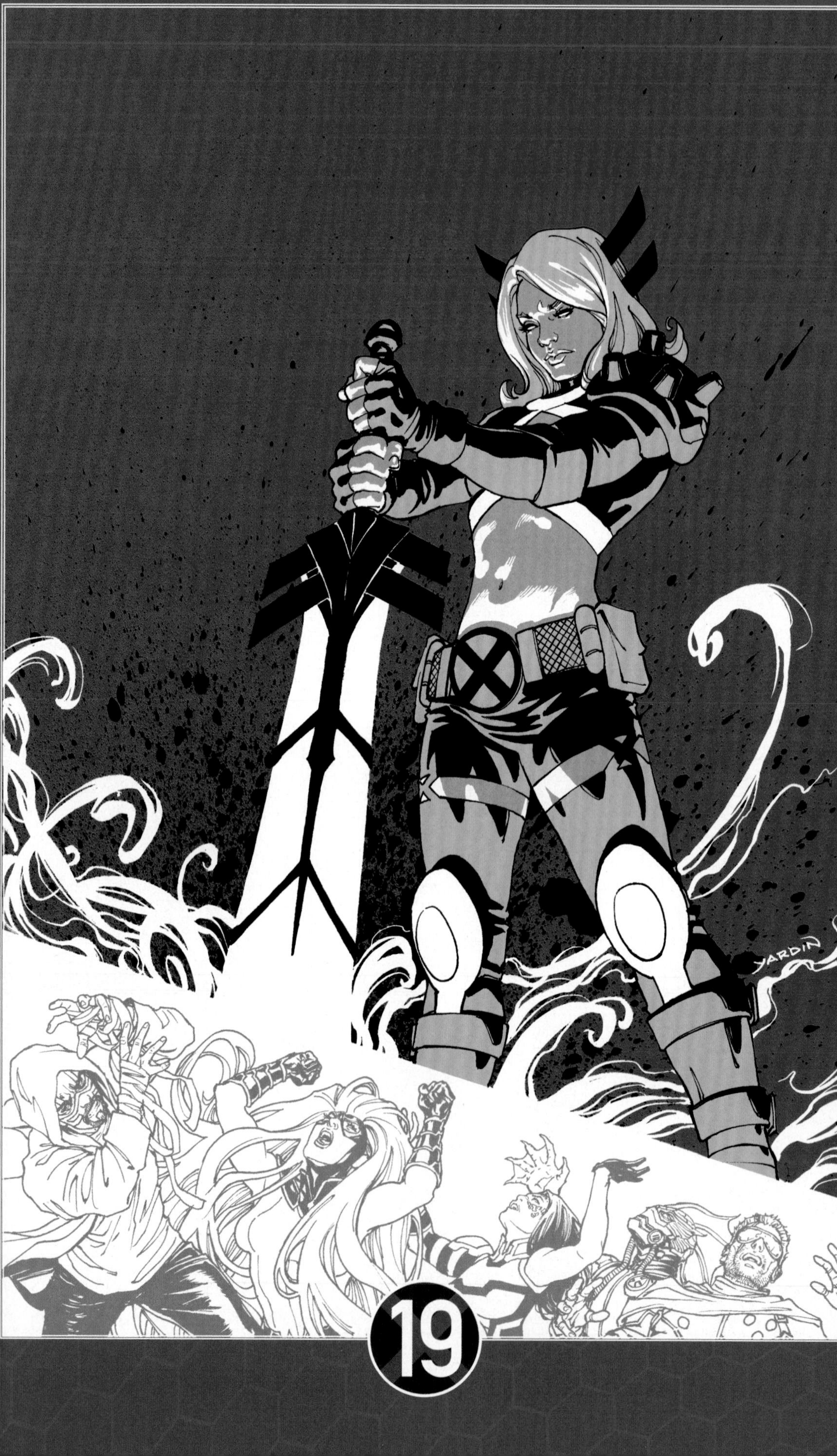
YARDIN
19

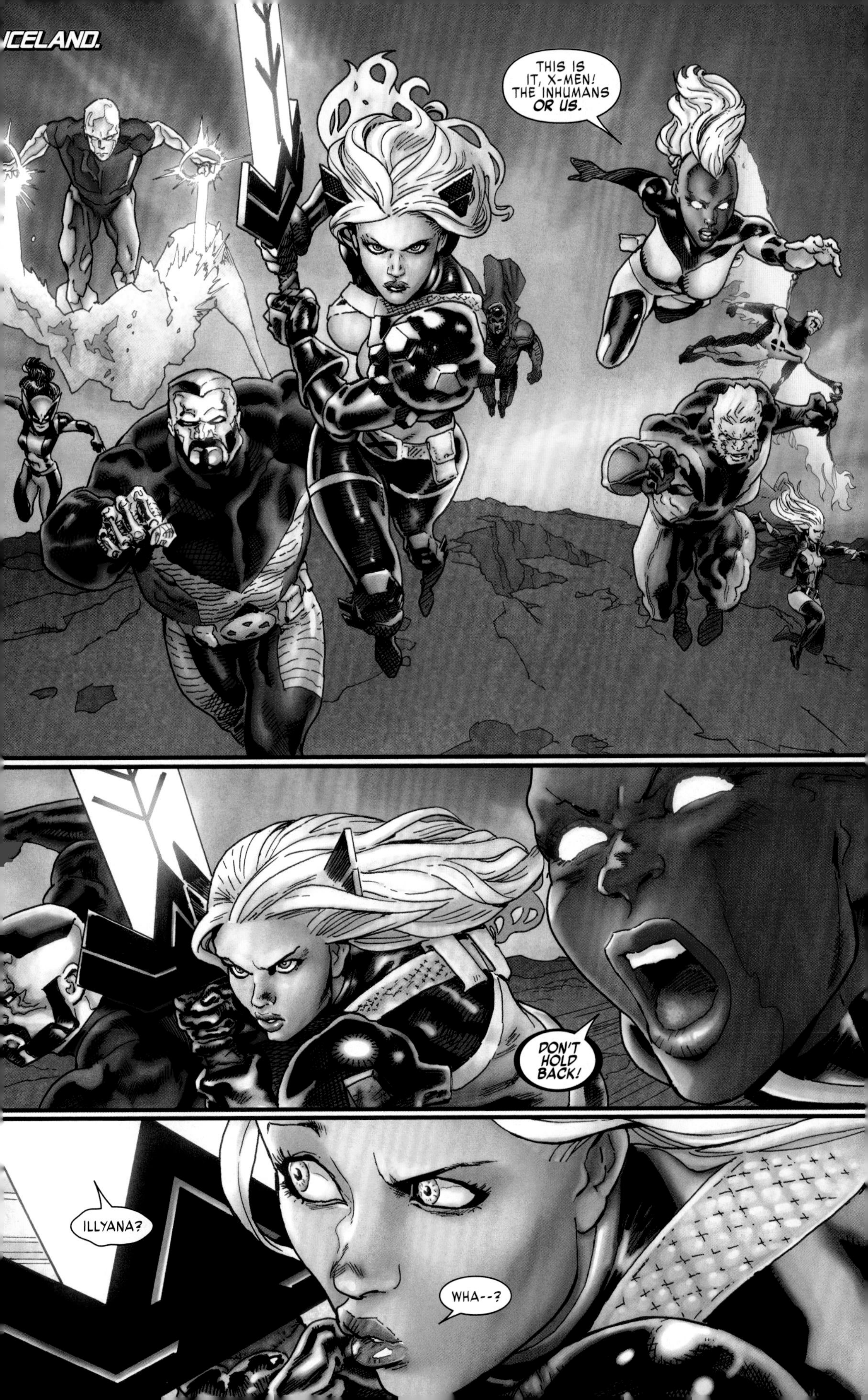

ICELAND.
THIS IS IT, X-MEN! THE INHUMANS OR US.
DON'T HOLD BACK!
ILLYANA?
WHA--?

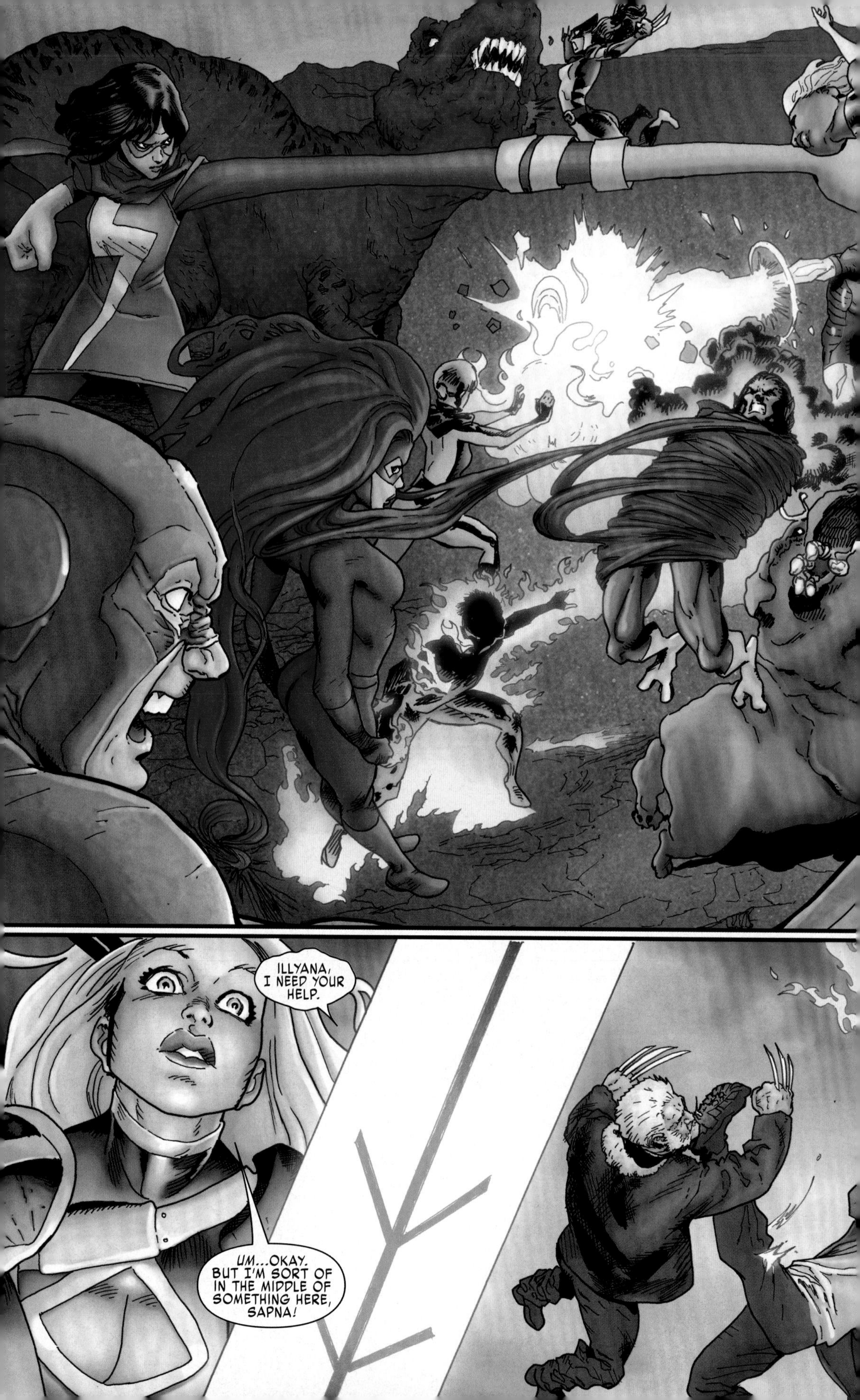
ILLYANA, I NEED YOUR HELP.
UM...OKAY. BUT I'M SORT OF IN THE MIDDLE OF SOMETHING HERE, SAPNA!

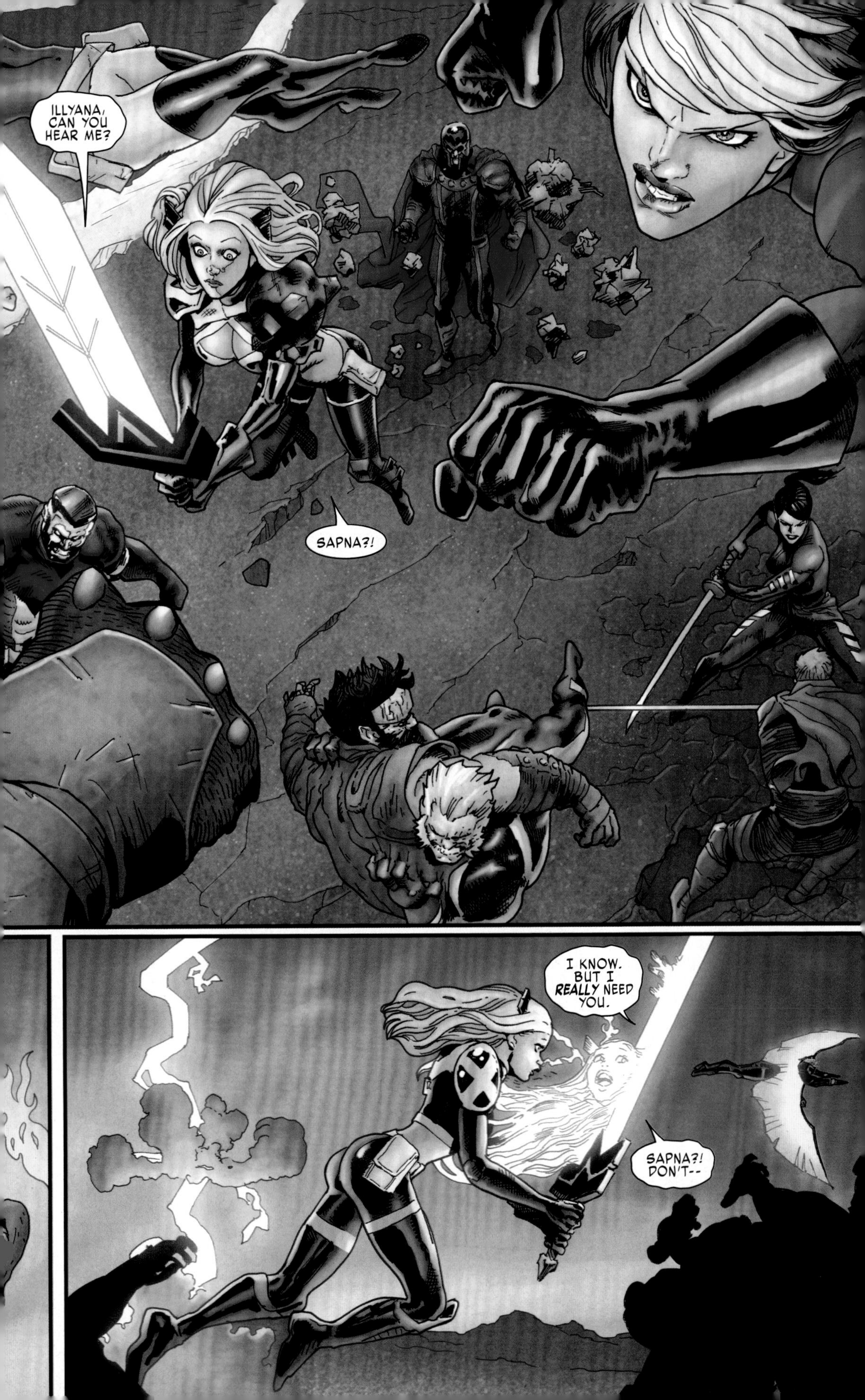
ILLYANA, CAN YOU HEAR ME?
SAPNA?!
I KNOW. BUT I *REALLY* NEED YOU.
SAPNA?! DON'T--

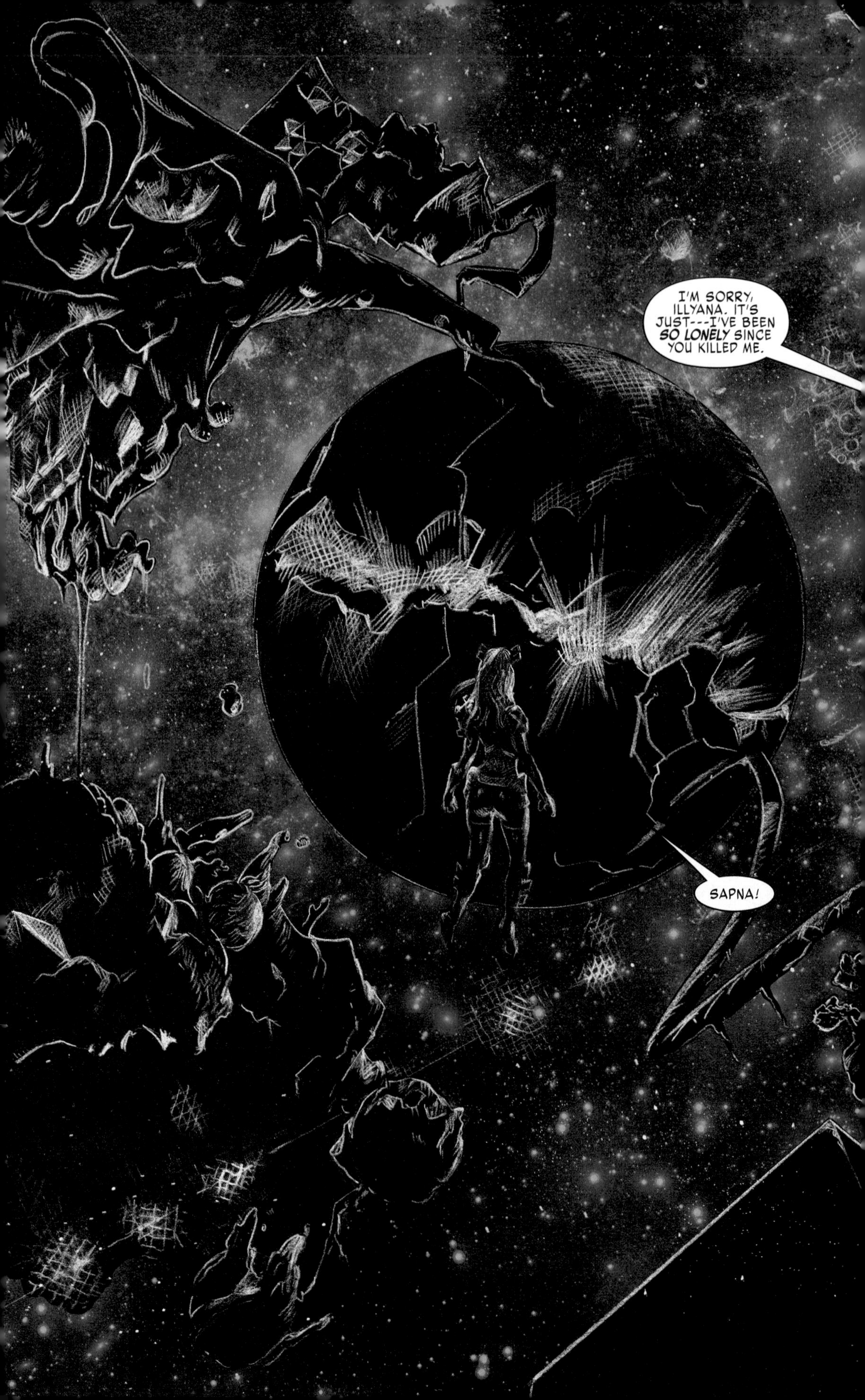
I'M SORRY, ILLYANA. IT'S JUST---I'VE BEEN SO LONELY SINCE YOU KILLED ME.
SAPNA!

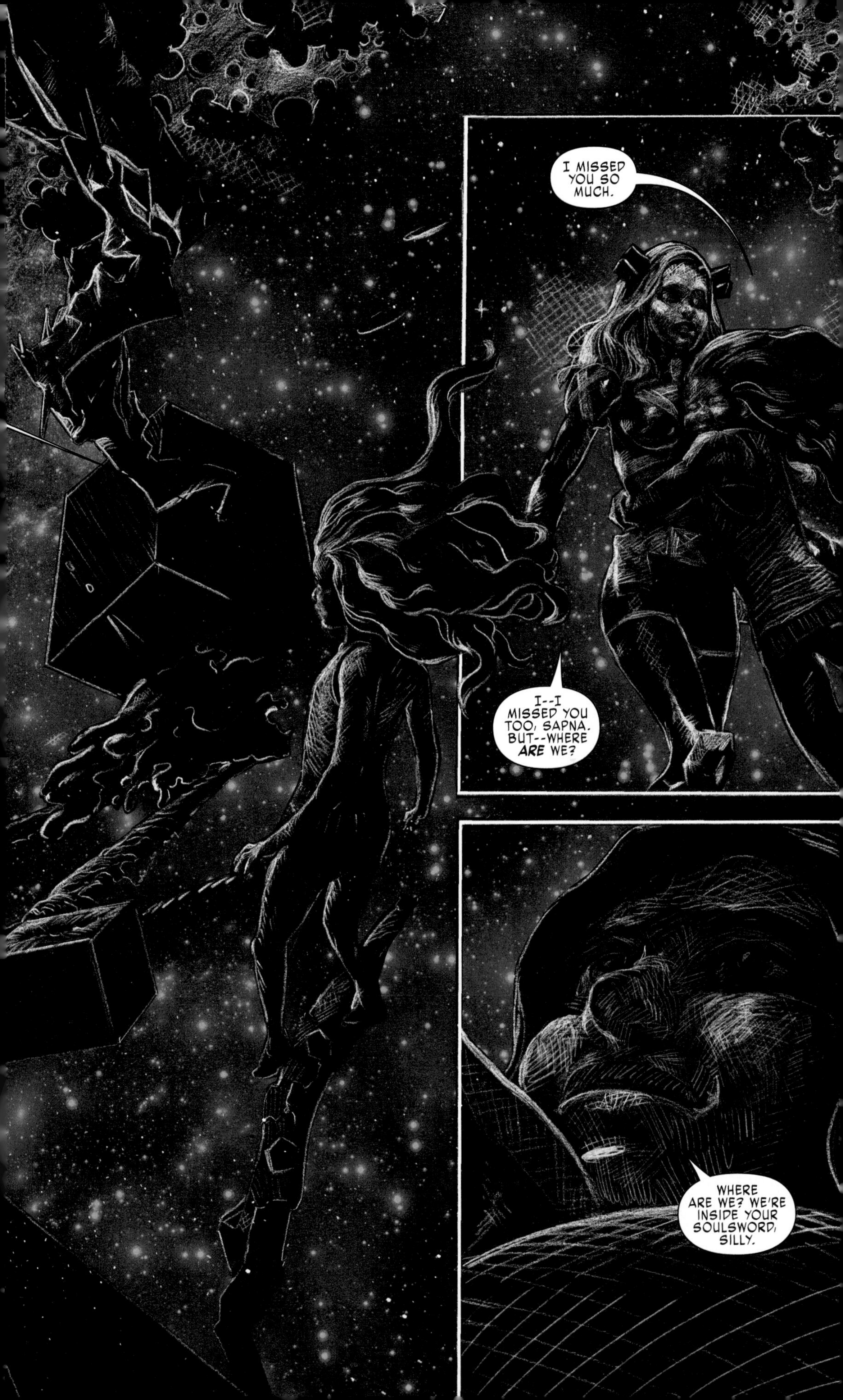
I MISSED YOU SO MUCH.
I--I MISSED YOU TOO, SAPNA. BUT--WHERE *ARE* WE?
WHERE ARE WE? WE'RE INSIDE YOUR SOULSWORD, SILLY.

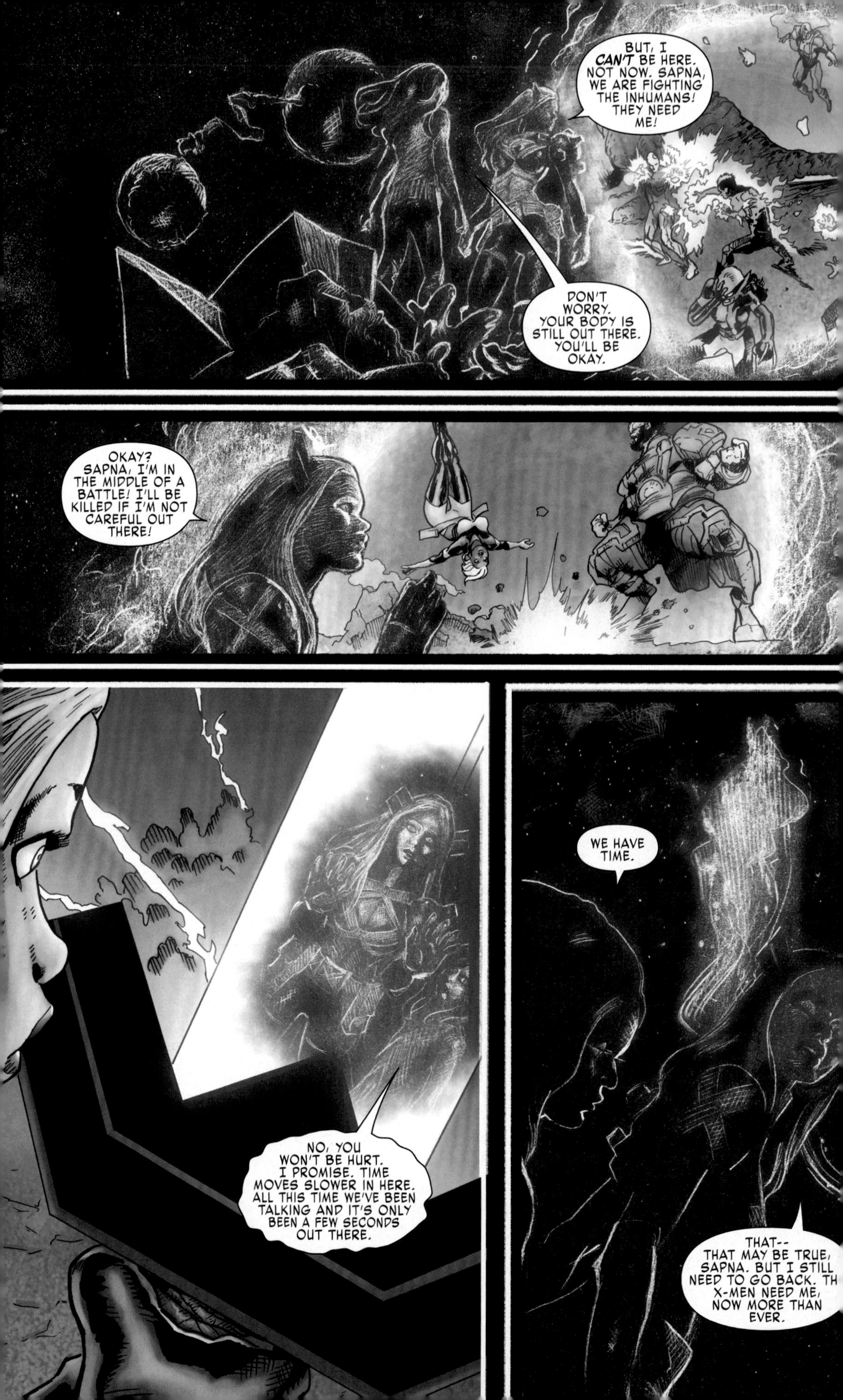
BUT, I CAN'T BE HERE. NOT NOW. SAPNA, WE ARE FIGHTING THE INHUMANS! THEY NEED ME!
DON'T WORRY. YOUR BODY IS STILL OUT THERE. YOU'LL BE OKAY.
OKAY? SAPNA, I'M IN THE MIDDLE OF A BATTLE! I'LL BE KILLED IF I'M NOT CAREFUL OUT THERE!
NO, YOU WON'T BE HURT. I PROMISE. TIME MOVES SLOWER IN HERE. ALL THIS TIME WE'VE BEEN TALKING AND IT'S ONLY BEEN A FEW SECONDS OUT THERE.
WE HAVE TIME.
THAT-- THAT MAY BE TRUE, SAPNA. BUT I STILL NEED TO GO BACK. TH X-MEN NEED ME, NOW MORE THAN EVER.

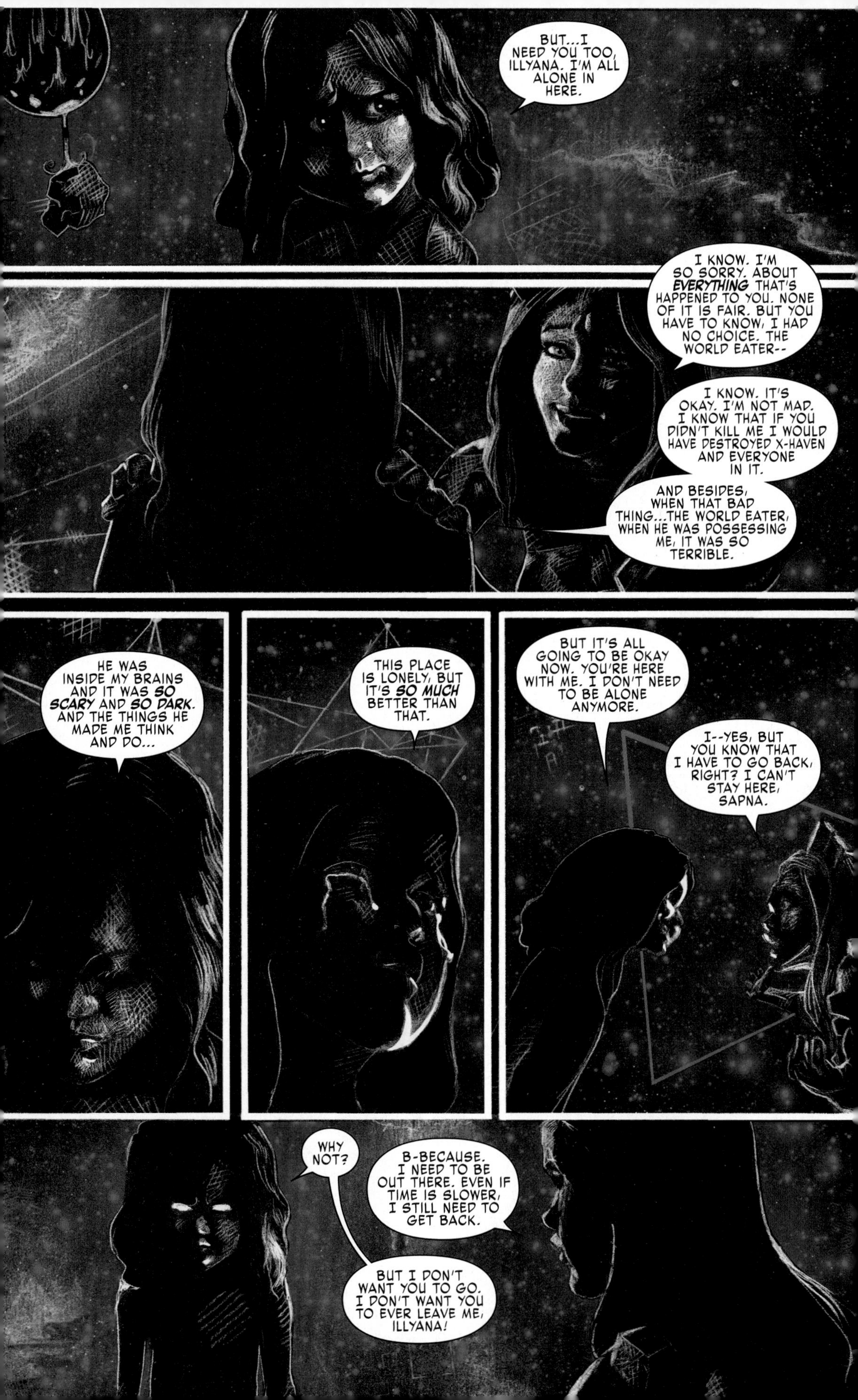
BUT...I NEED YOU TOO, ILLYANA. I'M ALL ALONE IN HERE.
I KNOW. I'M SO SORRY. ABOUT EVERYTHING THAT'S HAPPENED TO YOU. NONE OF IT IS FAIR. BUT YOU HAVE TO KNOW, I HAD NO CHOICE. THE WORLD EATER--
I KNOW. IT'S OKAY. I'M NOT MAD. I KNOW THAT IF YOU DIDN'T KILL ME I WOULD HAVE DESTROYED X-HAVEN AND EVERYONE IN IT.
AND BESIDES, WHEN THAT BAD THING...THE WORLD EATER, WHEN HE WAS POSSESSING ME, IT WAS SO TERRIBLE.
HE WAS INSIDE MY BRAINS AND IT WAS SO SCARY AND SO DARK. AND THE THINGS HE MADE ME THINK AND DO...
THIS PLACE IS LONELY, BUT IT'S SO MUCH BETTER THAN THAT.
BUT IT'S ALL GOING TO BE OKAY NOW. YOU'RE HERE WITH ME. I DON'T NEED TO BE ALONE ANYMORE.
I--YES, BUT YOU KNOW THAT I HAVE TO GO BACK, RIGHT? I CAN'T STAY HERE, SAPNA.
WHY NOT?
B-BECAUSE. I NEED TO BE OUT THERE. EVEN IF TIME IS SLOWER, I STILL NEED TO GET BACK.
BUT I DON'T WANT YOU TO GO. I DON'T WANT YOU TO EVER LEAVE ME, ILLYANA!

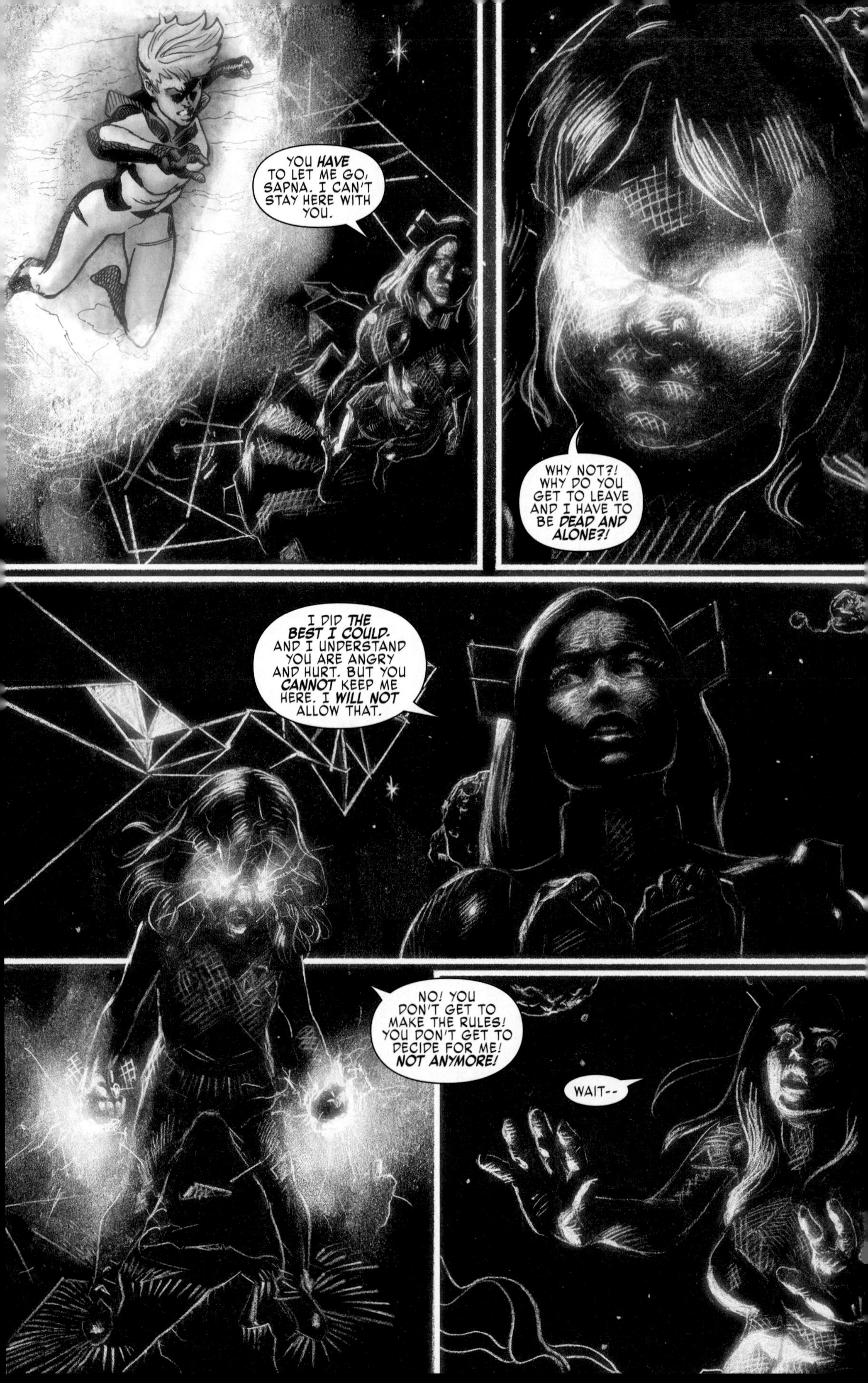
YOU HAVE TO LET ME GO, SAPNA. I CAN'T STAY HERE WITH YOU.
WHY NOT?! WHY DO YOU GET TO LEAVE AND I HAVE TO BE DEAD AND ALONE?!
I DID THE BEST I COULD. AND I UNDERSTAND YOU ARE ANGRY AND HURT. BUT YOU CANNOT KEEP ME HERE. I WILL NOT ALLOW THAT.
NO! YOU DON'T GET TO MAKE THE RULES! YOU DON'T GET TO DECIDE FOR ME! NOT ANYMORE!
WAIT--

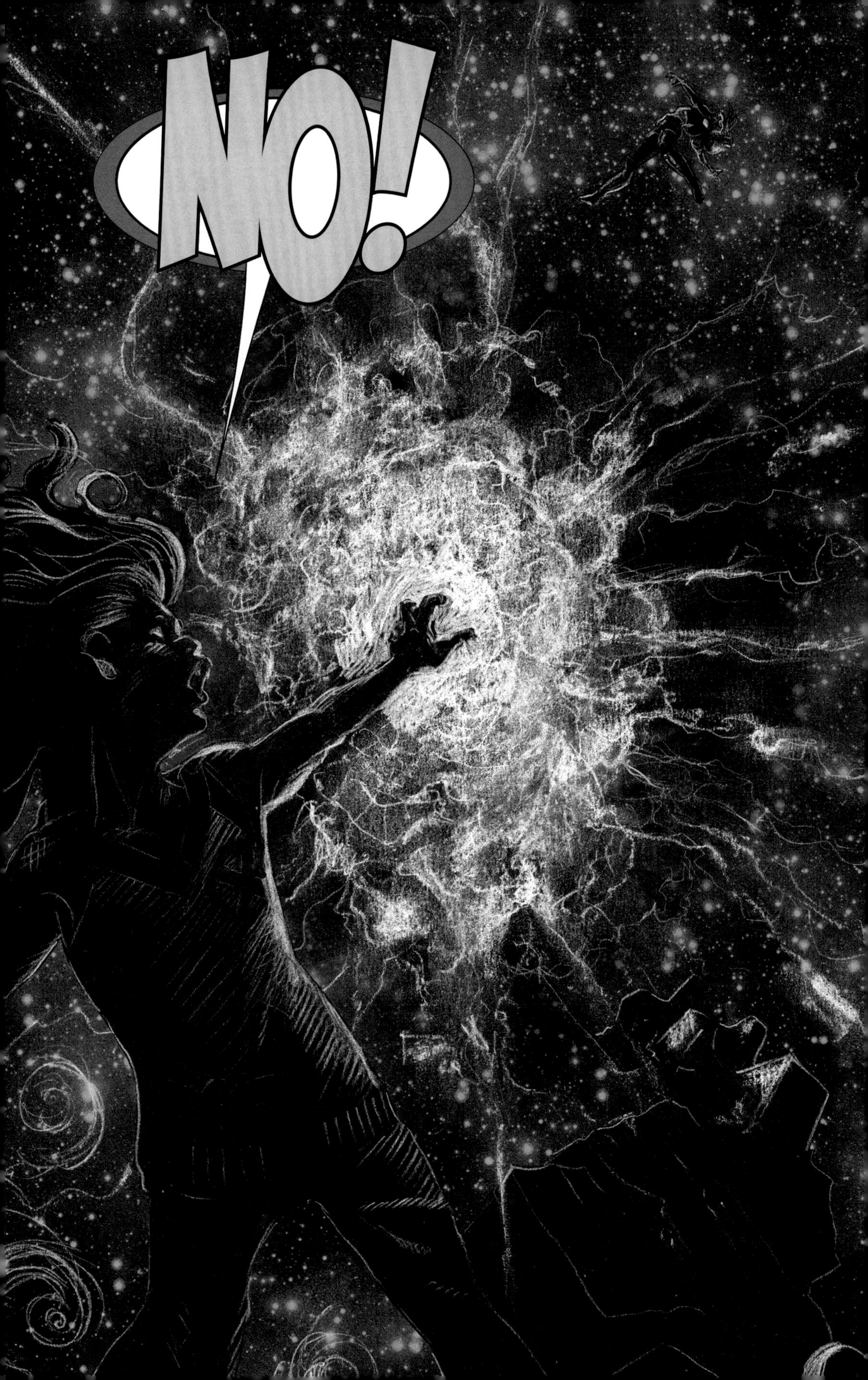
NO!

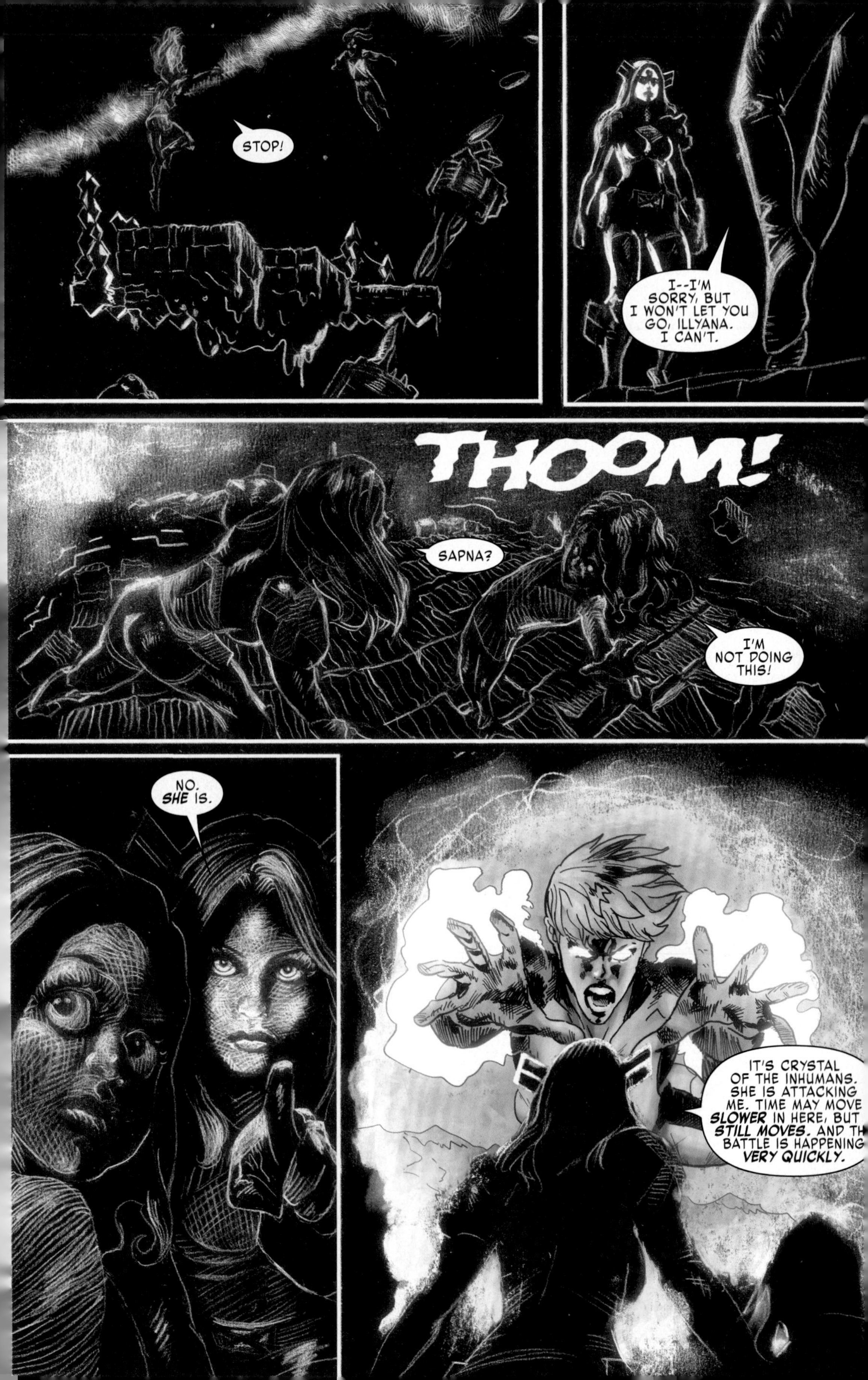

STOP!
I--I'M SORRY, BUT I WON'T LET YOU GO, ILLYANA. I CAN'T.
THOOM!
SAPNA?
I'M NOT DOING THIS!
NO. SHE IS.
IT'S CRYSTAL OF THE INHUMANS. SHE IS ATTACKING ME. TIME MAY MOVE SLOWER IN HERE, BUT STILL MOVES. AND TH BATTLE IS HAPPENING VERY QUICKLY.

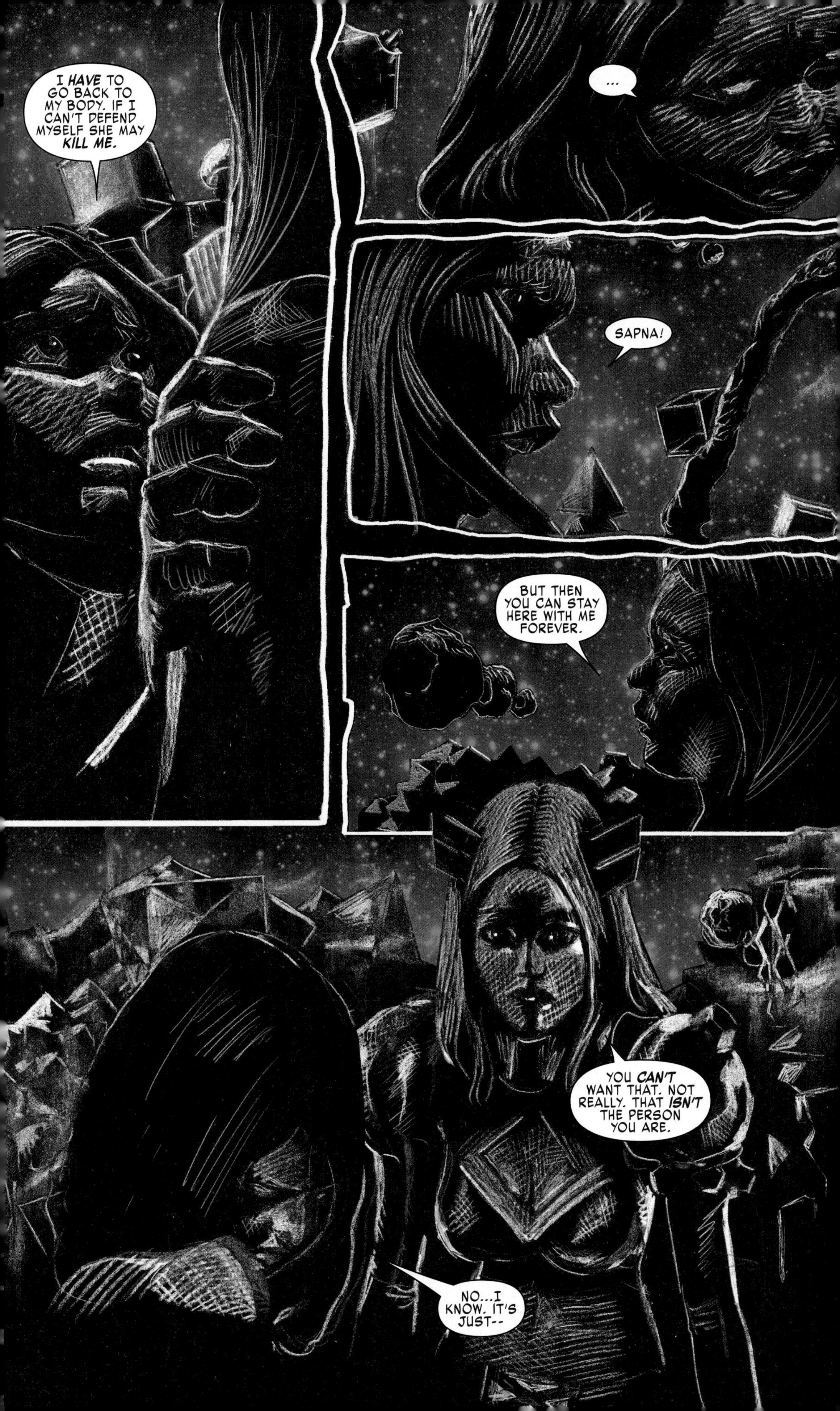
I HAVE TO GO BACK TO MY BODY. IF I CAN'T DEFEND MYSELF SHE MAY KILL ME.
...
SAPNA!
BUT THEN YOU CAN STAY HERE WITH ME FOREVER.
YOU CAN'T WANT THAT. NOT REALLY. THAT ISN'T THE PERSON YOU ARE.
NO...I KNOW. IT'S JUST--

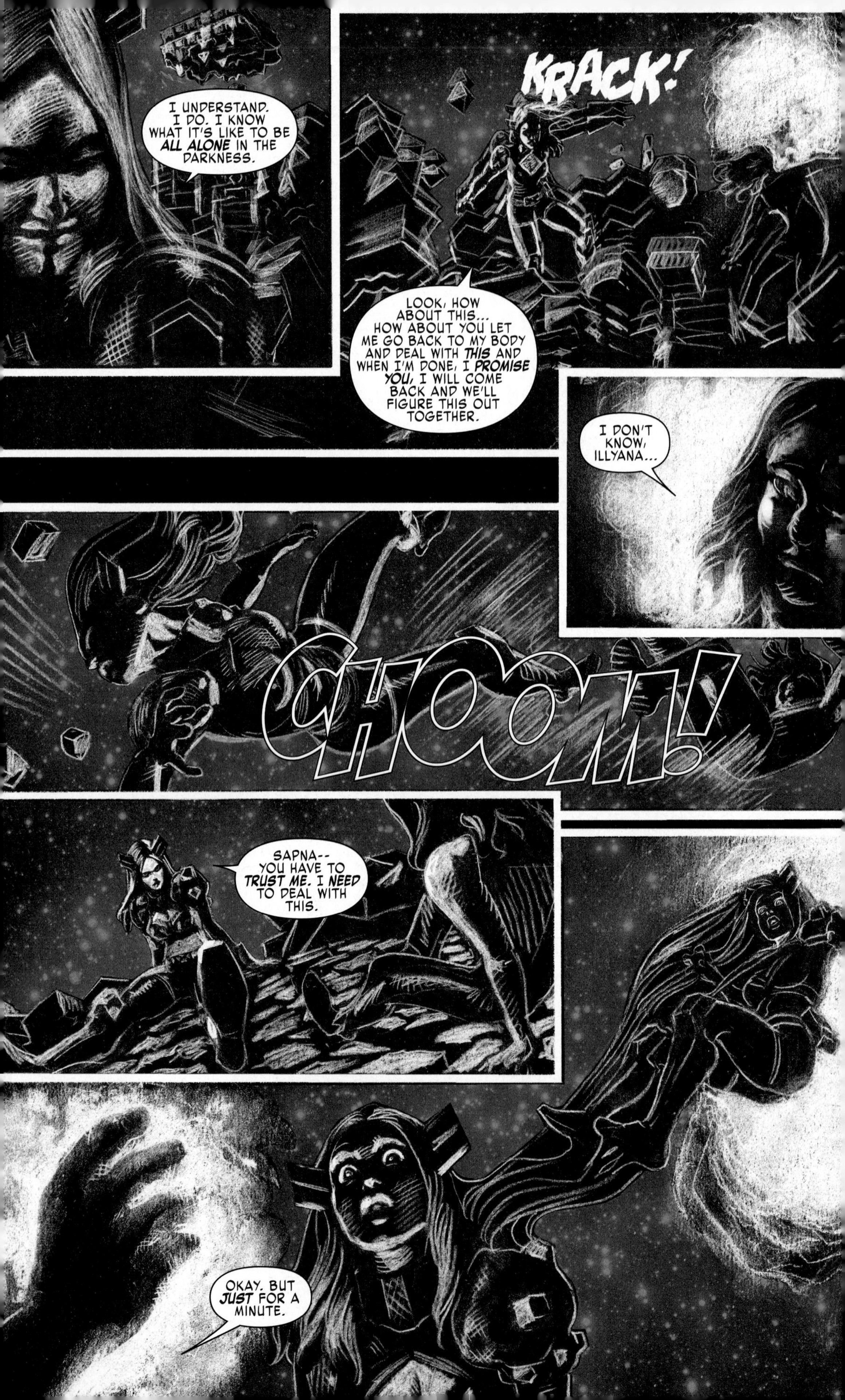
I UNDERSTAND. I DO. I KNOW WHAT IT'S LIKE TO BE ALL ALONE IN THE DARKNESS.
KRACK!
LOOK, HOW ABOUT THIS... HOW ABOUT YOU LET ME GO BACK TO MY BODY AND DEAL WITH THIS AND WHEN I'M DONE, I PROMISE YOU, I WILL COME BACK AND WE'LL FIGURE THIS OUT TOGETHER.
I DON'T KNOW, ILLYANA...
CHOOM!
SAPNA-- YOU HAVE TO TRUST ME. I NEED TO DEAL WITH THIS.
OKAY. BUT JUST FOR A MINUTE.

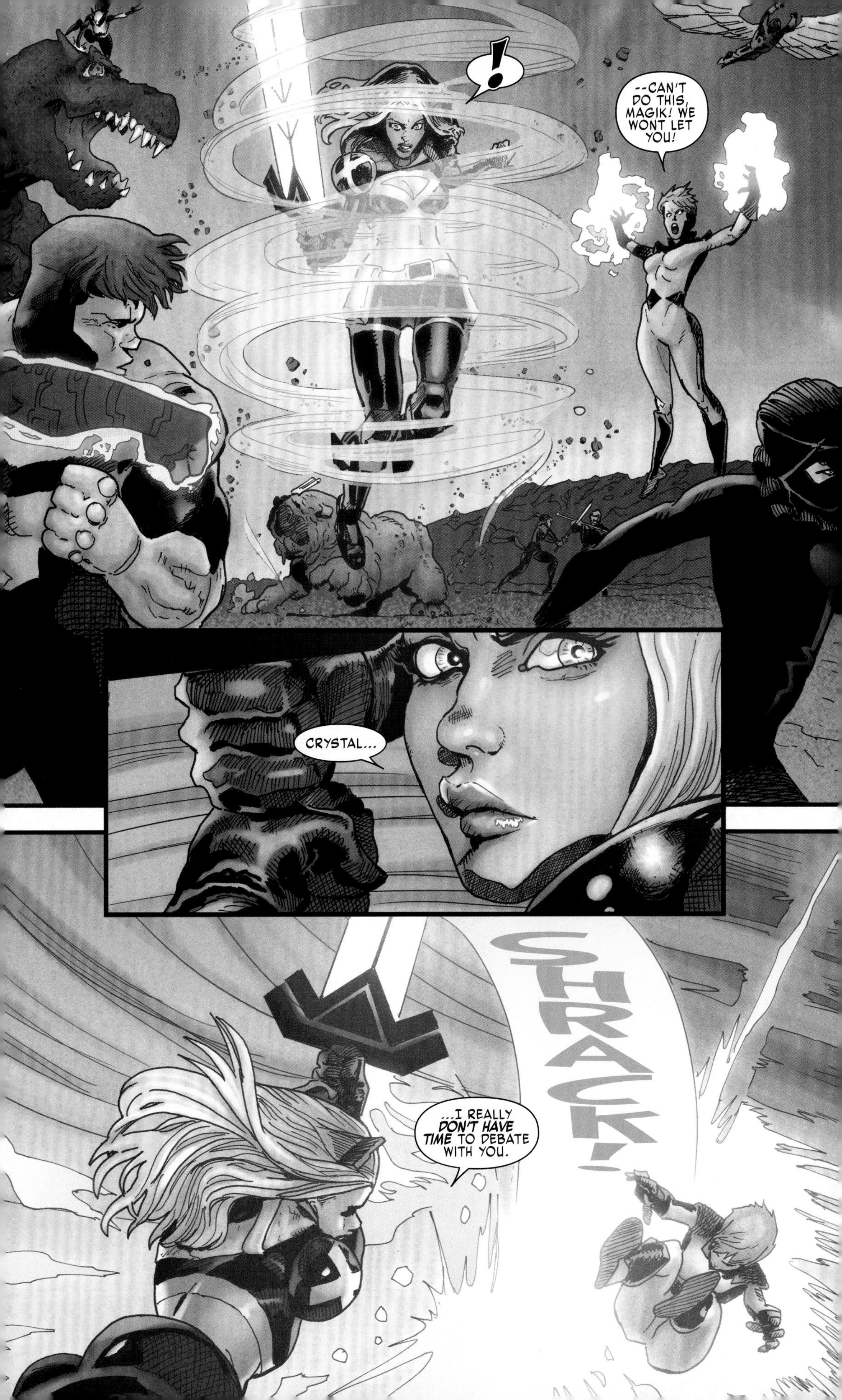
!
--CAN'T DO THIS, MAGIK! WE WONT LET YOU!
CRYSTAL...
SHRACK!
...I REALLY DON'T HAVE TIME TO DEBATE WITH YOU.

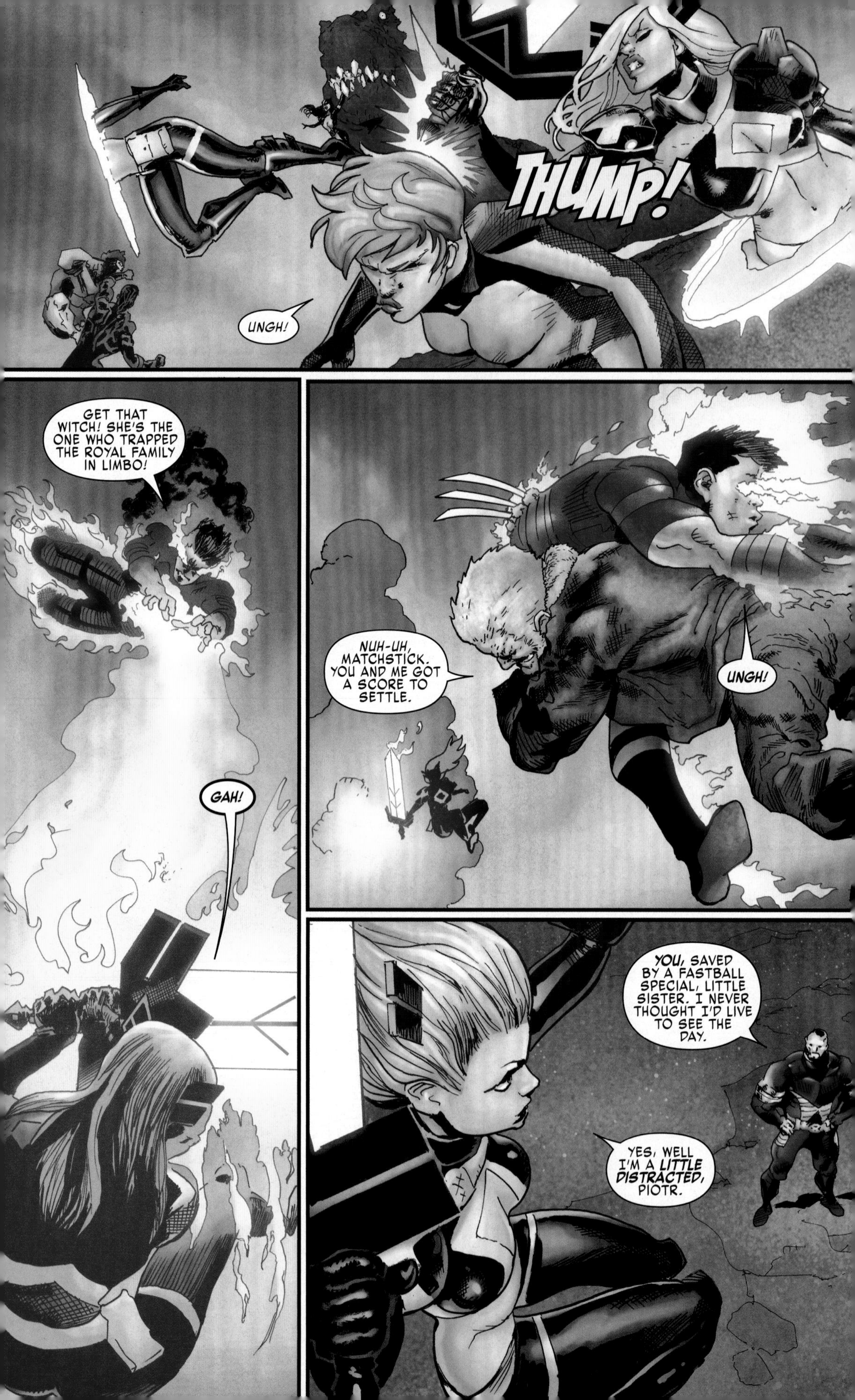
THUMP!
UNGH!
GET THAT WITCH! SHE'S THE ONE WHO TRAPPED THE ROYAL FAMILY IN LIMBO!
GAH!
NUH-UH, MATCHSTICK. YOU AND ME GOT A SCORE TO SETTLE.
UNGH!
YOU, SAVED BY A FASTBALL SPECIAL, LITTLE SISTER. I NEVER THOUGHT I'D LIVE TO SEE THE DAY.
YES, WELL I'M A LITTLE DISTRACTED, PIOTR.

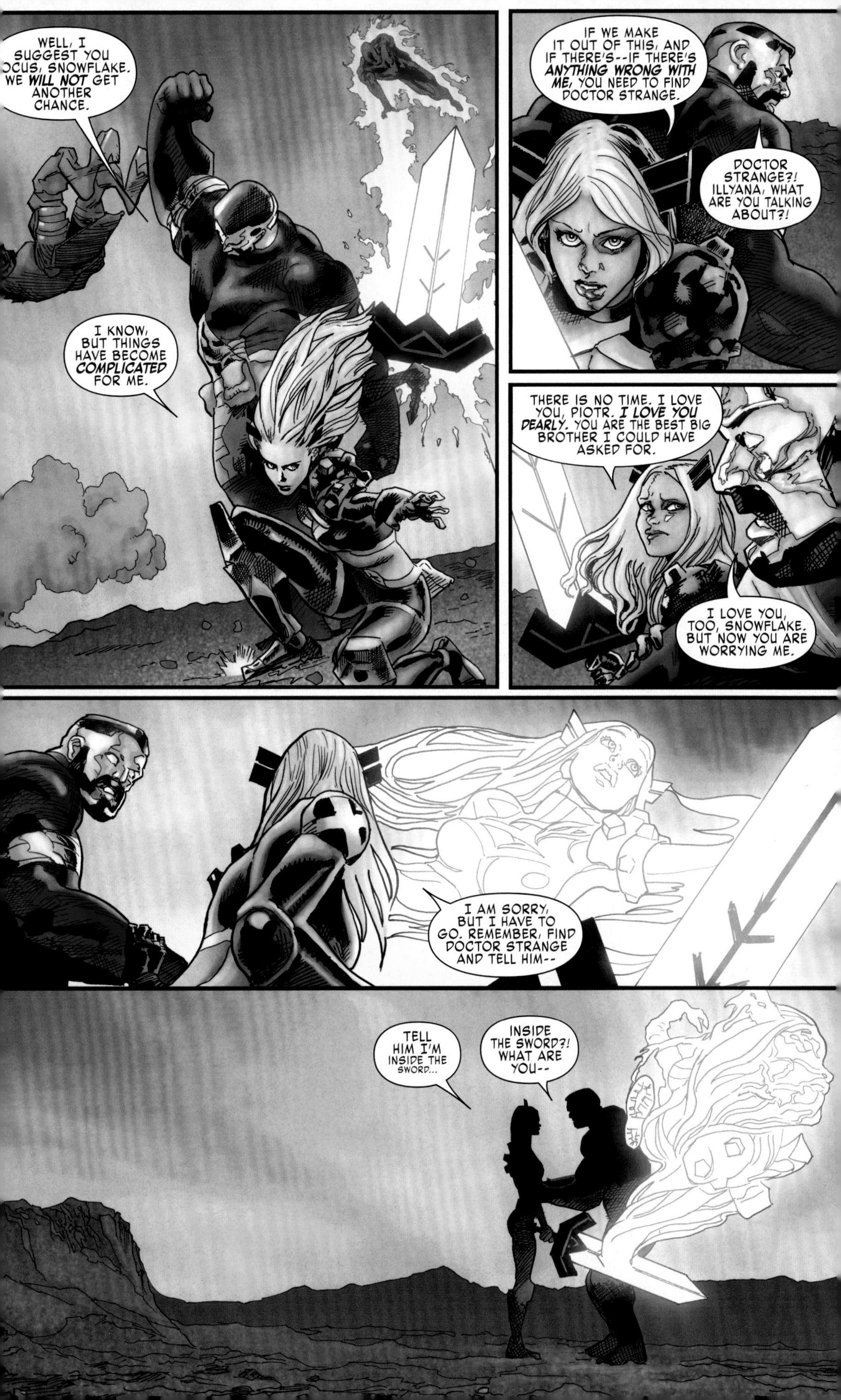

WELL, I SUGGEST YOU FOCUS, SNOWFLAKE. WE WILL NOT GET ANOTHER CHANCE.
I KNOW, BUT THINGS HAVE BECOME COMPLICATED FOR ME.
IF WE MAKE IT OUT OF THIS, AND IF THERE'S--IF THERE'S ANYTHING WRONG WITH ME, YOU NEED TO FIND DOCTOR STRANGE.
DOCTOR STRANGE?! ILLYANA, WHAT ARE YOU TALKING ABOUT?!
THERE IS NO TIME. I LOVE YOU, PIOTR. I LOVE YOU DEARLY. YOU ARE THE BEST BIG BROTHER I COULD HAVE ASKED FOR.
I LOVE YOU, TOO, SNOWFLAKE. BUT NOW YOU ARE WORRYING ME.
I AM SORRY, BUT I HAVE TO GO. REMEMBER, FIND DOCTOR STRANGE AND TELL HIM--
TELL HIM I'M INSIDE THE SWORD...
INSIDE THE SWORD?! WHAT ARE YOU--

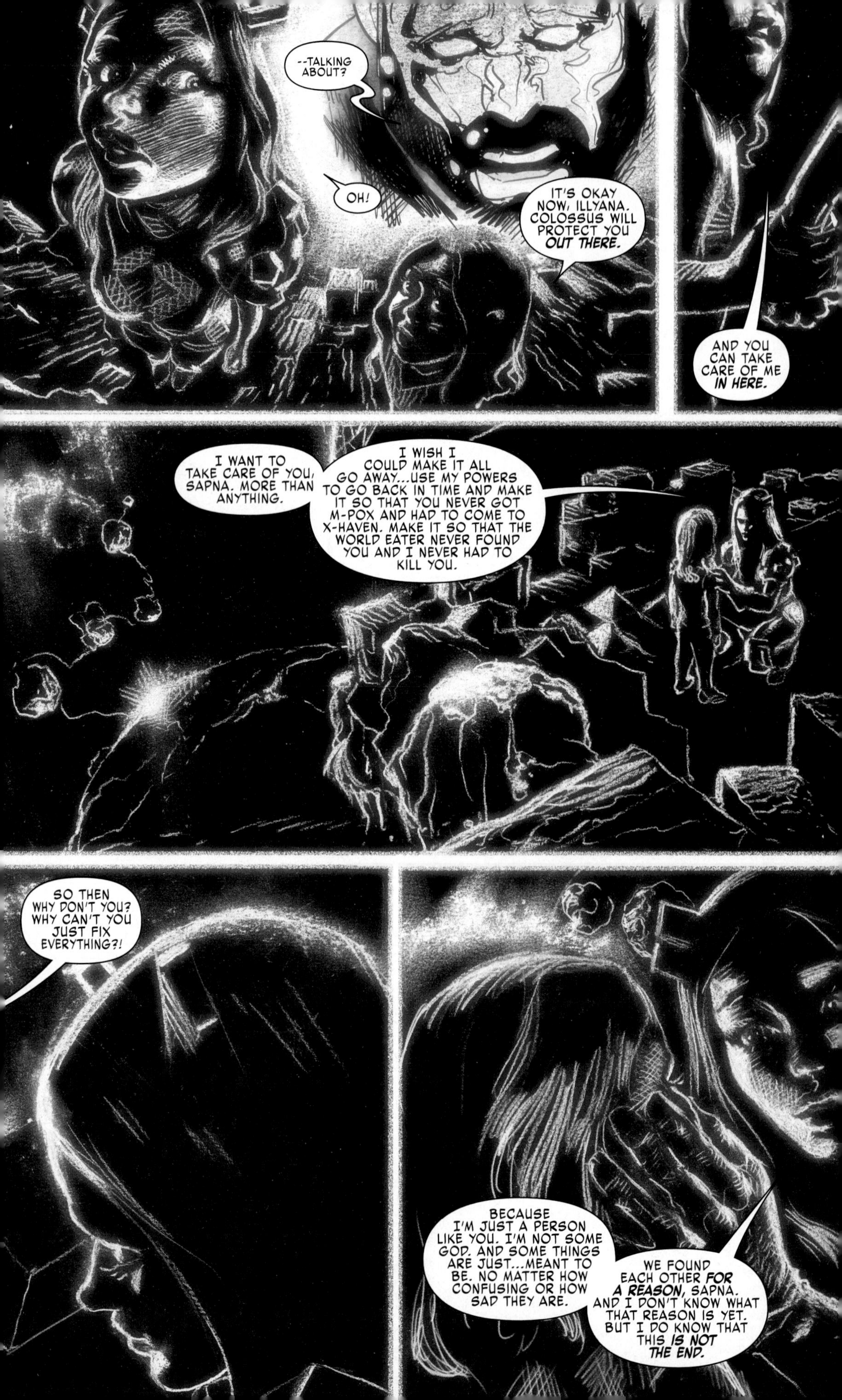
--TALKING ABOUT?
OH!
IT'S OKAY NOW, ILLYANA. COLOSSUS WILL PROTECT YOU *OUT THERE.*
AND YOU CAN TAKE CARE OF ME *IN HERE.*
I WANT TO TAKE CARE OF YOU, SAPNA. MORE THAN ANYTHING.
I WISH I COULD MAKE IT ALL GO AWAY...USE MY POWERS TO GO BACK IN TIME AND MAKE IT SO THAT YOU NEVER GOT M-POX AND HAD TO COME TO X-HAVEN. MAKE IT SO THAT THE WORLD EATER NEVER FOUND YOU AND I NEVER HAD TO KILL YOU.
SO THEN WHY DON'T YOU? WHY CAN'T YOU JUST FIX EVERYTHING?!
BECAUSE I'M JUST A PERSON LIKE YOU. I'M NOT SOME GOD. AND SOME THINGS ARE JUST...MEANT TO BE. NO MATTER HOW CONFUSING OR HOW SAD THEY ARE.
WE FOUND EACH OTHER *FOR A REASON,* SAPNA. AND I DON'T KNOW WHAT THAT REASON IS YET. BUT I DO KNOW THAT THIS *IS NOT THE END.*

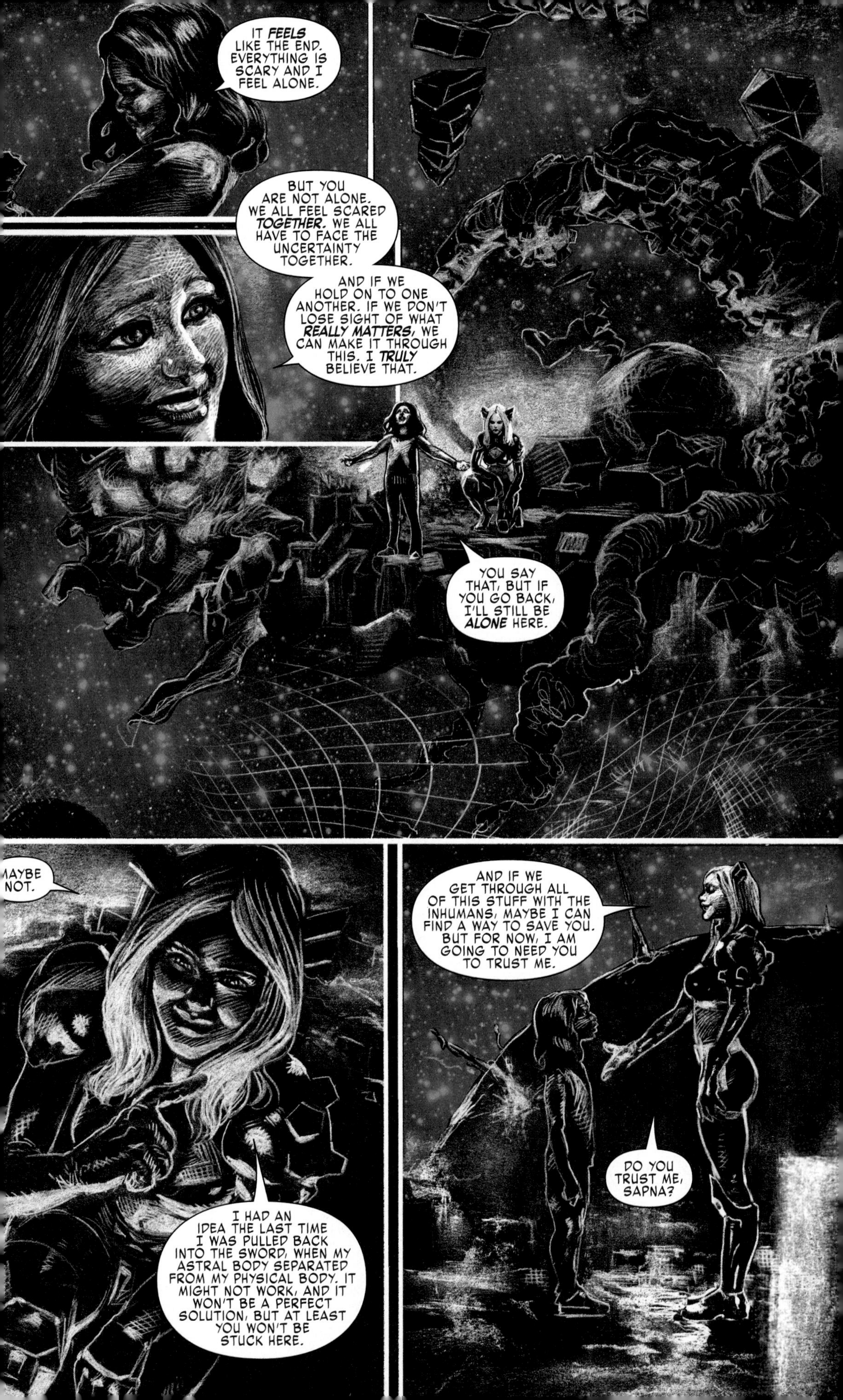
IT FEELS LIKE THE END. EVERYTHING IS SCARY AND I FEEL ALONE.
BUT YOU ARE NOT ALONE. WE ALL FEEL SCARED TOGETHER. WE ALL HAVE TO FACE THE UNCERTAINTY TOGETHER.
AND IF WE HOLD ON TO ONE ANOTHER. IF WE DON'T LOSE SIGHT OF WHAT REALLY MATTERS, WE CAN MAKE IT THROUGH THIS. I TRULY BELIEVE THAT.
YOU SAY THAT, BUT IF YOU GO BACK, I'LL STILL BE ALONE HERE.
MAYBE NOT.
I HAD AN IDEA THE LAST TIME I WAS PULLED BACK INTO THE SWORD, WHEN MY ASTRAL BODY SEPARATED FROM MY PHYSICAL BODY. IT MIGHT NOT WORK, AND IT WON'T BE A PERFECT SOLUTION, BUT AT LEAST YOU WON'T BE STUCK HERE.
AND IF WE GET THROUGH ALL OF THIS STUFF WITH THE INHUMANS, MAYBE I CAN FIND A WAY TO SAVE YOU. BUT FOR NOW, I AM GOING TO NEED YOU TO TRUST ME.
DO YOU TRUST ME, SAPNA?

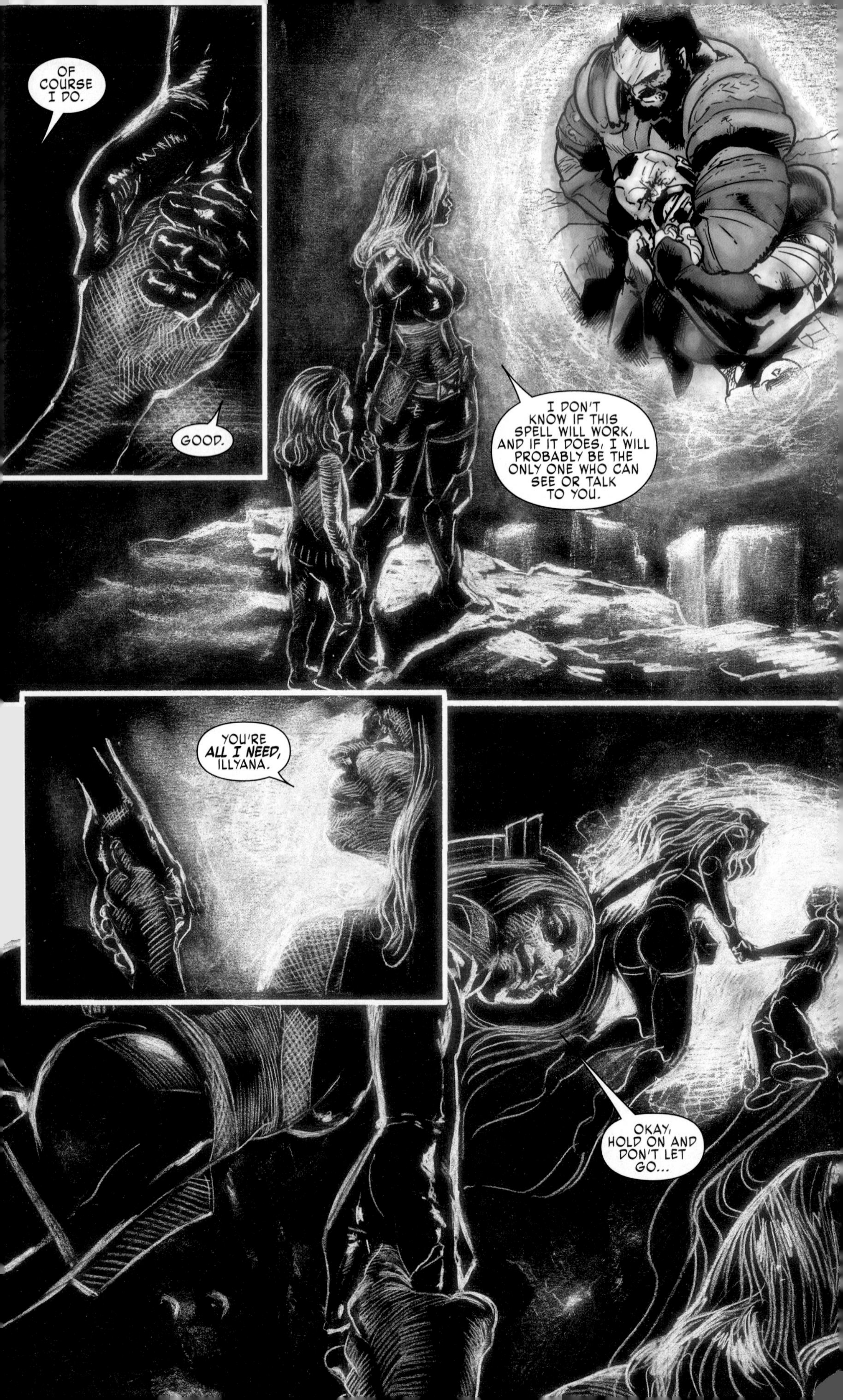

OF COURSE I DO.
GOOD.
I DON'T KNOW IF THIS SPELL WILL WORK, AND IF IT DOES, I WILL PROBABLY BE THE ONLY ONE WHO CAN SEE OR TALK TO YOU.
YOU'RE ALL I NEED, ILLYANA.
OKAY, HOLD ON AND DON'T LET GO...

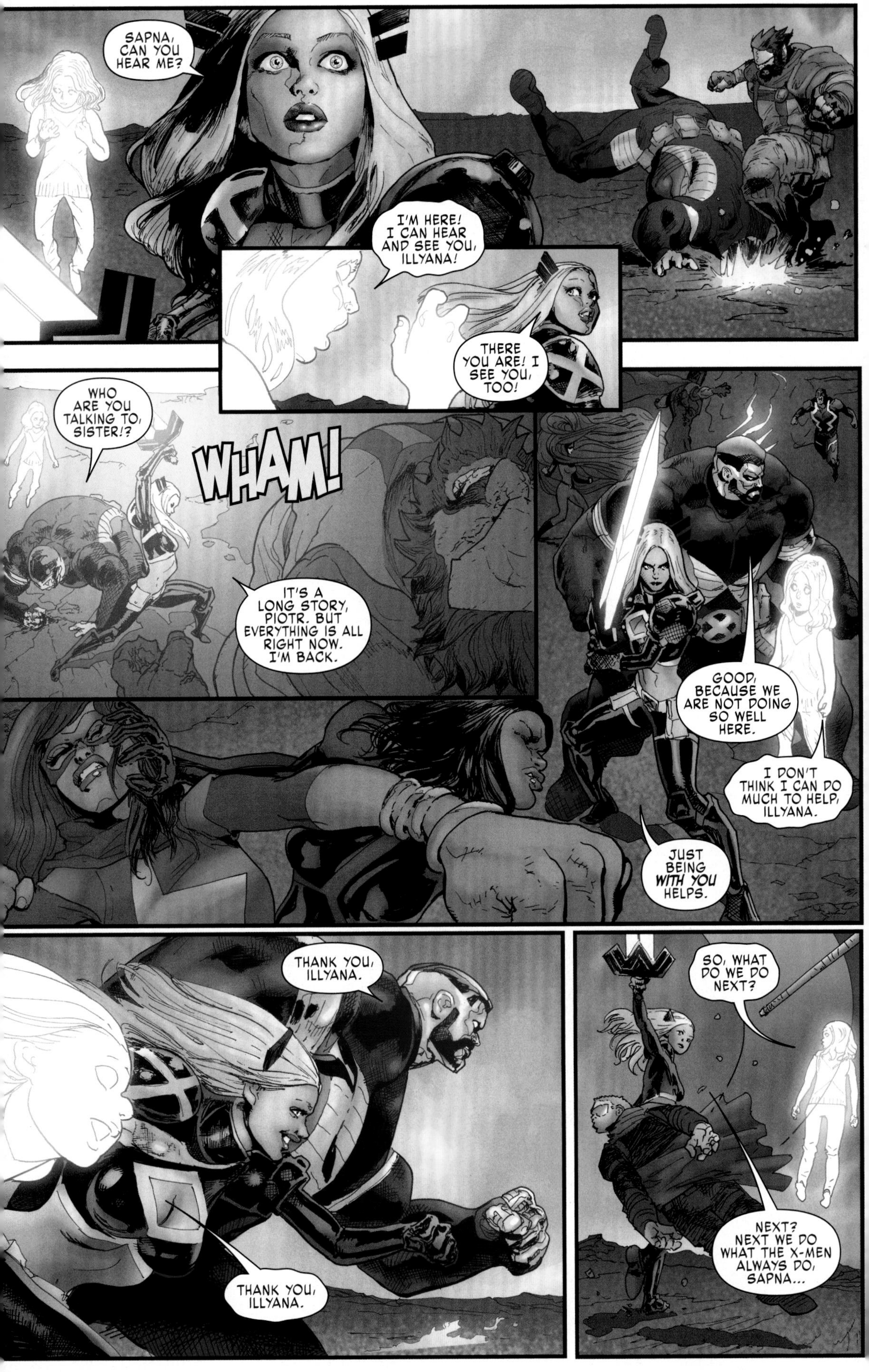
SAPNA, CAN YOU HEAR ME?
I'M HERE! I CAN HEAR AND SEE YOU, ILLYANA!
THERE YOU ARE! I SEE YOU, TOO!
WHO ARE YOU TALKING TO, SISTER!?
WHAM!
IT'S A LONG STORY, PIOTR. BUT EVERYTHING IS ALL RIGHT NOW. I'M BACK.
GOOD, BECAUSE WE ARE NOT DOING SO WELL HERE.
I DON'T THINK I CAN DO MUCH TO HELP, ILLYANA.
JUST BEING WITH YOU HELPS.
THANK YOU, ILLYANA.
THANK YOU, ILLYANA.
SO, WHAT DO WE DO NEXT?
NEXT? NEXT WE DO WHAT THE X-MEN ALWAYS DO, SAPNA...

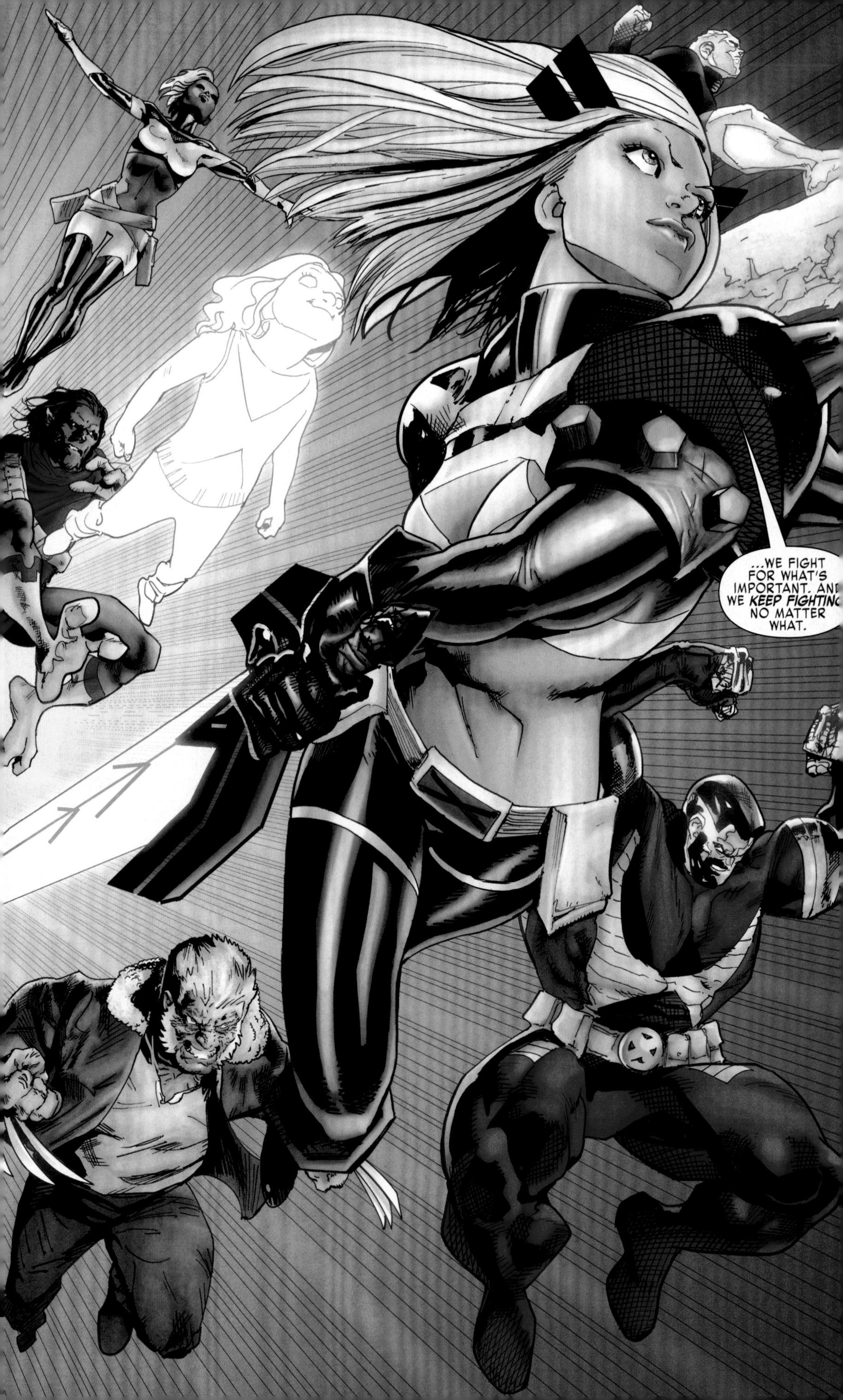
...WE FIGHT FOR WHAT'S IMPORTANT. AND WE KEEP FIGHTING NO MATTER WHAT.

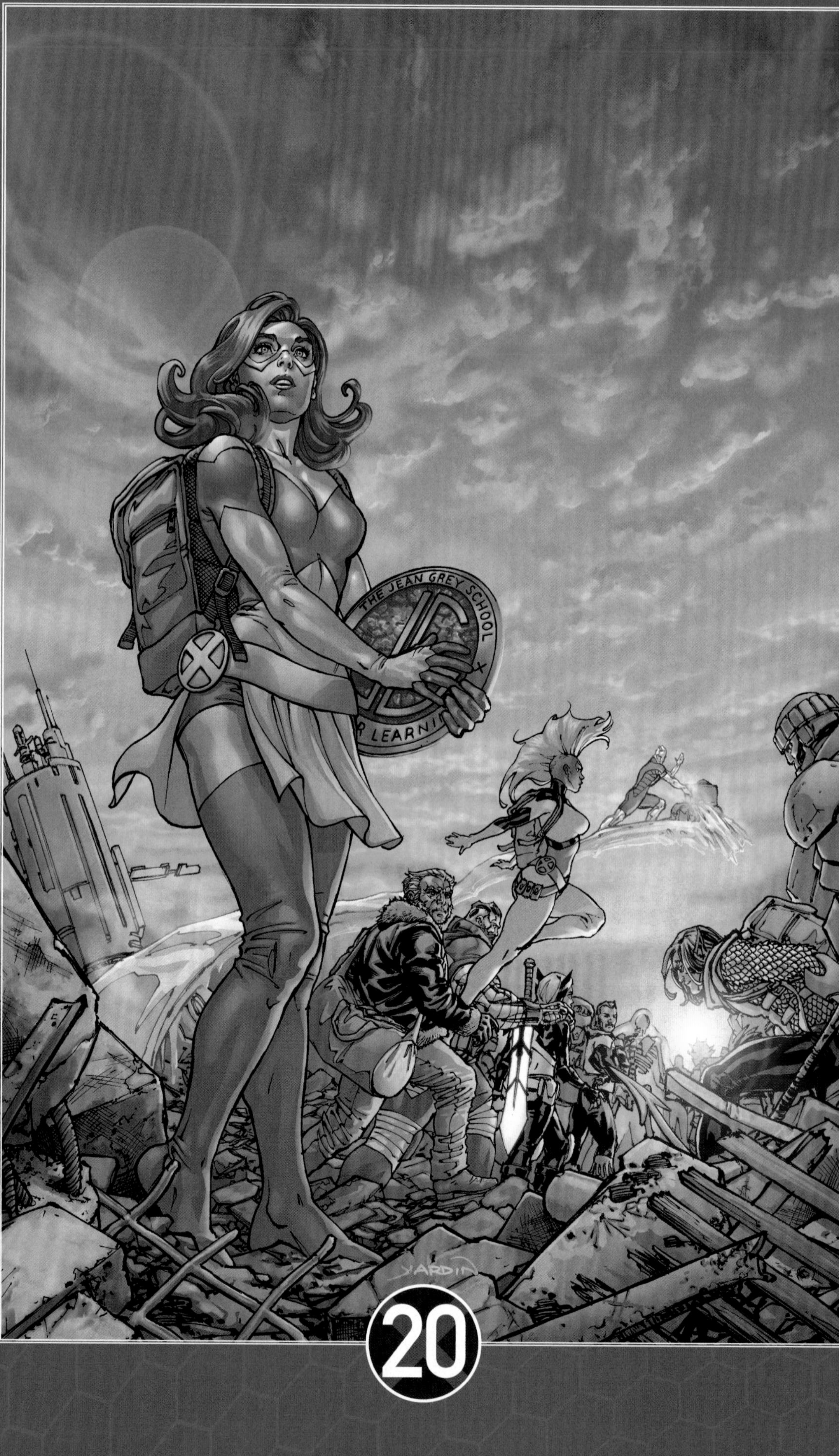
THE JEAN GREY SCHOOL
R LEARNI
JARDIN
20

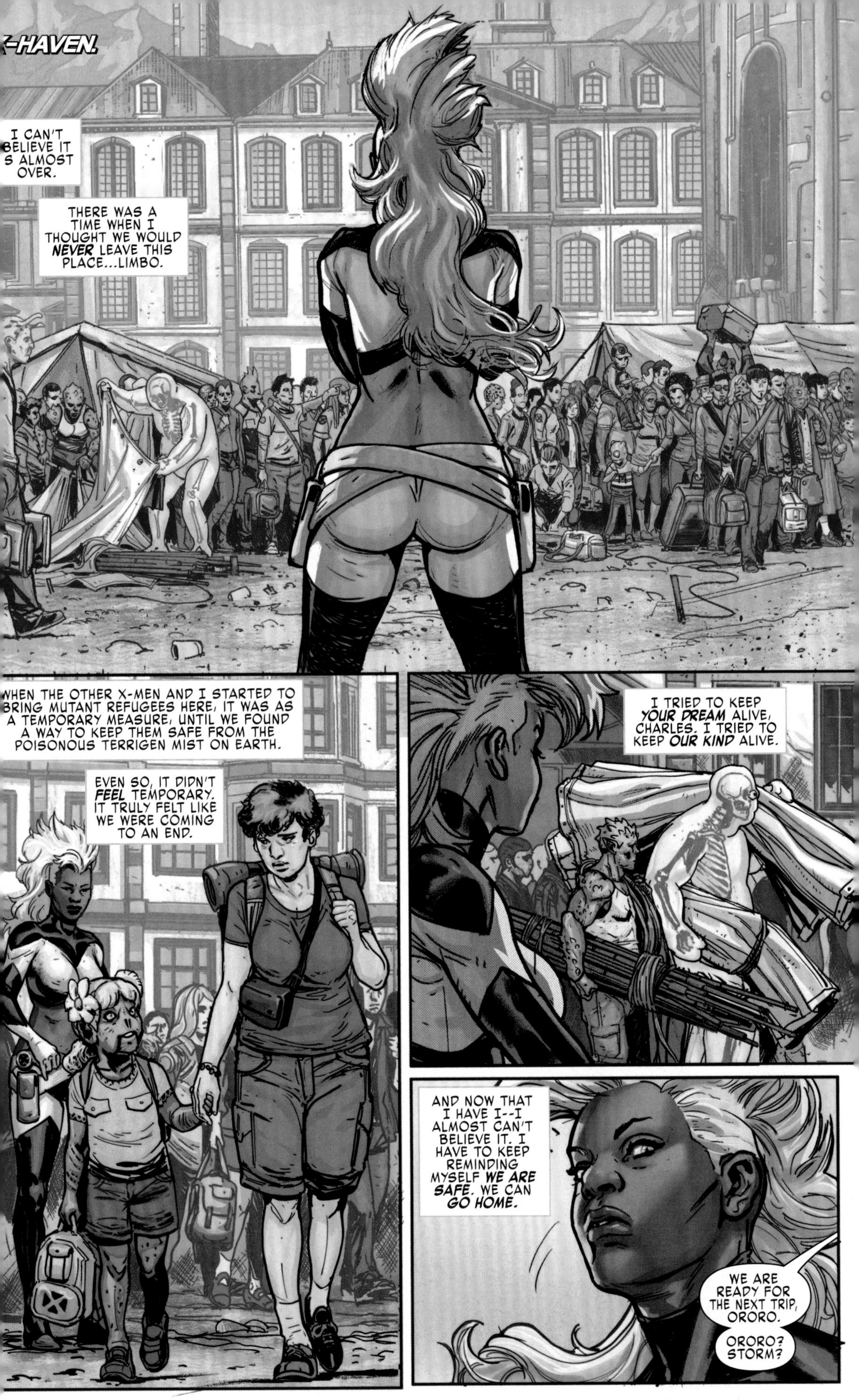

-HAVEN.
I CAN'T BELIEVE IT S ALMOST OVER.
THERE WAS A TIME WHEN I THOUGHT WE WOULD NEVER LEAVE THIS PLACE...LIMBO.
WHEN THE OTHER X-MEN AND I STARTED TO BRING MUTANT REFUGEES HERE, IT WAS AS A TEMPORARY MEASURE, UNTIL WE FOUND A WAY TO KEEP THEM SAFE FROM THE POISONOUS TERRIGEN MIST ON EARTH.
EVEN SO, IT DIDN'T FEEL TEMPORARY. IT TRULY FELT LIKE WE WERE COMING TO AN END.
I TRIED TO KEEP YOUR DREAM ALIVE, CHARLES. I TRIED TO KEEP OUR KIND ALIVE.
AND NOW THAT I HAVE I--I ALMOST CAN'T BELIEVE IT. I HAVE TO KEEP REMINDING MYSELF WE ARE SAFE. WE CAN GO HOME.
WE ARE READY FOR THE NEXT TRIP, ORORO.
ORORO? STORM?

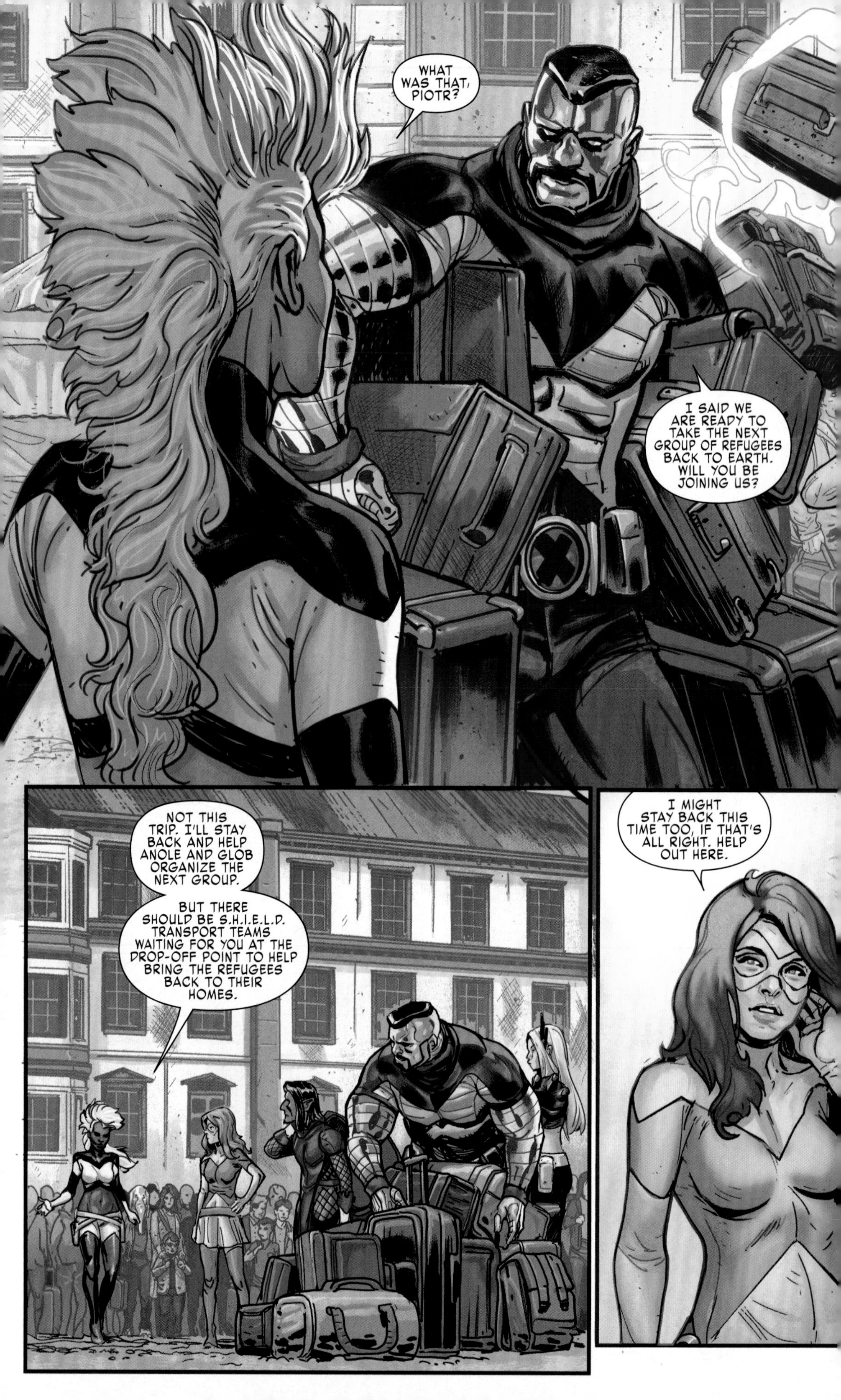
WHAT WAS THAT, PIOTR?
I SAID WE ARE READY TO TAKE THE NEXT GROUP OF REFUGEES BACK TO EARTH. WILL YOU BE JOINING US?
NOT THIS TRIP. I'LL STAY BACK AND HELP ANOLE AND GLOB ORGANIZE THE NEXT GROUP.
BUT THERE SHOULD BE S.H.I.E.L.D. TRANSPORT TEAMS WAITING FOR YOU AT THE DROP-OFF POINT TO HELP BRING THE REFUGEES BACK TO THEIR HOMES.
I MIGHT STAY BACK THIS TIME TOO, IF THAT'S ALL RIGHT. HELP OUT HERE.

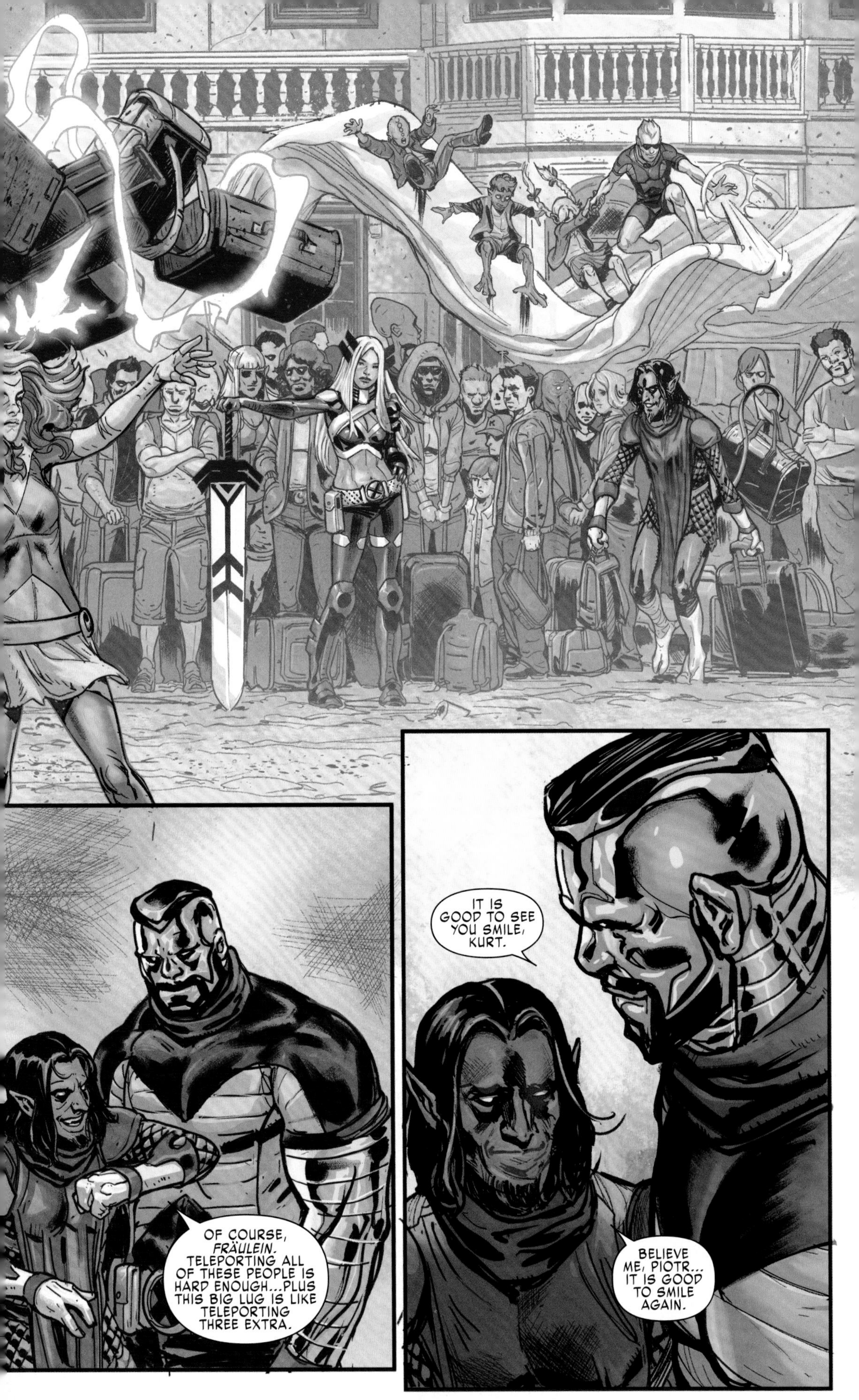

OF COURSE, *FRÄULEIN*. TELEPORTING ALL OF THESE PEOPLE IS HARD ENOUGH...PLUS THIS BIG LUG IS LIKE TELEPORTING THREE EXTRA.
IT IS GOOD TO SEE YOU SMILE, KURT.
BELIEVE ME, PIOTR... IT IS GOOD TO SMILE AGAIN.

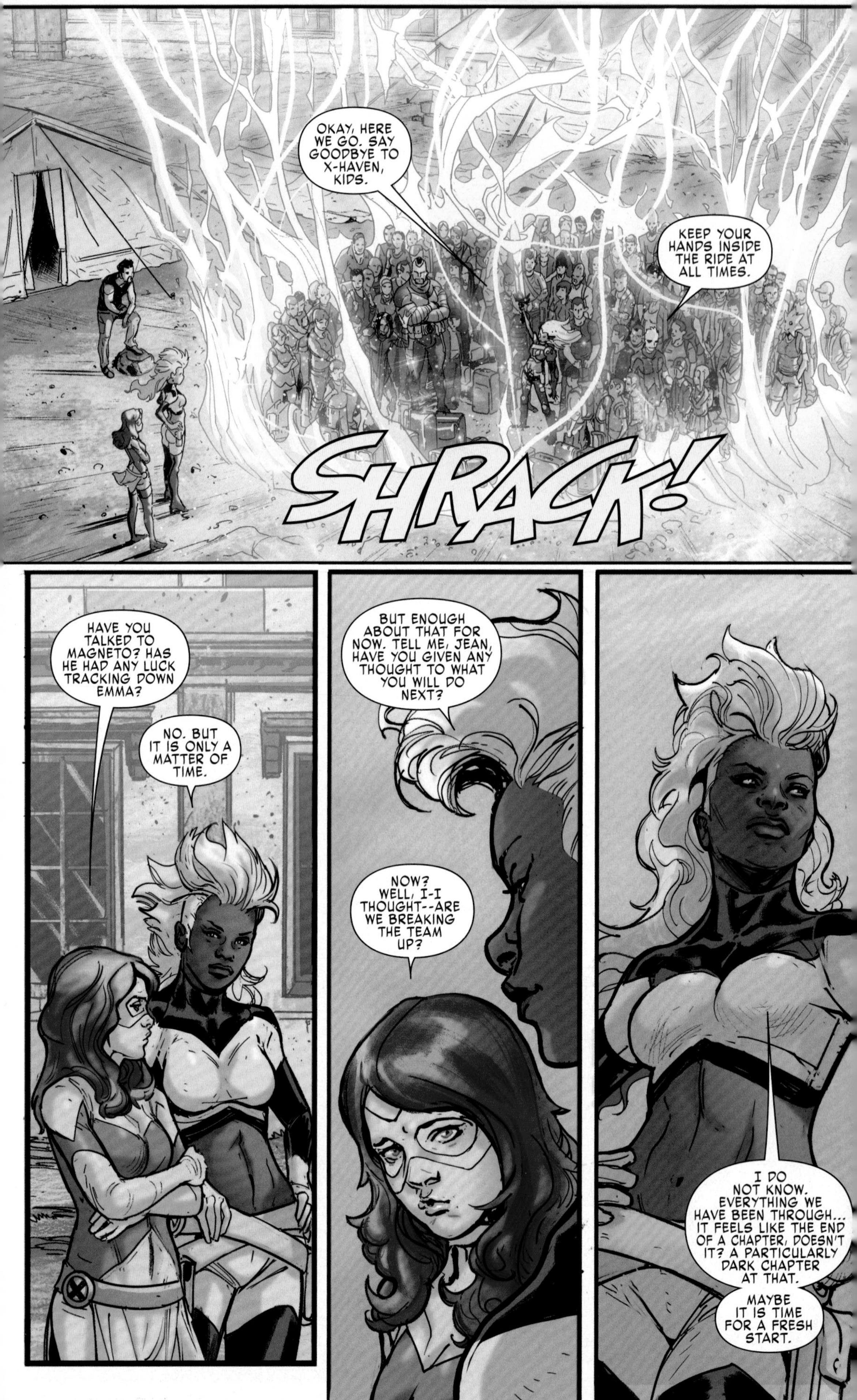
OKAY, HERE WE GO. SAY GOODBYE TO X-HAVEN, KIDS.
KEEP YOUR HANDS INSIDE THE RIDE AT ALL TIMES.
SHRACK!
HAVE YOU TALKED TO MAGNETO? HAS HE HAD ANY LUCK TRACKING DOWN EMMA?
NO. BUT IT IS ONLY A MATTER OF TIME.
BUT ENOUGH ABOUT THAT FOR NOW. TELL ME, JEAN, HAVE YOU GIVEN ANY THOUGHT TO WHAT YOU WILL DO NEXT?
NOW? WELL, I-I THOUGHT--ARE WE BREAKING THE TEAM UP?
I DO NOT KNOW. EVERYTHING WE HAVE BEEN THROUGH... IT FEELS LIKE THE END OF A CHAPTER, DOESN'T IT? A PARTICULARLY DARK CHAPTER AT THAT.
MAYBE IT IS TIME FOR A FRESH START.

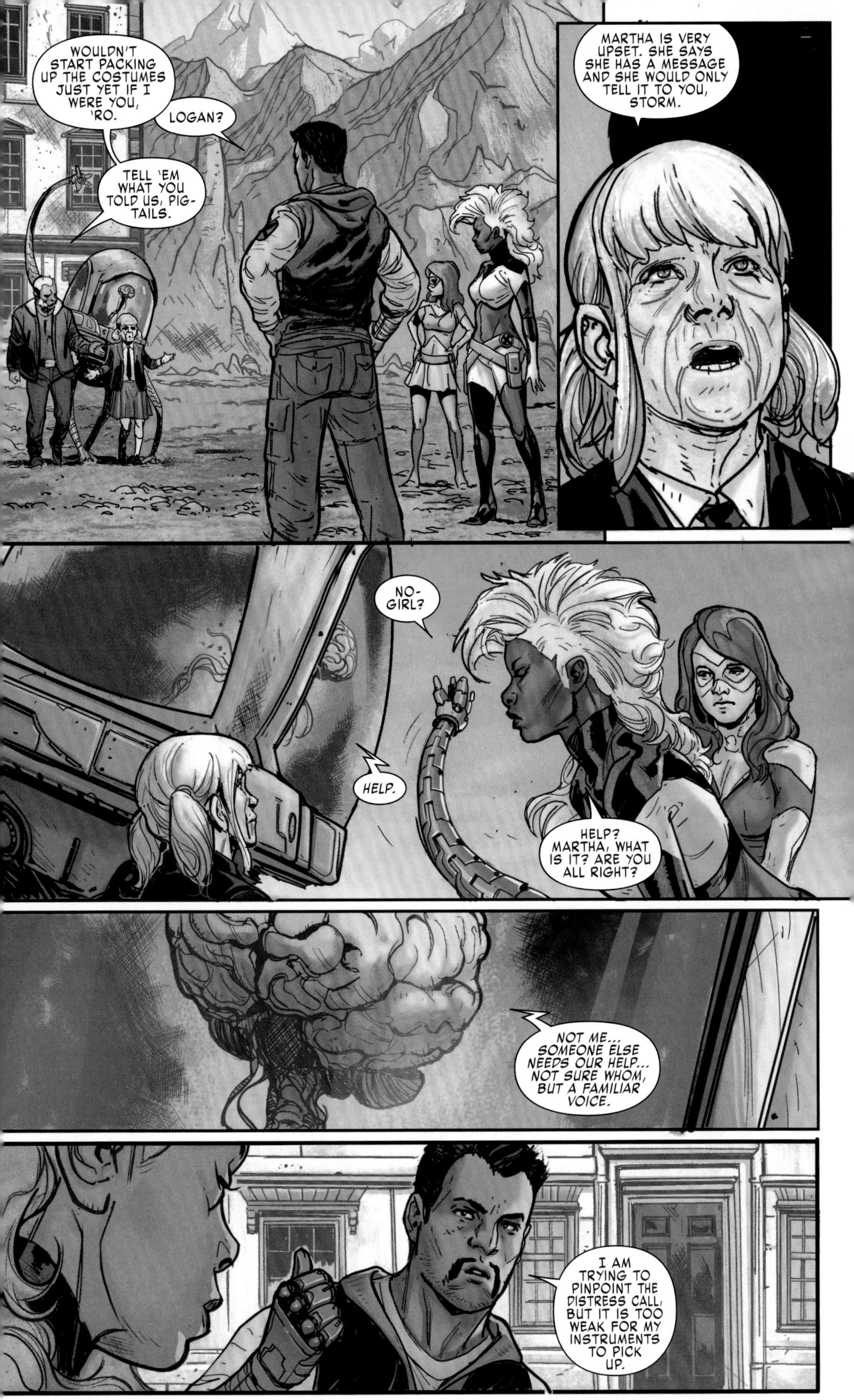
WOULDN'T START PACKING UP THE COSTUMES JUST YET IF I WERE YOU, 'RO.
LOGAN?
TELL 'EM WHAT YOU TOLD US, PIG-TAILS.
MARTHA IS VERY UPSET. SHE SAYS SHE HAS A MESSAGE AND SHE WOULD ONLY TELL IT TO YOU, STORM.
NO-GIRL?
HELP.
HELP? MARTHA, WHAT IS IT? ARE YOU ALL RIGHT?
NOT ME... SOMEONE ELSE NEEDS OUR HELP... NOT SURE WHOM, BUT A FAMILIAR VOICE.
I AM TRYING TO PINPOINT THE DISTRESS CALL, BUT IT IS TOO WEAK FOR MY INSTRUMENTS TO PICK UP.

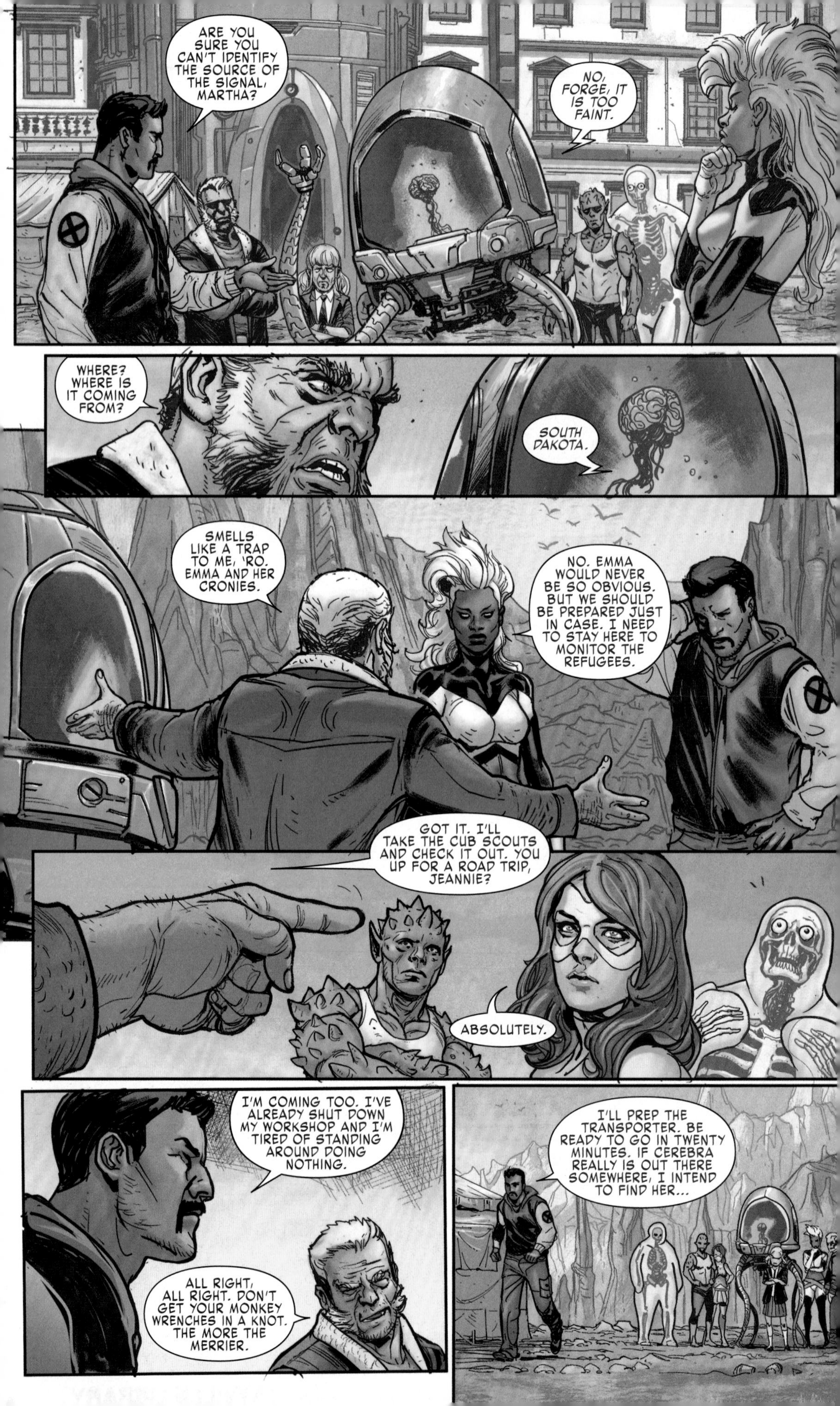
ARE YOU SURE YOU CAN'T IDENTIFY THE SOURCE OF THE SIGNAL, MARTHA?
NO, FORGE, IT IS TOO FAINT.
WHERE? WHERE IS IT COMING FROM?
SOUTH DAKOTA.
SMELLS LIKE A TRAP TO ME, 'RO. EMMA AND HER CRONIES.
NO. EMMA WOULD NEVER BE SO OBVIOUS. BUT WE SHOULD BE PREPARED JUST IN CASE. I NEED TO STAY HERE TO MONITOR THE REFUGEES.
GOT IT. I'LL TAKE THE CUB SCOUTS AND CHECK IT OUT. YOU UP FOR A ROAD TRIP, JEANNIE?
ABSOLUTELY.
I'M COMING TOO. I'VE ALREADY SHUT DOWN MY WORKSHOP AND I'M TIRED OF STANDING AROUND DOING NOTHING.
ALL RIGHT, ALL RIGHT. DON'T GET YOUR MONKEY WRENCHES IN A KNOT. THE MORE THE MERRIER.
I'LL PREP THE TRANSPORTER. BE READY TO GO IN TWENTY MINUTES. IF CEREBRA REALLY IS OUT THERE SOMEWHERE, I INTEND TO FIND HER...

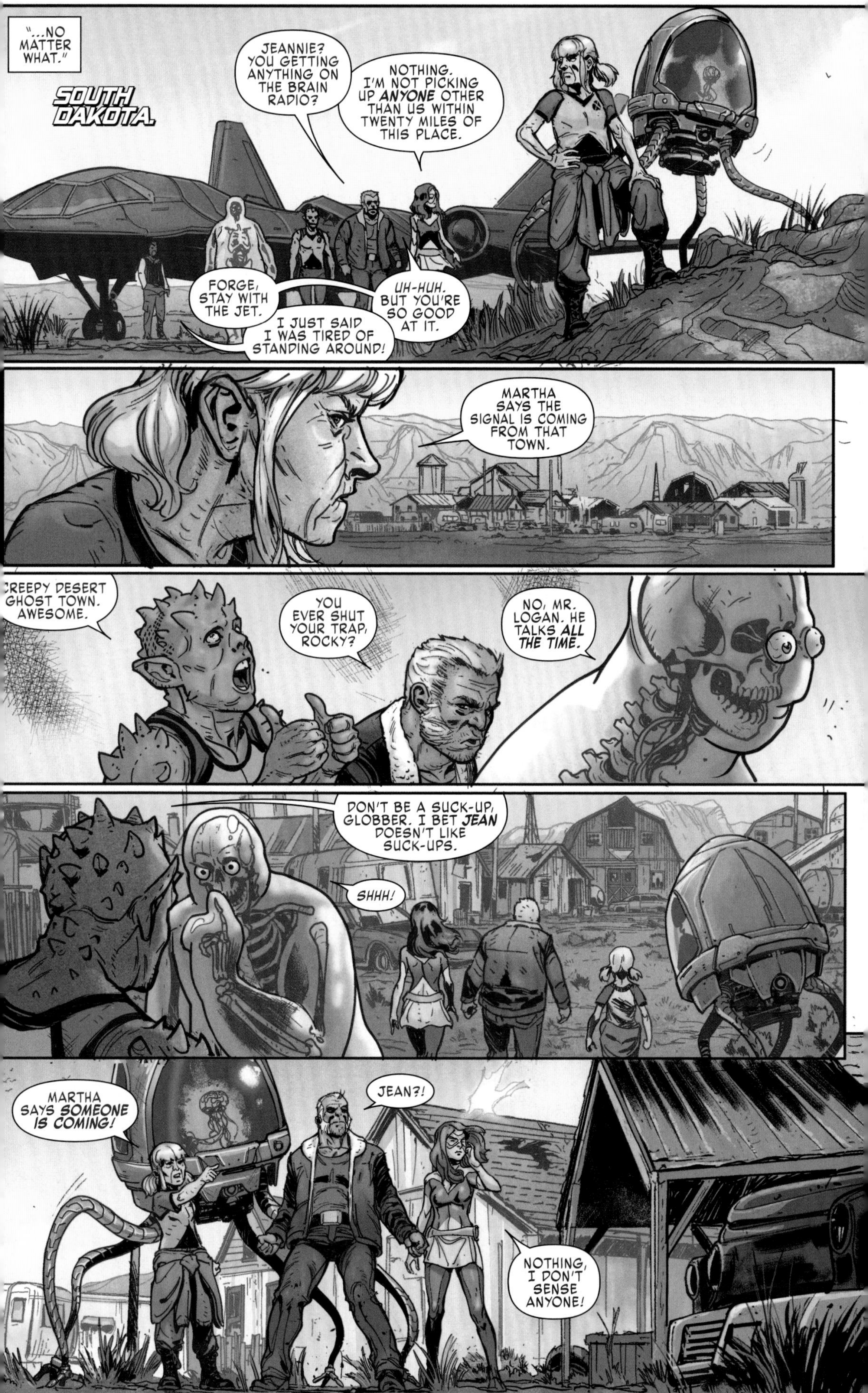
"...NO MATTER WHAT."
SOUTH DAKOTA.
JEANNIE? YOU GETTING ANYTHING ON THE BRAIN RADIO?
NOTHING. I'M NOT PICKING UP ANYONE OTHER THAN US WITHIN TWENTY MILES OF THIS PLACE.
FORGE, STAY WITH THE JET.
UH-HUH. BUT YOU'RE SO GOOD AT IT.
I JUST SAID I WAS TIRED OF STANDING AROUND!
MARTHA SAYS THE SIGNAL IS COMING FROM THAT TOWN.
CREEPY DESERT GHOST TOWN. AWESOME.
YOU EVER SHUT YOUR TRAP, ROCKY?
NO, MR. LOGAN. HE TALKS ALL THE TIME.
DON'T BE A SUCK-UP, GLOBBER. I BET JEAN DOESN'T LIKE SUCK-UPS.
SHHH!
MARTHA SAYS SOMEONE IS COMING!
JEAN?!
NOTHING, I DON'T SENSE ANYONE!

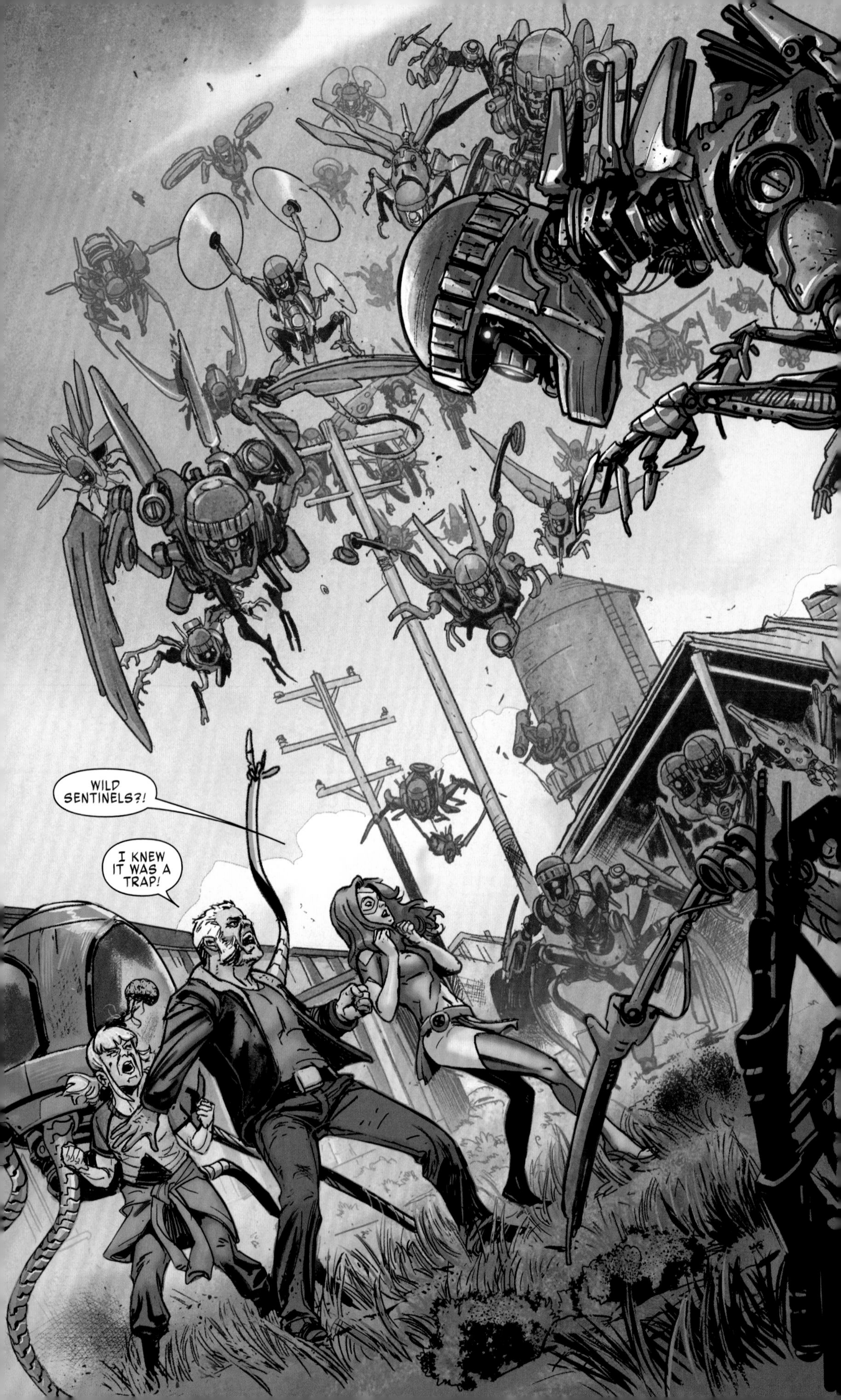
WILD SENTINELS?!
I KNEW IT WAS A TRAP!

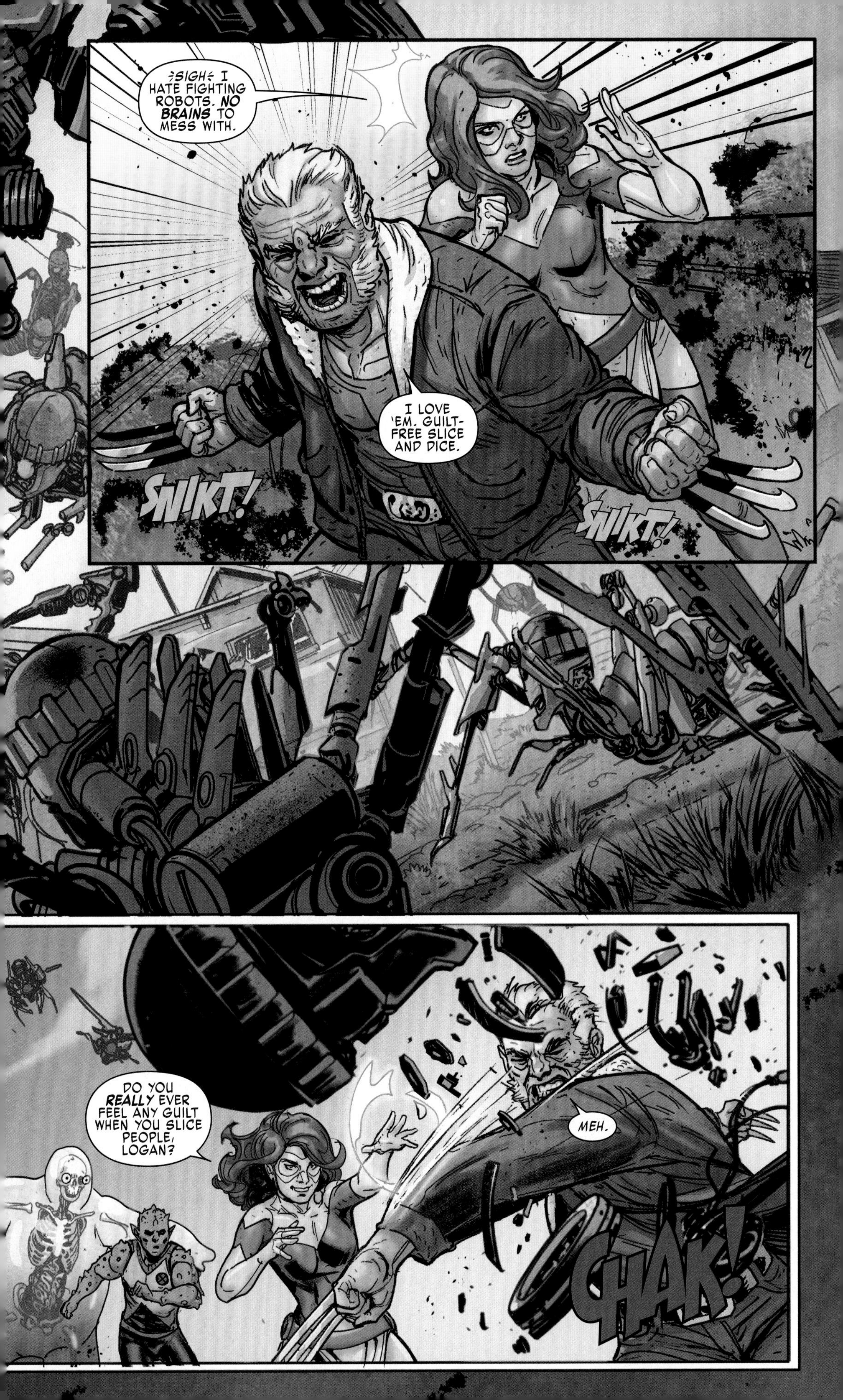

⇝SIGH⇜ I HATE FIGHTING ROBOTS. NO BRAINS TO MESS WITH.
I LOVE 'EM. GUILT-FREE SLICE AND DICE.
SNIKT!
SNIKT!
DO YOU REALLY EVER FEEL ANY GUILT WHEN YOU SLICE PEOPLE, LOGAN?
MEH.
CHAK!

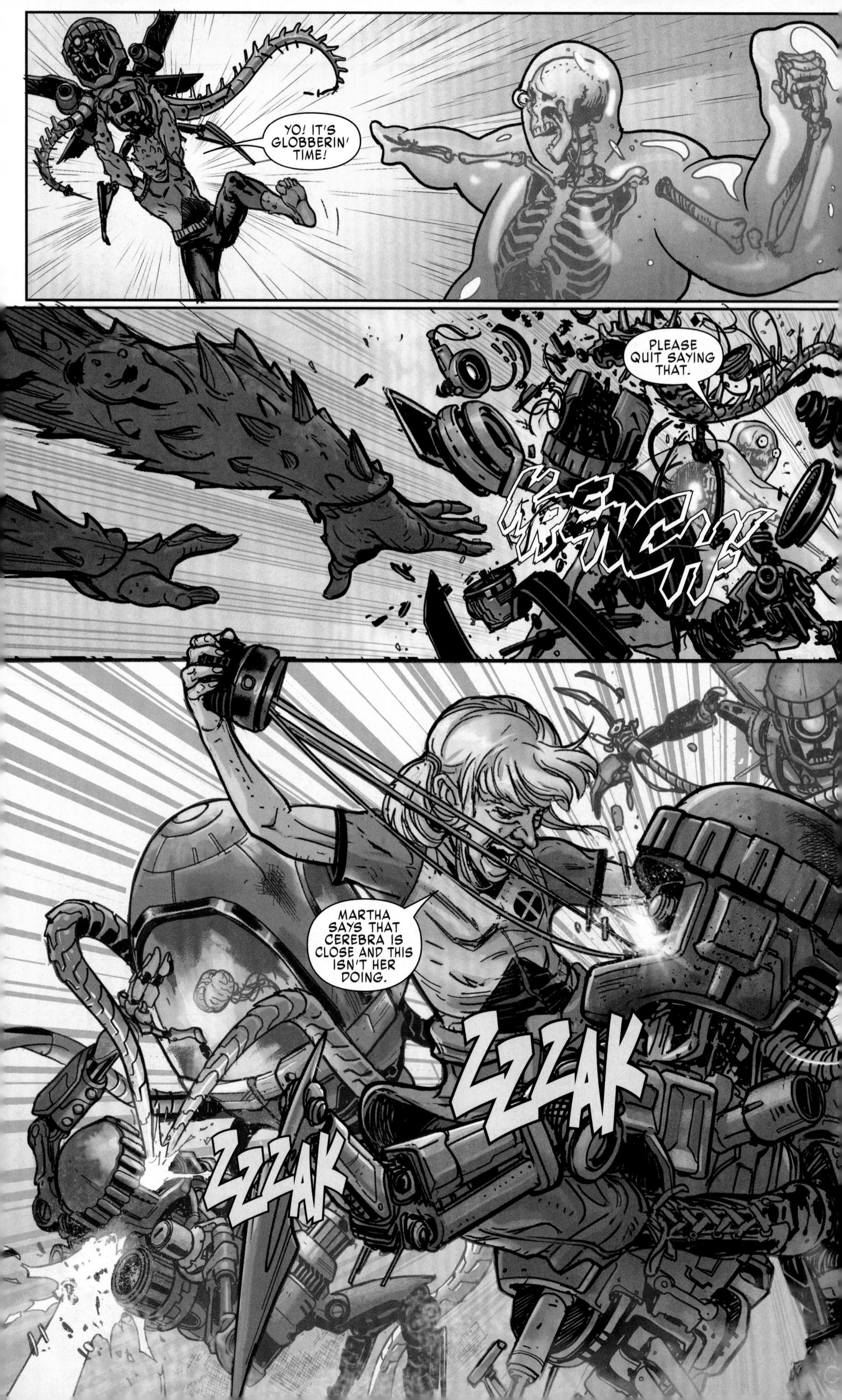
YO! IT'S GLOBBERIN' TIME!
PLEASE QUIT SAYING THAT.
MARTHA SAYS THAT CEREBRA IS CLOSE AND THIS ISN'T HER DOING.
ZZZAK
ZZZAK

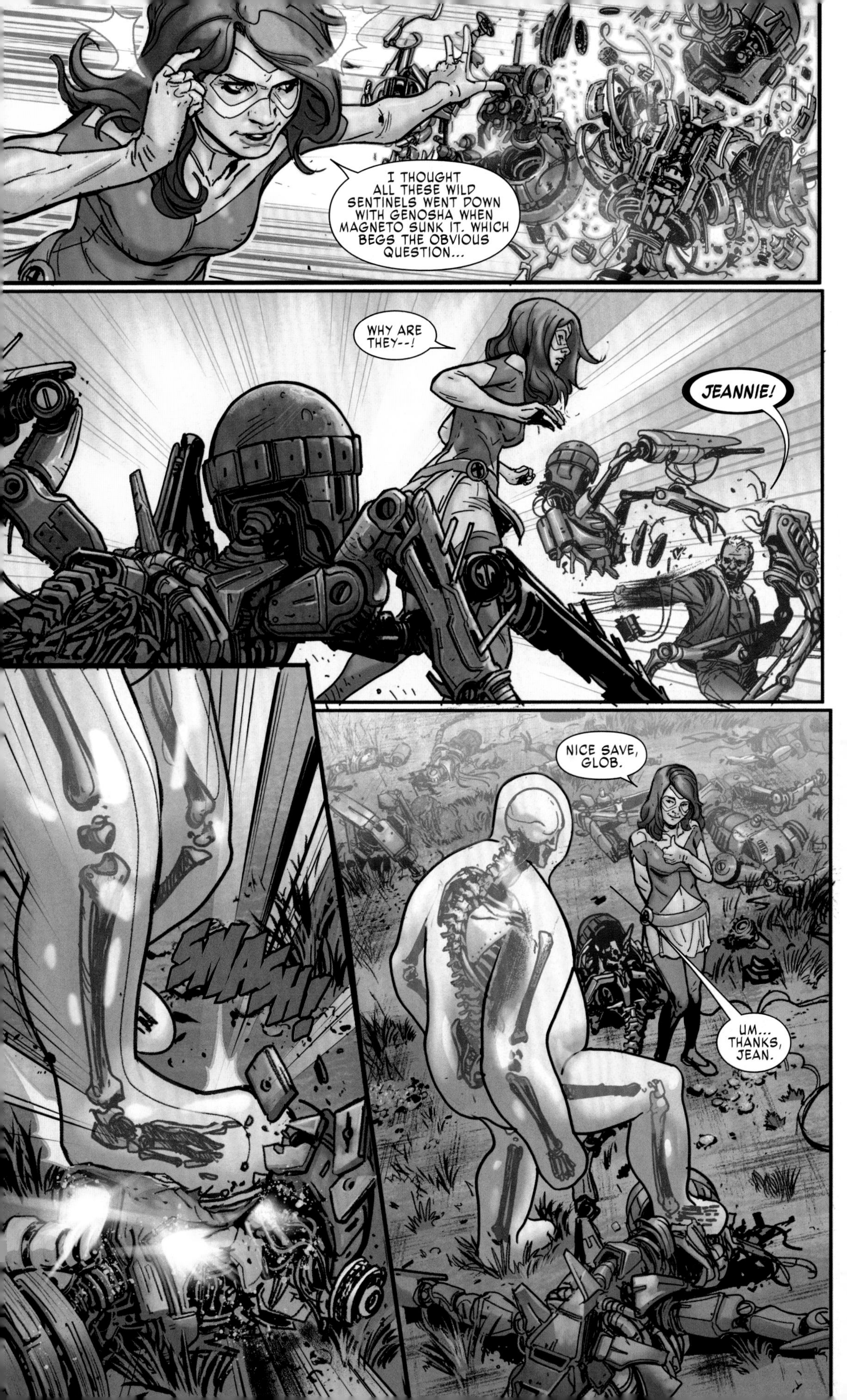

I THOUGHT ALL THESE WILD SENTINELS WENT DOWN WITH GENOSHA WHEN MAGNETO SUNK IT. WHICH BEGS THE OBVIOUS QUESTION...
WHY ARE THEY--!
JEANNIE!
SMASH!
NICE SAVE, GLOB.
UM... THANKS, JEAN.

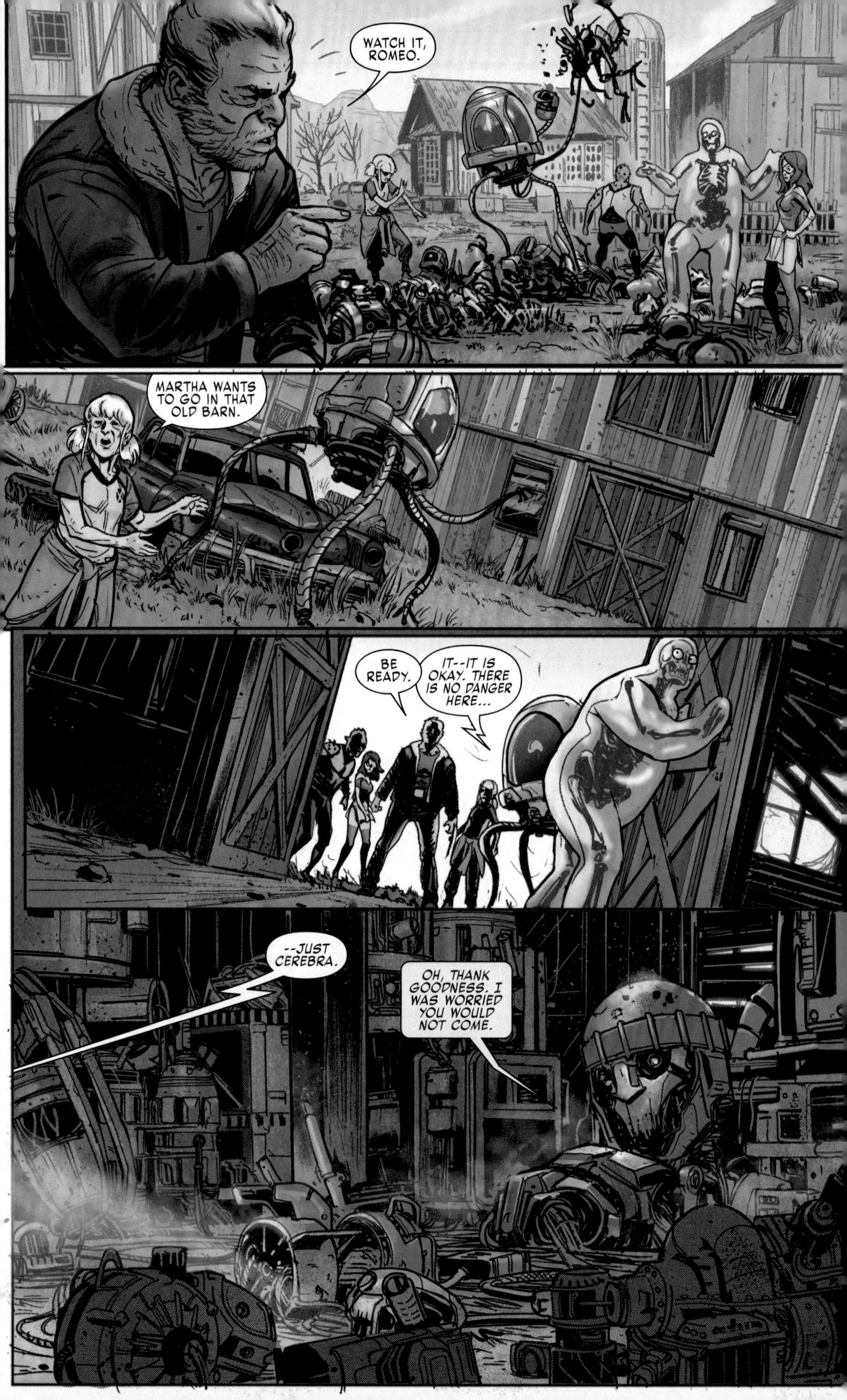
WATCH IT, ROMEO.
MARTHA WANTS TO GO IN THAT OLD BARN.
BE READY.
IT--IT IS OKAY. THERE IS NO DANGER HERE...
--JUST CEREBRA.
OH, THANK GOODNESS. I WAS WORRIED YOU WOULD NOT COME.

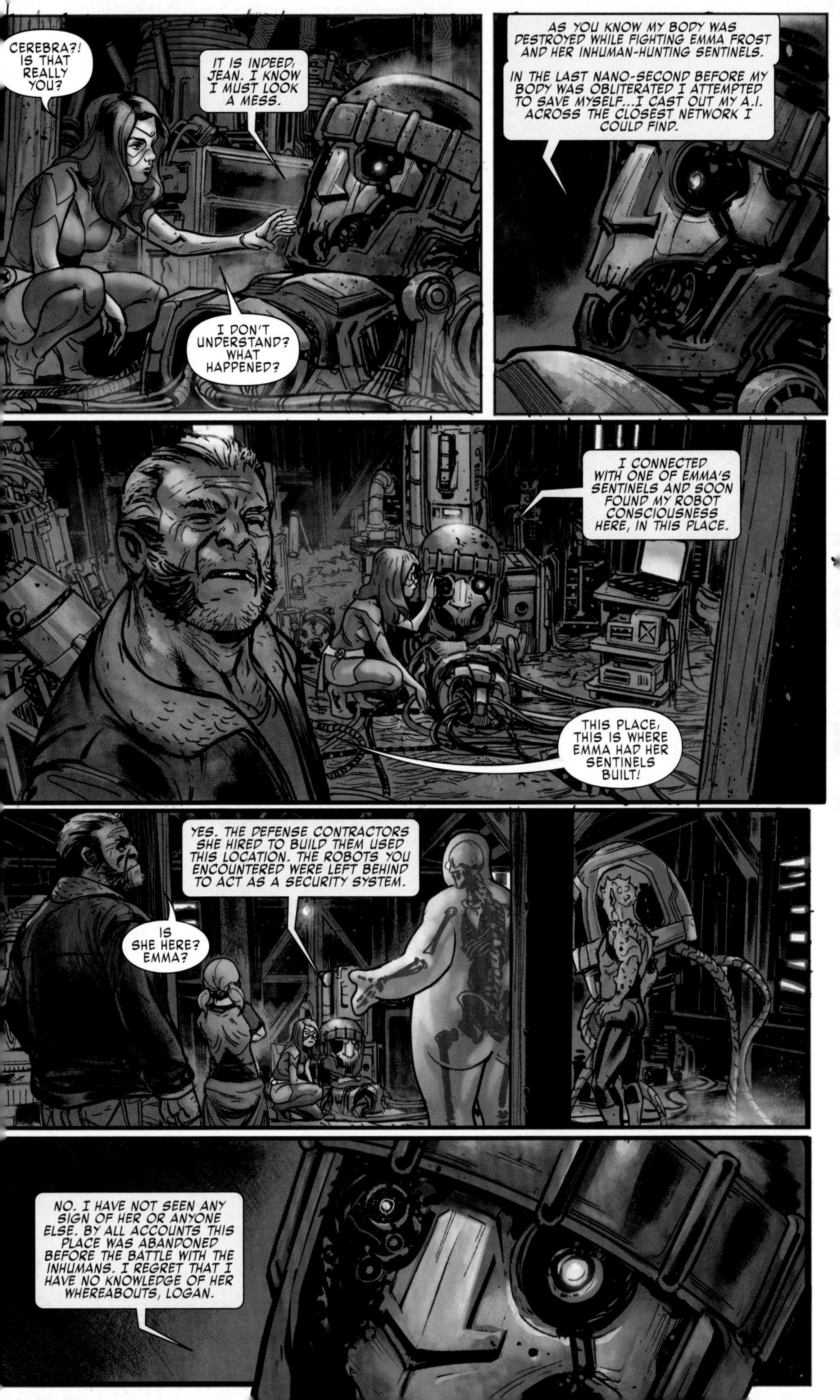

CEREBRA?! IS THAT REALLY YOU?
IT IS INDEED, JEAN. I KNOW I MUST LOOK A MESS.
I DON'T UNDERSTAND? WHAT HAPPENED?
AS YOU KNOW MY BODY WAS DESTROYED WHILE FIGHTING EMMA FROST AND HER INHUMAN-HUNTING SENTINELS.
IN THE LAST NANO-SECOND BEFORE MY BODY WAS OBLITERATED I ATTEMPTED TO SAVE MYSELF...I CAST OUT MY A.I. ACROSS THE CLOSEST NETWORK I COULD FIND.
I CONNECTED WITH ONE OF EMMA'S SENTINELS AND SOON FOUND MY ROBOT CONSCIOUSNESS HERE, IN THIS PLACE.
THIS PLACE, THIS IS WHERE EMMA HAD HER SENTINELS BUILT!
IS SHE HERE? EMMA?
YES. THE DEFENSE CONTRACTORS SHE HIRED TO BUILD THEM USED THIS LOCATION. THE ROBOTS YOU ENCOUNTERED WERE LEFT BEHIND TO ACT AS A SECURITY SYSTEM.
NO. I HAVE NOT SEEN ANY SIGN OF HER OR ANYONE ELSE. BY ALL ACCOUNTS THIS PLACE WAS ABANDONED BEFORE THE BATTLE WITH THE INHUMANS. I REGRET THAT I HAVE NO KNOWLEDGE OF HER WHEREABOUTS, LOGAN.

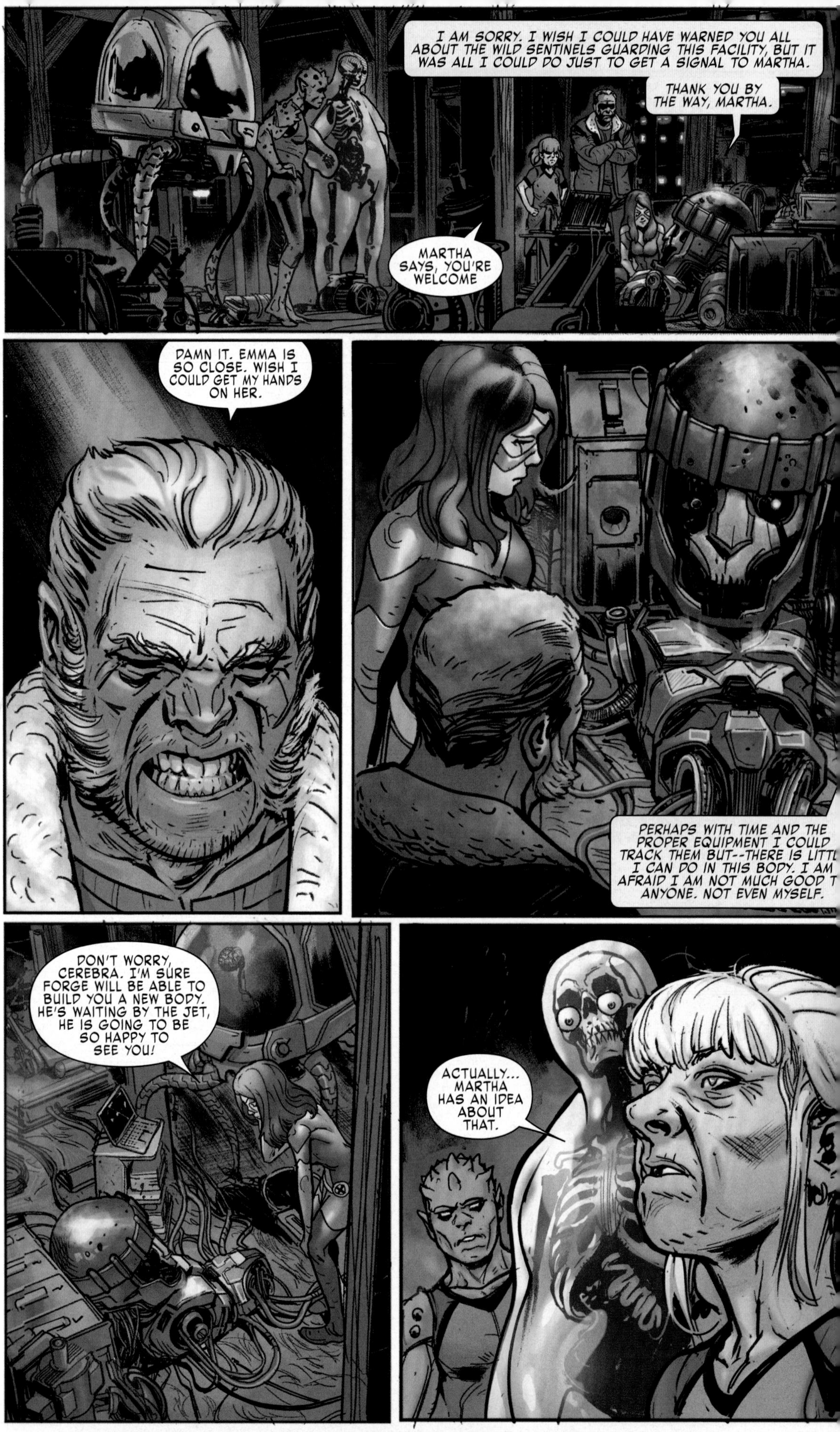
I AM SORRY. I WISH I COULD HAVE WARNED YOU ALL ABOUT THE WILD SENTINELS GUARDING THIS FACILITY, BUT IT WAS ALL I COULD DO JUST TO GET A SIGNAL TO MARTHA.
THANK YOU BY THE WAY, MARTHA.
MARTHA SAYS, YOU'RE WELCOME
DAMN IT. EMMA IS SO CLOSE. WISH I COULD GET MY HANDS ON HER.
PERHAPS WITH TIME AND THE PROPER EQUIPMENT I COULD TRACK THEM BUT--THERE IS LITTL I CAN DO IN THIS BODY. I AM AFRAID I AM NOT MUCH GOOD T ANYONE. NOT EVEN MYSELF.
DON'T WORRY, CEREBRA. I'M SURE FORGE WILL BE ABLE TO BUILD YOU A NEW BODY. HE'S WAITING BY THE JET, HE IS GOING TO BE SO HAPPY TO SEE YOU!
ACTUALLY... MARTHA HAS AN IDEA ABOUT THAT.

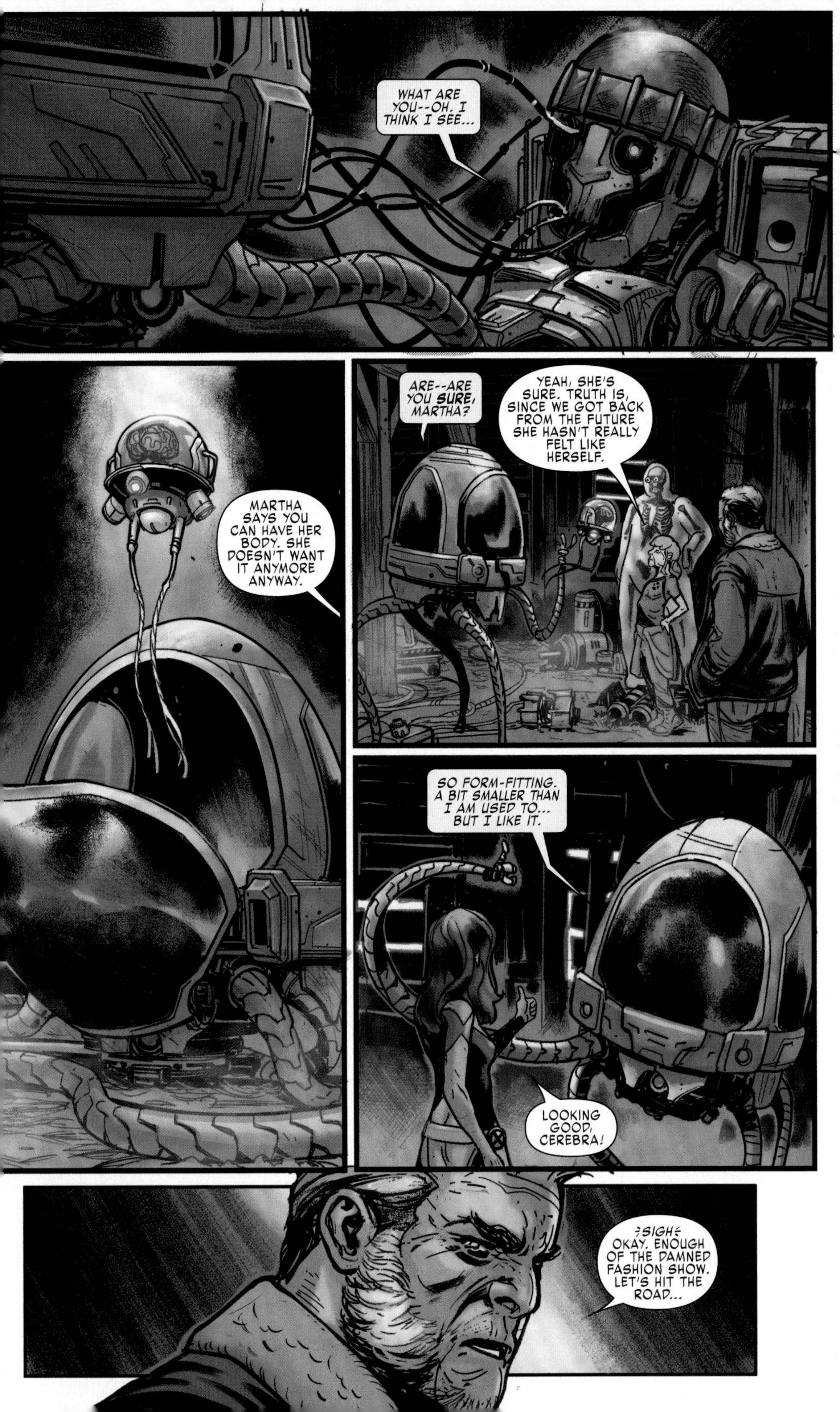

WHAT ARE YOU--OH. I THINK I SEE...
MARTHA SAYS YOU CAN HAVE HER BODY. SHE DOESN'T WANT IT ANYMORE ANYWAY.
ARE--ARE YOU **SURE**, MARTHA?
YEAH, SHE'S SURE. TRUTH IS, SINCE WE GOT BACK FROM THE FUTURE SHE HASN'T REALLY FELT LIKE HERSELF.
SO FORM-FITTING. A BIT SMALLER THAN I AM USED TO... BUT I LIKE IT.
LOOKING GOOD, CEREBRA!
SIGH OKAY. ENOUGH OF THE DAMNED FASHION SHOW. LET'S HIT THE ROAD...

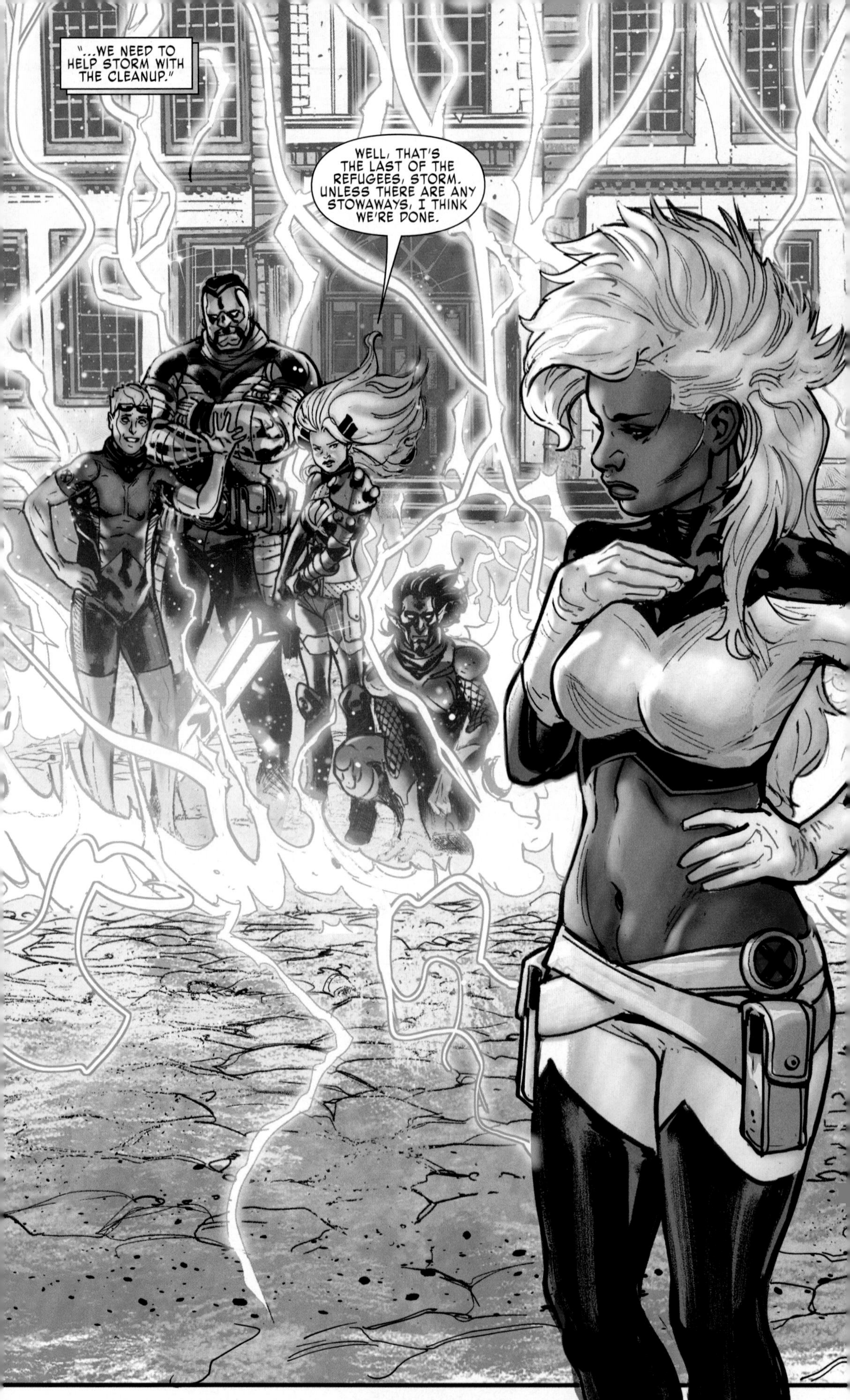
"...WE NEED TO HELP STORM WITH THE CLEANUP."
WELL, THAT'S THE LAST OF THE REFUGEES, STORM. UNLESS THERE ARE ANY STOWAWAYS, I THINK WE'RE DONE.

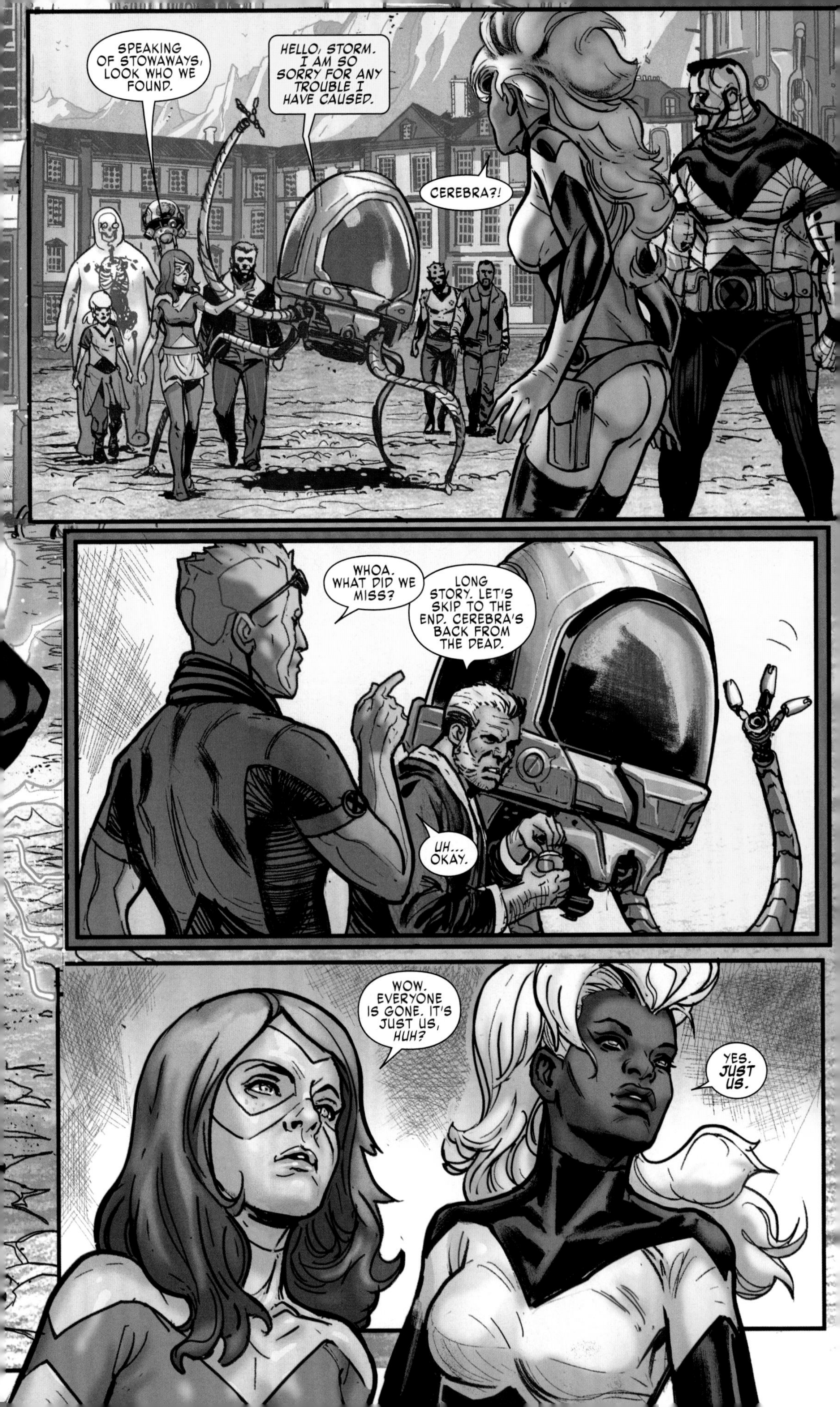
SPEAKING OF STOWAWAYS, LOOK WHO WE FOUND.
HELLO, STORM. I AM SO SORRY FOR ANY TROUBLE I HAVE CAUSED.
CEREBRA?!
WHOA. WHAT DID WE MISS?
LONG STORY. LET'S SKIP TO THE END. CEREBRA'S BACK FROM THE DEAD.
UH... OKAY.
WOW. EVERYONE IS GONE. IT'S JUST US, HUH?
YES. JUST US.

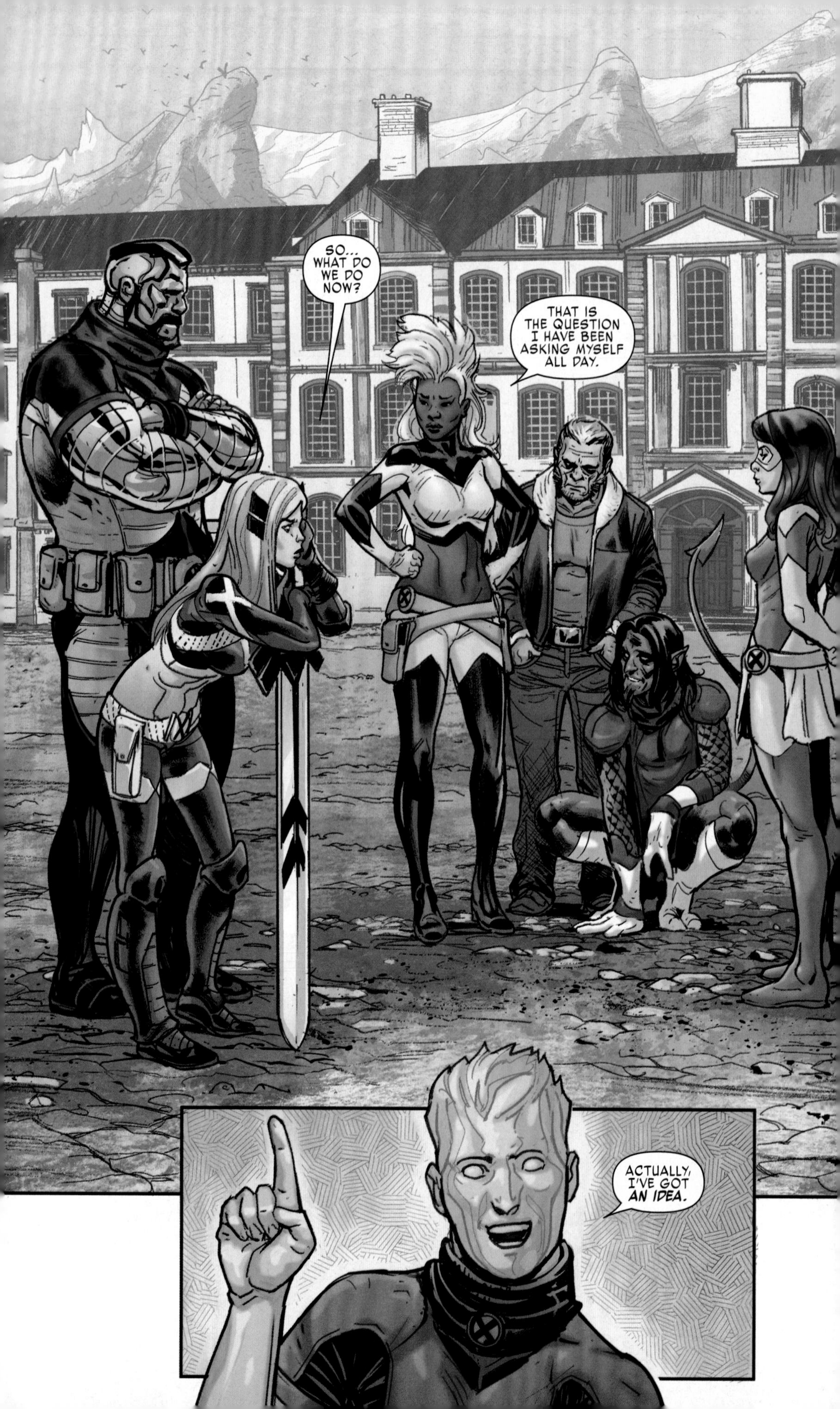
SO... WHAT DO WE DO NOW?
THAT IS THE QUESTION I HAVE BEEN ASKING MYSELF ALL DAY.
ACTUALLY, I'VE GOT **AN IDEA.**

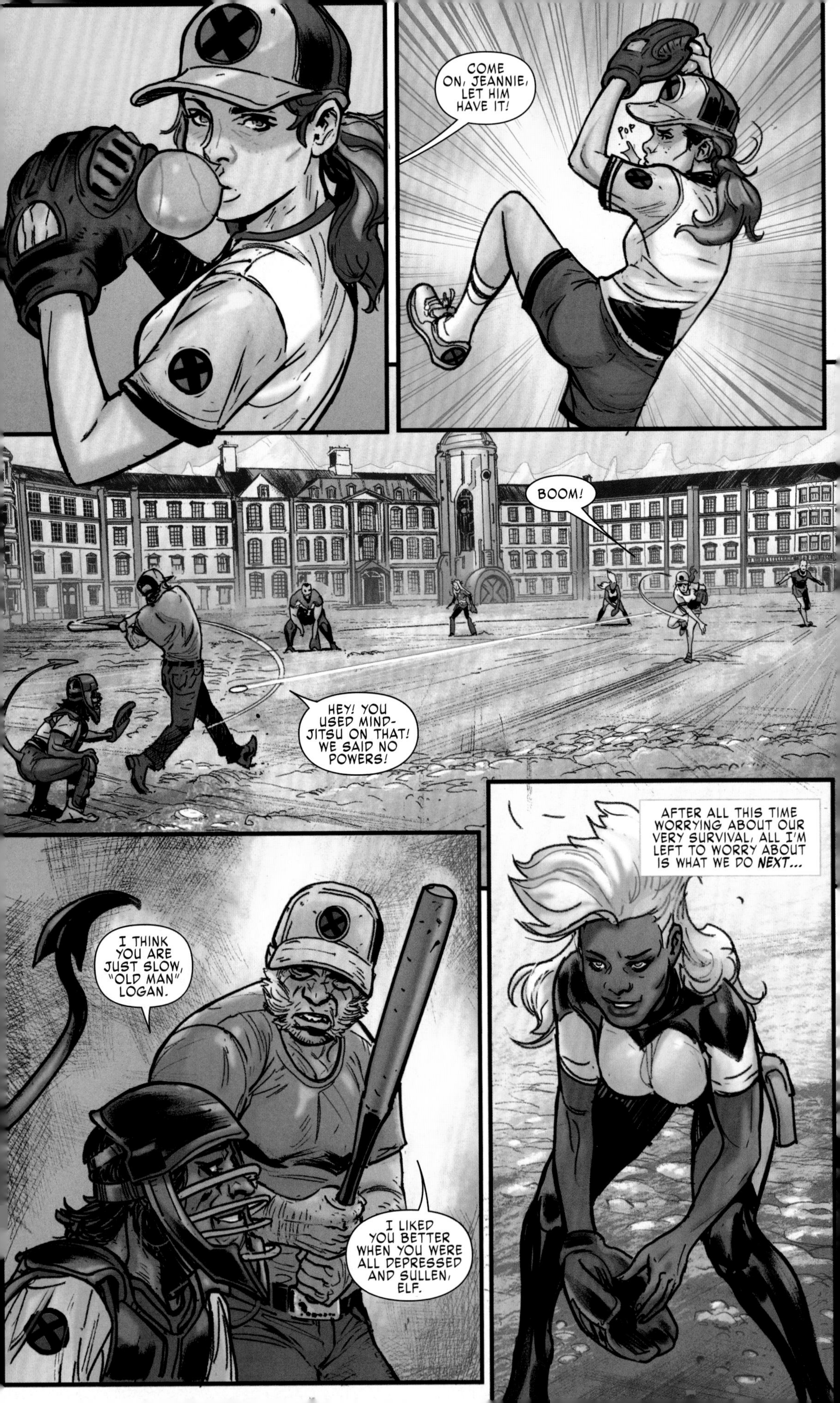
COME ON, JEANNIE, LET HIM HAVE IT!
POP
BOOM!
HEY! YOU USED MIND-JITSU ON THAT! WE SAID NO POWERS!
AFTER ALL THIS TIME WORRYING ABOUT OUR VERY SURVIVAL, ALL I'M LEFT TO WORRY ABOUT IS WHAT WE DO NEXT...
I THINK YOU ARE JUST SLOW, "OLD MAN" LOGAN.
I LIKED YOU BETTER WHEN YOU WERE ALL DEPRESSED AND SULLEN, ELF.

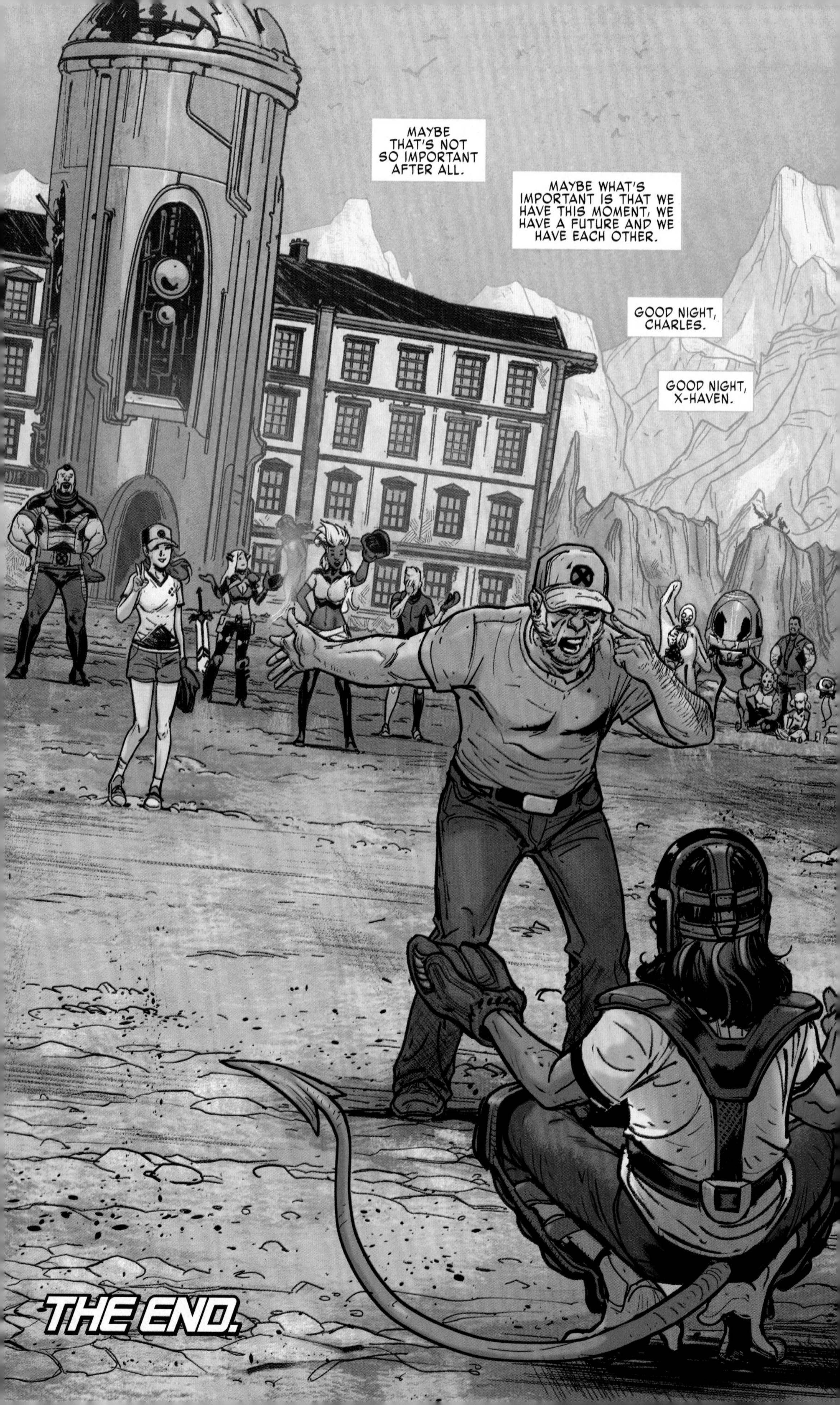
MAYBE THAT'S NOT SO IMPORTANT AFTER ALL.
MAYBE WHAT'S IMPORTANT IS THAT WE HAVE THIS MOMENT, WE HAVE A FUTURE AND WE HAVE EACH OTHER.
GOOD NIGHT, CHARLES.
GOOD NIGHT, X-HAVEN.
THE END.

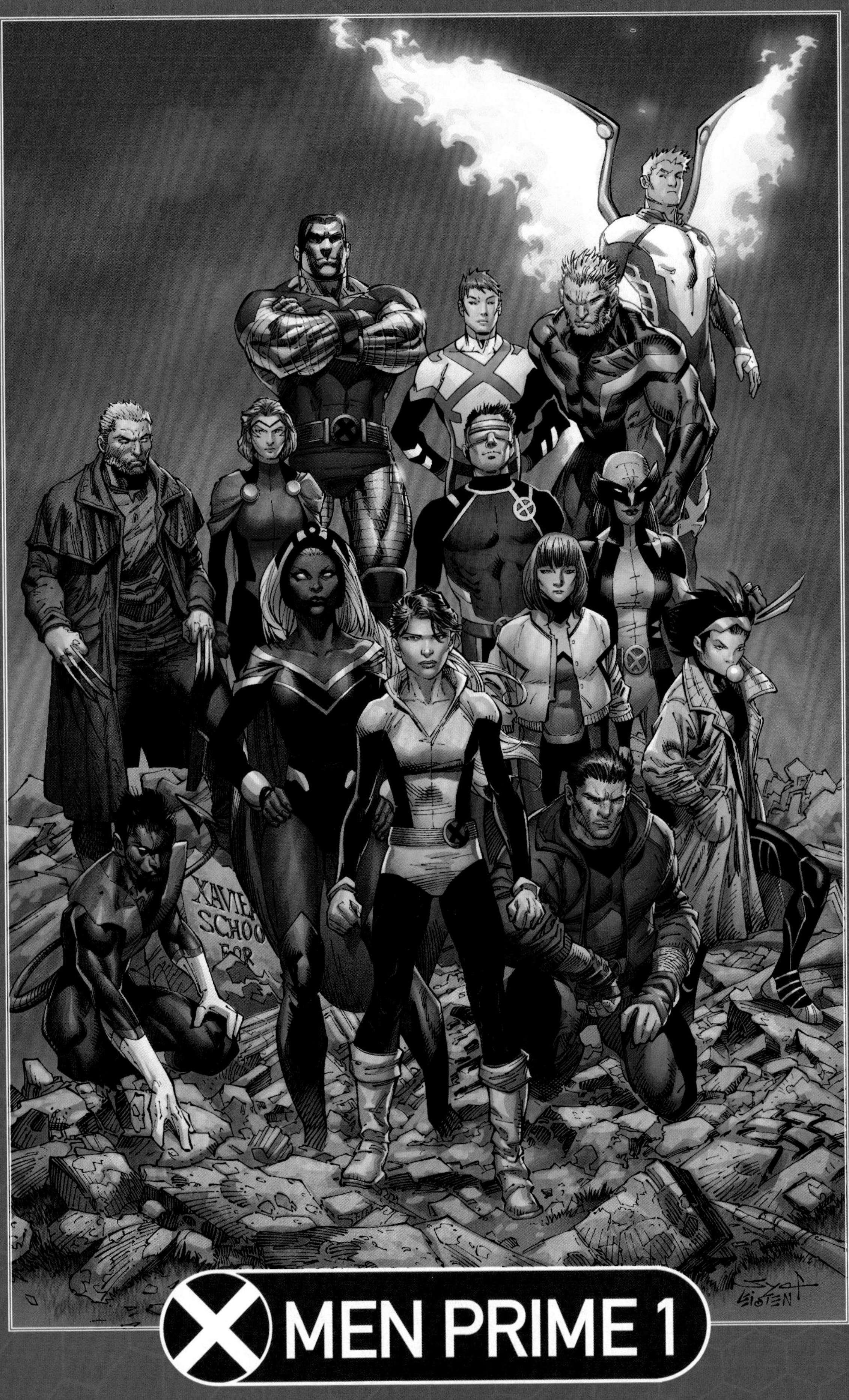
MEN PRIME 1

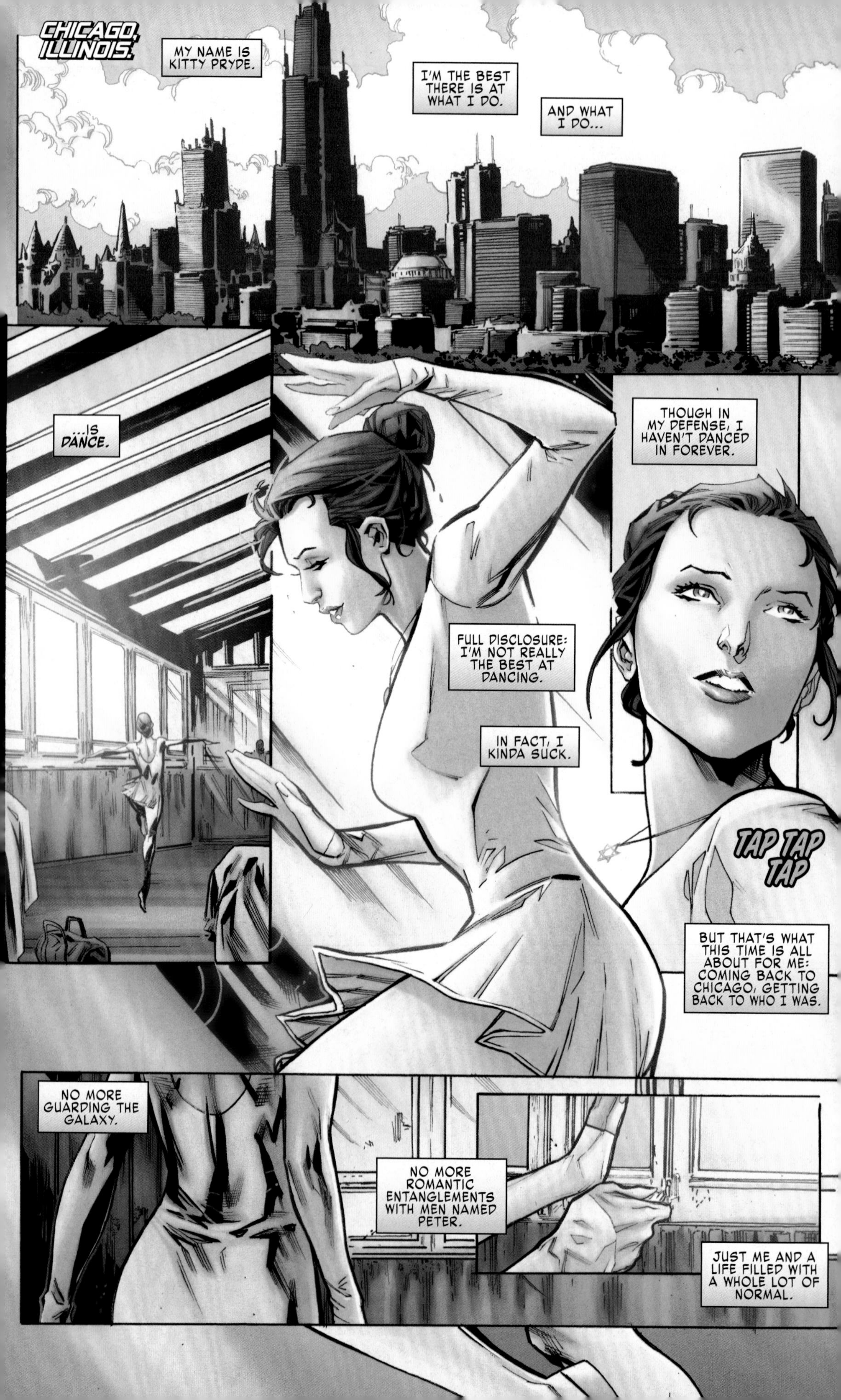
CHICAGO, ILLINOIS.
MY NAME IS KITTY PRYDE.
I'M THE BEST THERE IS AT WHAT I DO.
AND WHAT I DO...
...IS DANCE.
THOUGH IN MY DEFENSE, I HAVEN'T DANCED IN FOREVER.
FULL DISCLOSURE: I'M NOT REALLY THE BEST AT DANCING.
IN FACT, I KINDA SUCK.
TAP TAP TAP
BUT THAT'S WHAT THIS TIME IS ALL ABOUT FOR ME: COMING BACK TO CHICAGO, GETTING BACK TO WHO I WAS.
NO MORE GUARDING THE GALAXY.
NO MORE ROMANTIC ENTANGLEMENTS WITH MEN NAMED PETER.
JUST ME AND A LIFE FILLED WITH A WHOLE LOT OF NORMAL.

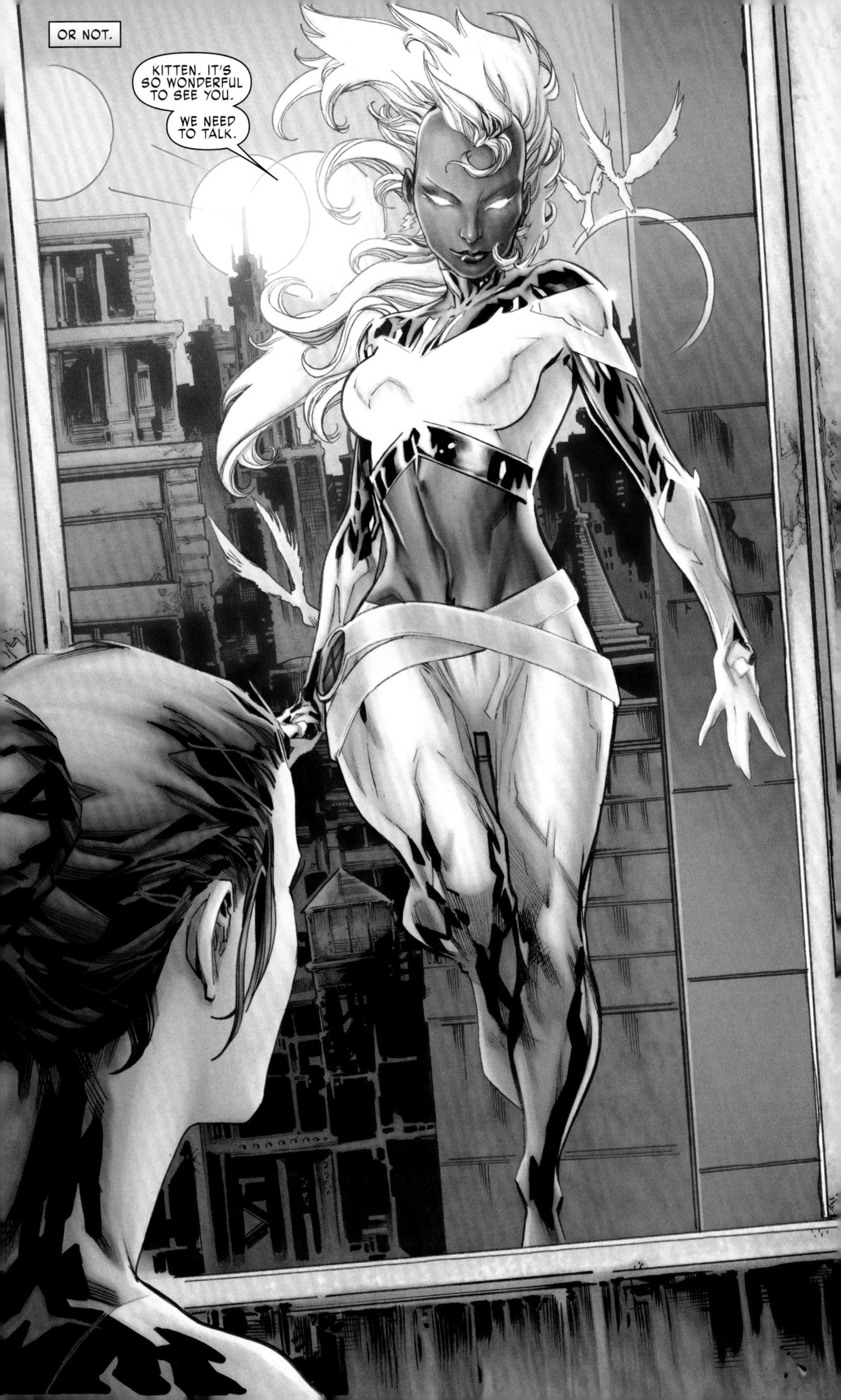
OR NOT.
KITTEN. IT'S SO WONDERFUL TO SEE YOU.
WE NEED TO TALK.

X-MEN PRIME

PREVIOUSLY IN *X-MEN*...

RETURNING TO EARTH AFTER A SERIES OF ADVENTURES WITH THE GUARDIANS OF THE GALAXY, FORMER X-MAN KITTY PRYDE DISCOVERS THAT SHE'S NOT THE ONLY ONE STARTING A NEW CHAPTER. IN THE AFTERMATH OF THEIR WAR WITH THE INHUMANS, THE X-MEN FIND THEMSELVES OUT FROM UNDER THE THREAT OF EXTINCTION AND WITH AN UNCERTAIN FUTURE STRETCHED OUT BEFORE THEM...

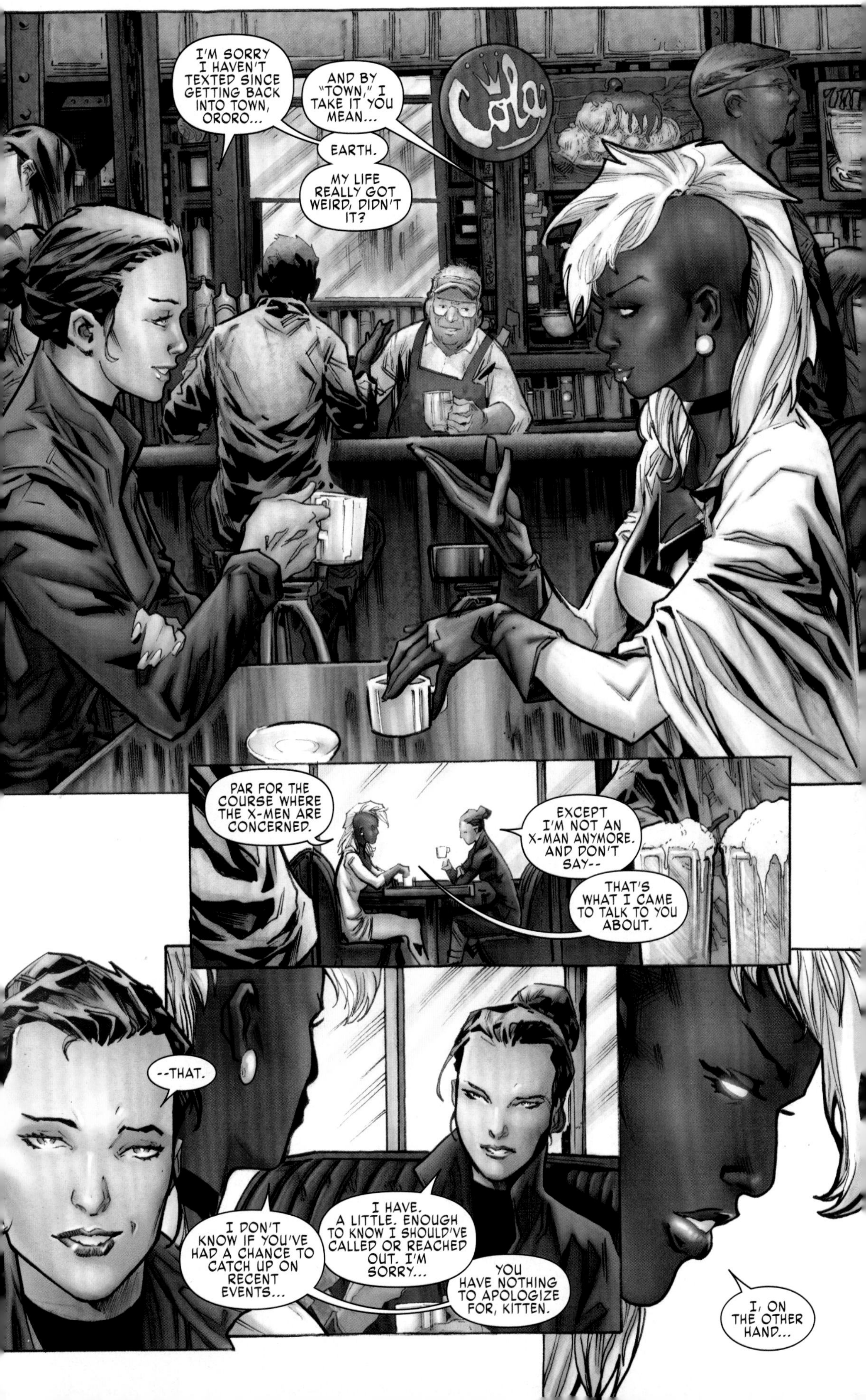

I'M SORRY I HAVEN'T TEXTED SINCE GETTING BACK INTO TOWN, ORORO...
AND BY "TOWN," I TAKE IT YOU MEAN...
EARTH.
MY LIFE REALLY GOT WEIRD, DIDN'T IT?
PAR FOR THE COURSE WHERE THE X-MEN ARE CONCERNED.
EXCEPT I'M NOT AN X-MAN ANYMORE. AND DON'T SAY--
THAT'S WHAT I CAME TO TALK TO YOU ABOUT.
--THAT.
I DON'T KNOW IF YOU'VE HAD A CHANCE TO CATCH UP ON RECENT EVENTS...
I HAVE. A LITTLE. ENOUGH TO KNOW I SHOULD'VE CALLED OR REACHED OUT. I'M SORRY...
YOU HAVE NOTHING TO APOLOGIZE FOR, KITTEN.
I, ON THE OTHER HAND...

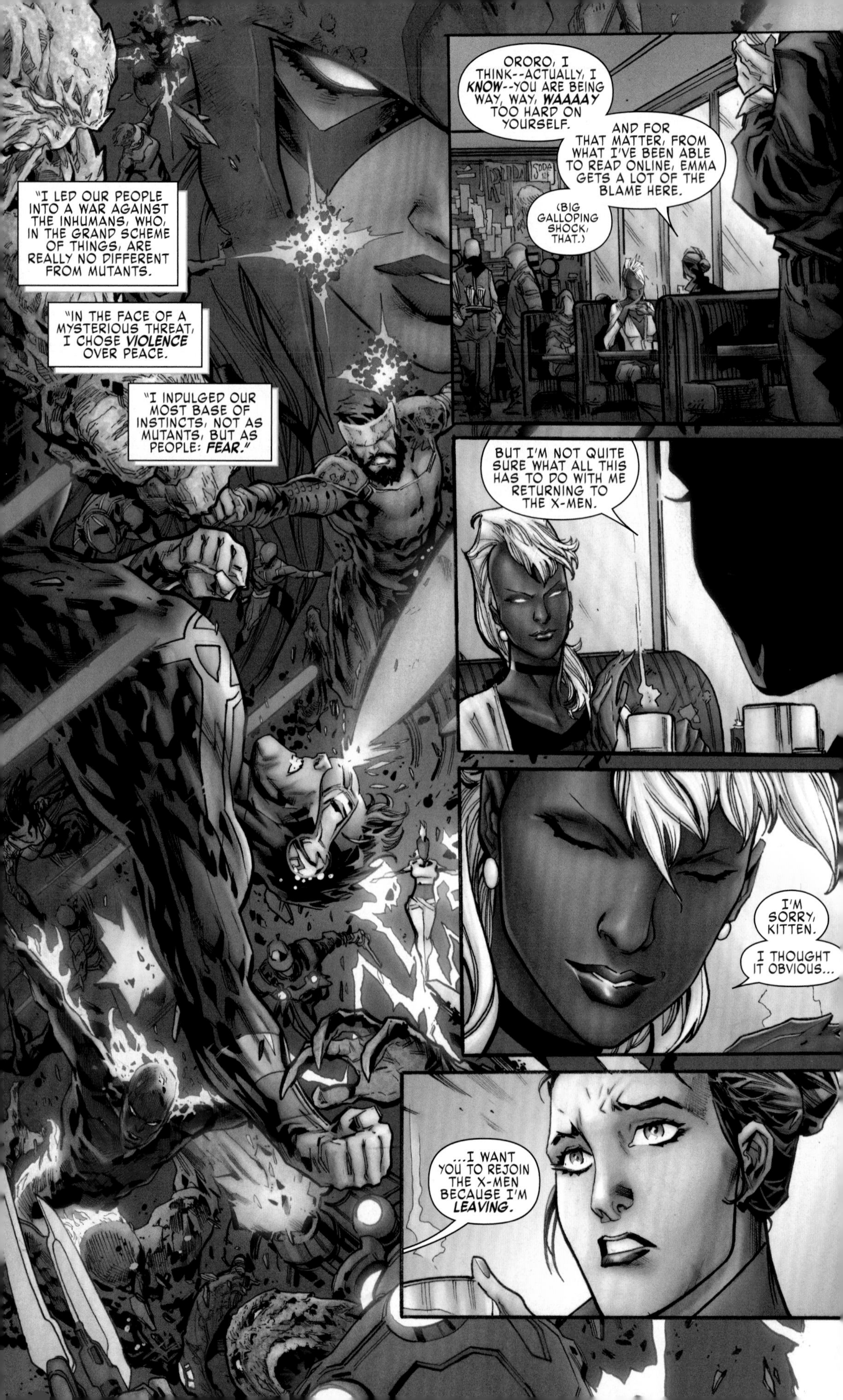
"I LED OUR PEOPLE INTO A WAR AGAINST THE INHUMANS, WHO, IN THE GRAND SCHEME OF THINGS, ARE REALLY NO DIFFERENT FROM MUTANTS.
"IN THE FACE OF A MYSTERIOUS THREAT, I CHOSE *VIOLENCE* OVER PEACE.
"I INDULGED OUR MOST BASE OF INSTINCTS, NOT AS MUTANTS, BUT AS PEOPLE: *FEAR.*"
ORORO, I THINK--ACTUALLY, I *KNOW*--YOU ARE BEING WAY, WAY, *WAAAAY* TOO HARD ON YOURSELF.
AND FOR THAT MATTER, FROM WHAT I'VE BEEN ABLE TO READ ONLINE, EMMA GETS A LOT OF THE BLAME HERE.
(BIG GALLOPING SHOCK, THAT.)
BUT I'M NOT QUITE SURE WHAT ALL THIS HAS TO DO WITH ME RETURNING TO THE X-MEN.
I'M SORRY, KITTEN.
I THOUGHT IT OBVIOUS...
...I WANT YOU TO REJOIN THE X-MEN BECAUSE I'M *LEAVING.*

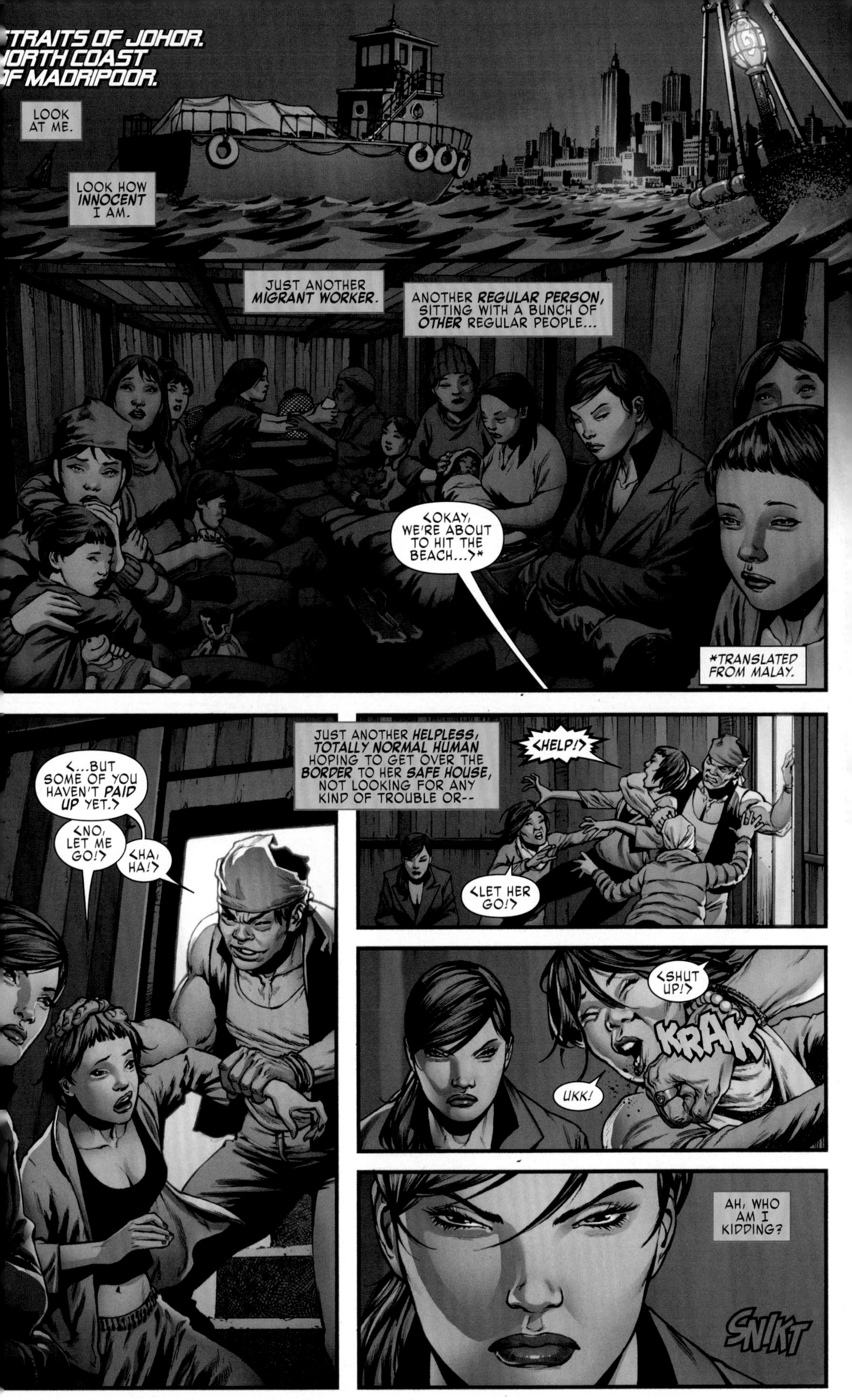

TRAITS OF JOHOR. ORTH COAST F MADRIPOOR.
LOOK AT ME.
LOOK HOW INNOCENT I AM.
JUST ANOTHER MIGRANT WORKER.
ANOTHER REGULAR PERSON, SITTING WITH A BUNCH OF OTHER REGULAR PEOPLE...
<OKAY, WE'RE ABOUT TO HIT THE BEACH...>*
*TRANSLATED FROM MALAY.
<...BUT SOME OF YOU HAVEN'T PAID UP YET.>
<NO, LET ME GO!>
<HA, HA!>
JUST ANOTHER HELPLESS, TOTALLY NORMAL HUMAN HOPING TO GET OVER THE BORDER TO HER SAFE HOUSE, NOT LOOKING FOR ANY KIND OF TROUBLE OR--
<HELP!>
<LET HER GO!>
<SHUT UP!>
KRAK
UKK!
AH, WHO AM I KIDDING?
SNIKT

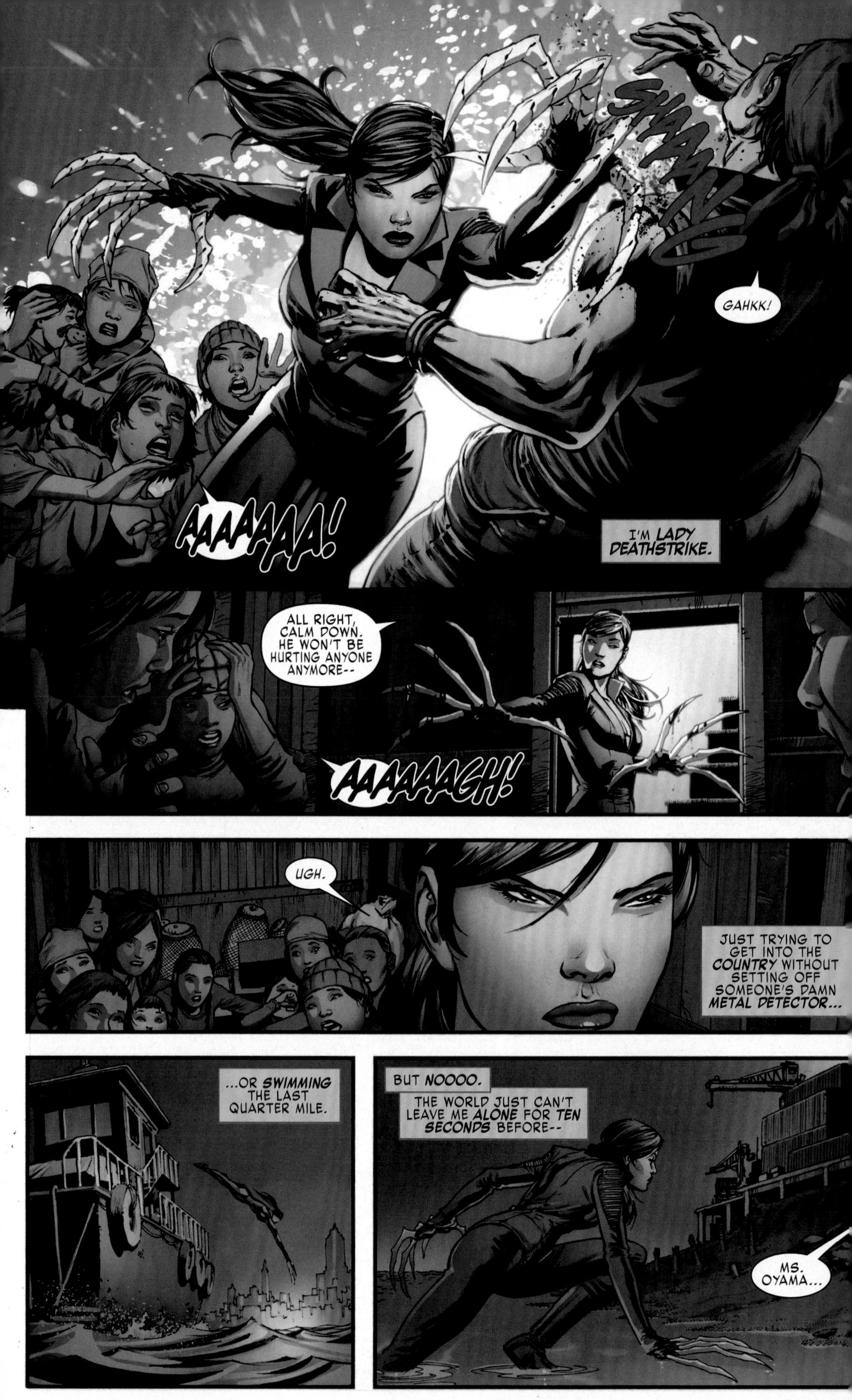
SHHAANG
GAHKK!
AAAAAAA!
I'M LADY DEATHSTRIKE.
ALL RIGHT, CALM DOWN. HE WON'T BE HURTING ANYONE ANYMORE--
AAAAAAGH!
UGH.
JUST TRYING TO GET INTO THE COUNTRY WITHOUT SETTING OFF SOMEONE'S DAMN METAL DETECTOR...
...OR SWIMMING THE LAST QUARTER MILE.
BUT NOOOO.
THE WORLD JUST CAN'T LEAVE ME ALONE FOR TEN SECONDS BEFORE--
MS. OYAMA...

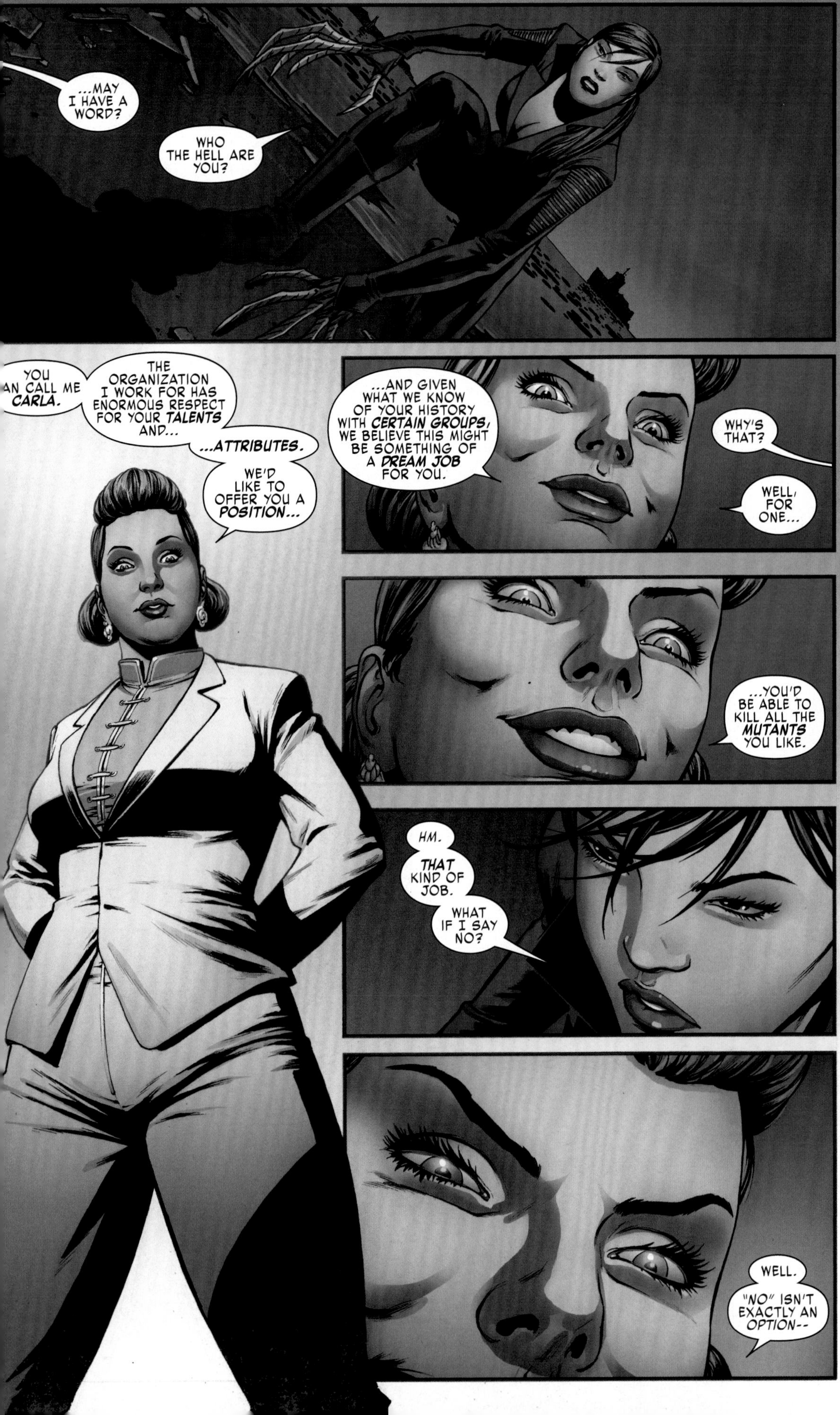

...MAY I HAVE A WORD?
WHO THE HELL ARE YOU?
YOU AN CALL ME CARLA.
THE ORGANIZATION I WORK FOR HAS ENORMOUS RESPECT FOR YOUR TALENTS AND...
...ATTRIBUTES.
WE'D LIKE TO OFFER YOU A POSITION...
...AND GIVEN WHAT WE KNOW OF YOUR HISTORY WITH CERTAIN GROUPS, WE BELIEVE THIS MIGHT BE SOMETHING OF A DREAM JOB FOR YOU.
WHY'S THAT?
WELL, FOR ONE...
...YOU'D BE ABLE TO KILL ALL THE MUTANTS YOU LIKE.
HM.
THAT KIND OF JOB.
WHAT IF I SAY NO?
WELL.
"NO" ISN'T EXACTLY AN OPTION--

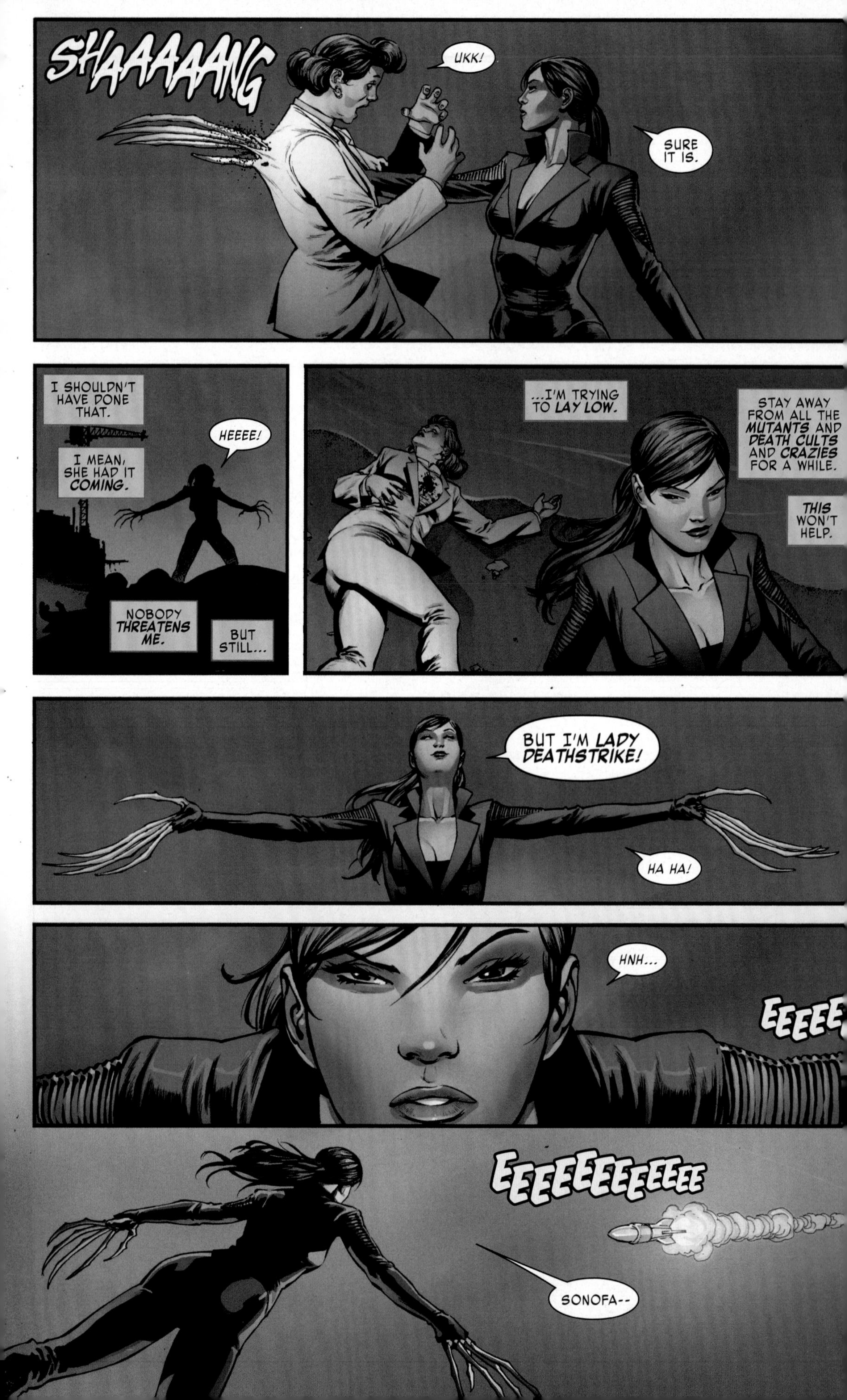

SHAAAAANG
UKK!
SURE IT IS.
I SHOULDN'T HAVE DONE THAT.
HEEEE!
I MEAN, SHE HAD IT COMING.
NOBODY THREATENS ME.
BUT STILL...
...I'M TRYING TO LAY LOW.
STAY AWAY FROM ALL THE MUTANTS AND DEATH CULTS AND CRAZIES FOR A WHILE.
THIS WON'T HELP.
BUT I'M LADY DEATHSTRIKE!
HA HA!
HNH...
EEEEE
EEEEEEEEEEEE
SONOFA--

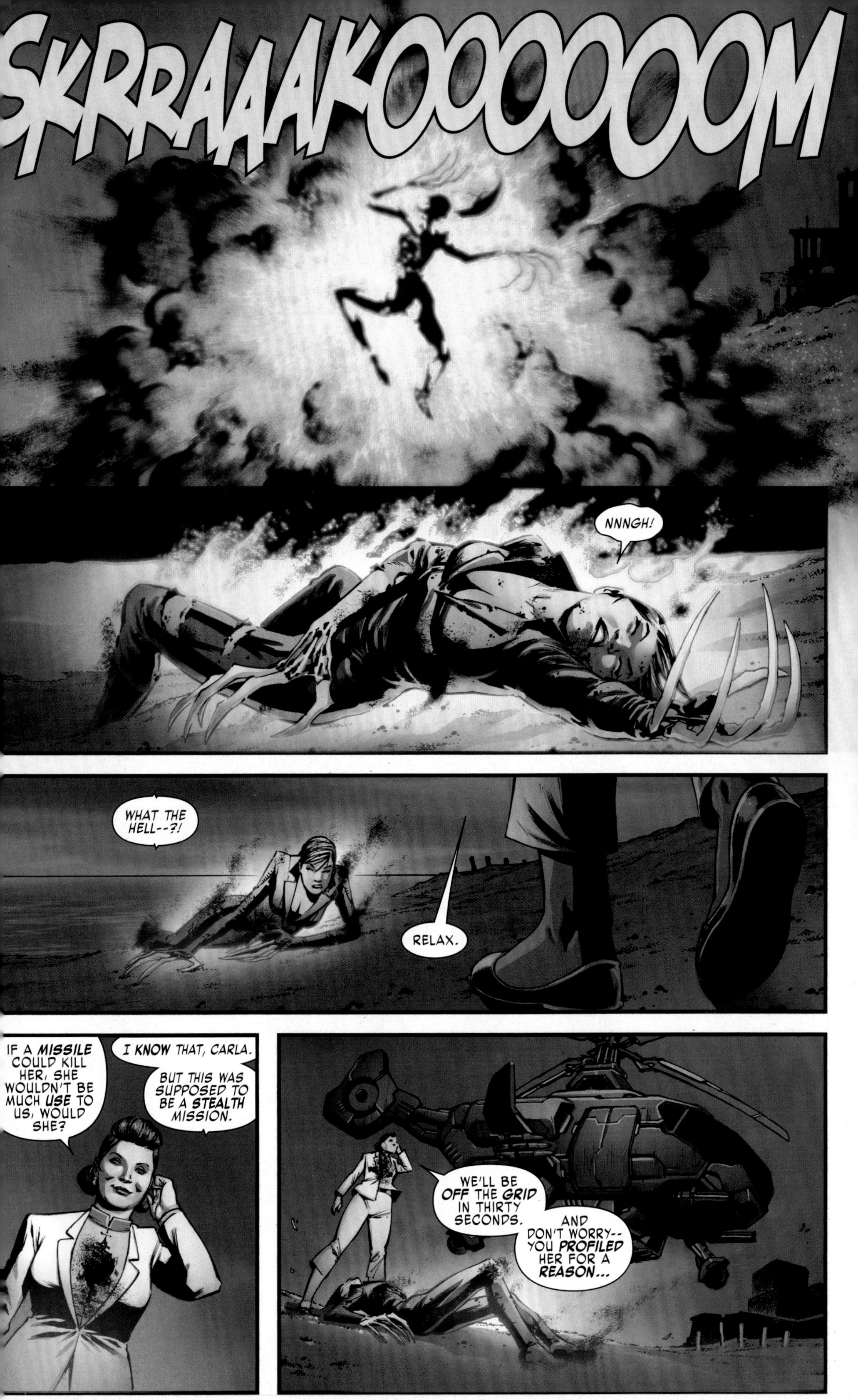
SKRRAAAKOOOOOOM
NNNGH!
WHAT THE HELL--?!
RELAX.
IF A MISSILE COULD KILL HER, SHE WOULDN'T BE MUCH USE TO US, WOULD SHE?
I KNOW THAT, CARLA.
BUT THIS WAS SUPPOSED TO BE A STEALTH MISSION.
WE'LL BE OFF THE GRID IN THIRTY SECONDS.
AND DON'T WORRY--YOU PROFILED HER FOR A REASON...

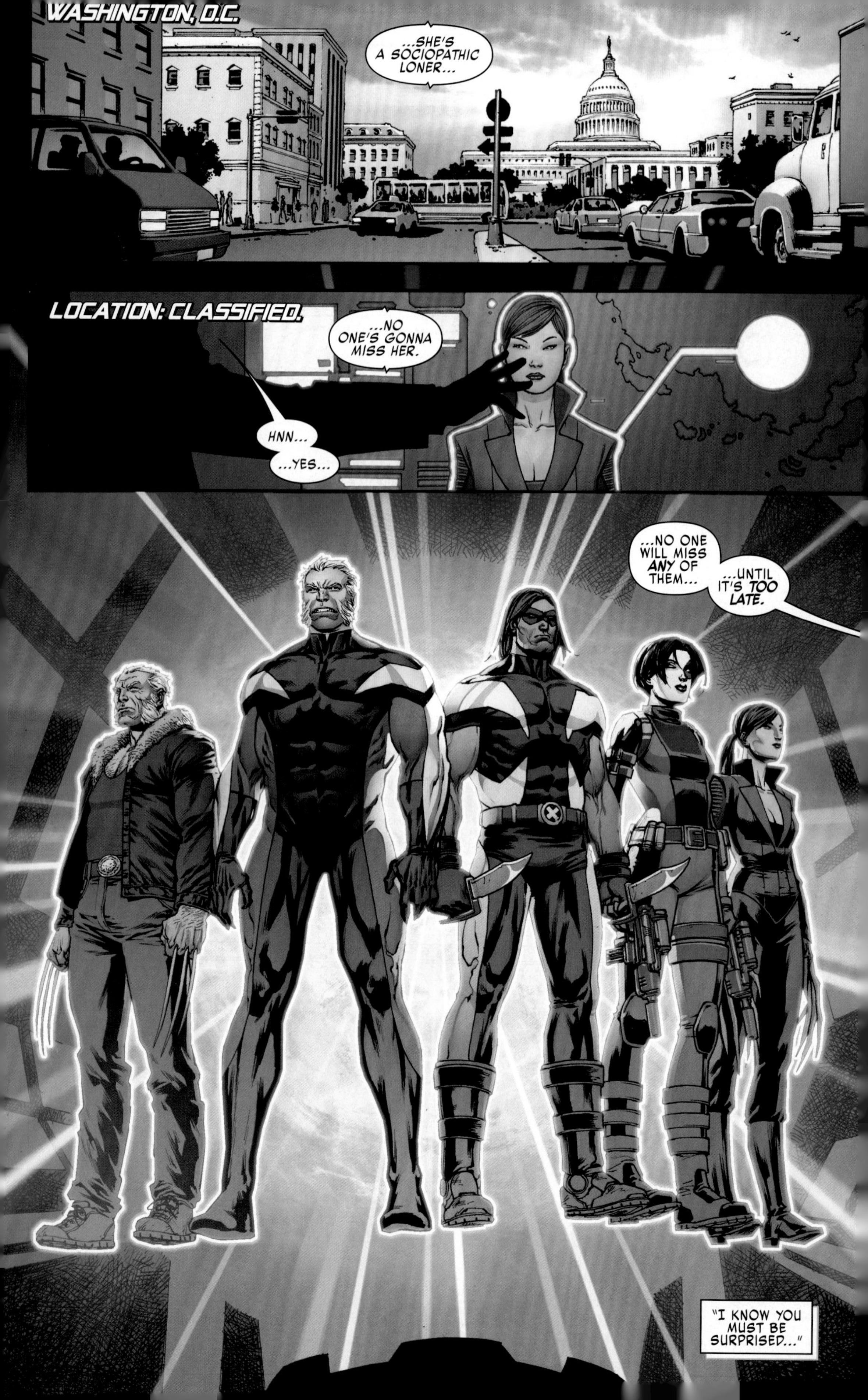
WASHINGTON, D.C.
...SHE'S A SOCIOPATHIC LONER...
LOCATION: CLASSIFIED.
...NO ONE'S GONNA MISS HER.
HNN...
...YES...
...NO ONE WILL MISS ANY OF THEM...
...UNTIL IT'S TOO LATE.
"I KNOW YOU MUST BE SURPRISED..."

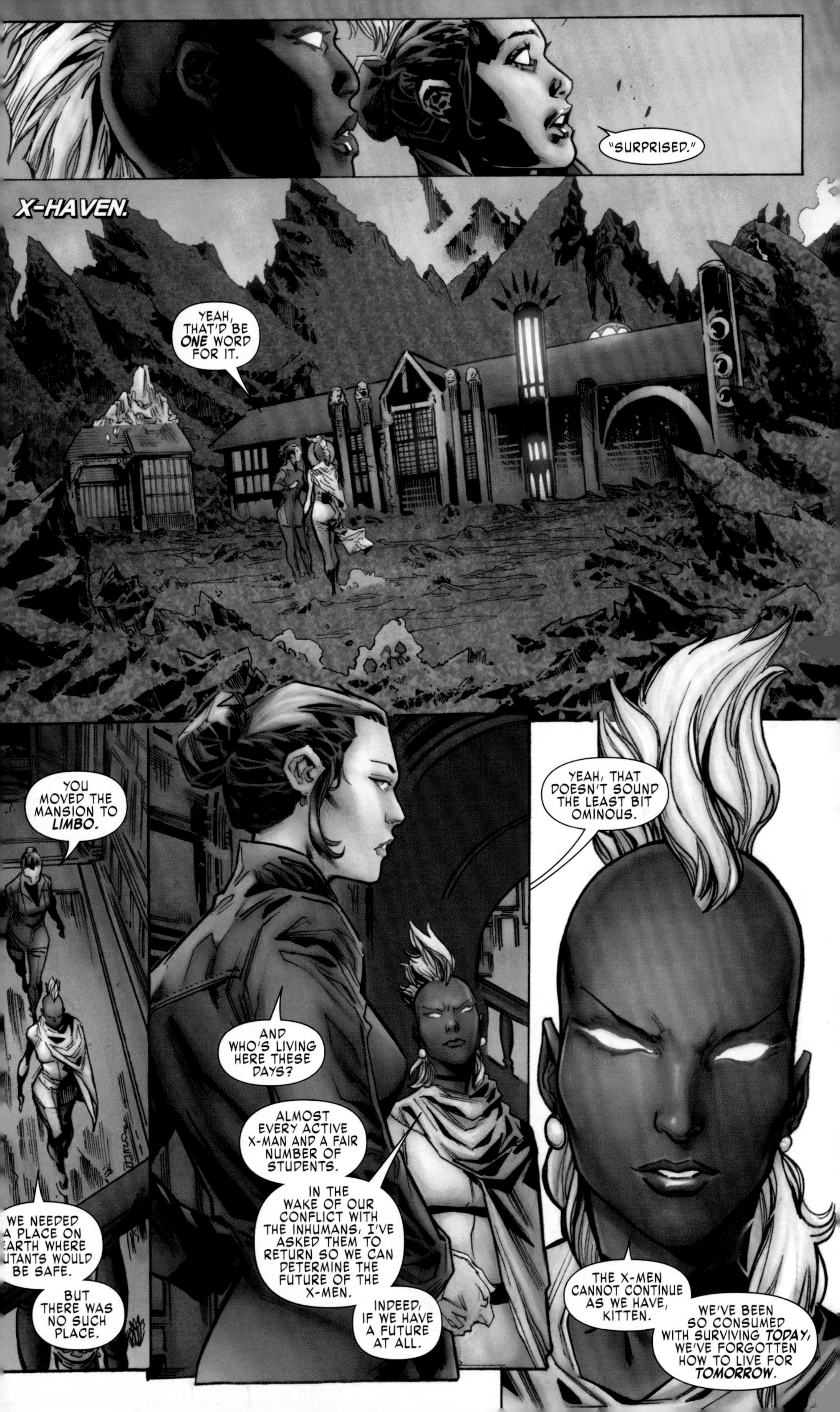
"SURPRISED."
X-HAVEN.
YEAH, THAT'D BE ONE WORD FOR IT.
YOU MOVED THE MANSION TO LIMBO.
WE NEEDED A PLACE ON EARTH WHERE UTANTS WOULD BE SAFE.
BUT THERE WAS NO SUCH PLACE.
AND WHO'S LIVING HERE THESE DAYS?
ALMOST EVERY ACTIVE X-MAN AND A FAIR NUMBER OF STUDENTS.
IN THE WAKE OF OUR CONFLICT WITH THE INHUMANS, I'VE ASKED THEM TO RETURN SO WE CAN DETERMINE THE FUTURE OF THE X-MEN.
INDEED, IF WE HAVE A FUTURE AT ALL.
YEAH, THAT DOESN'T SOUND THE LEAST BIT OMINOUS.
THE X-MEN CANNOT CONTINUE AS WE HAVE, KITTEN.
WE'VE BEEN SO CONSUMED WITH SURVIVING TODAY, WE'VE FORGOTTEN HOW TO LIVE FOR TOMORROW.

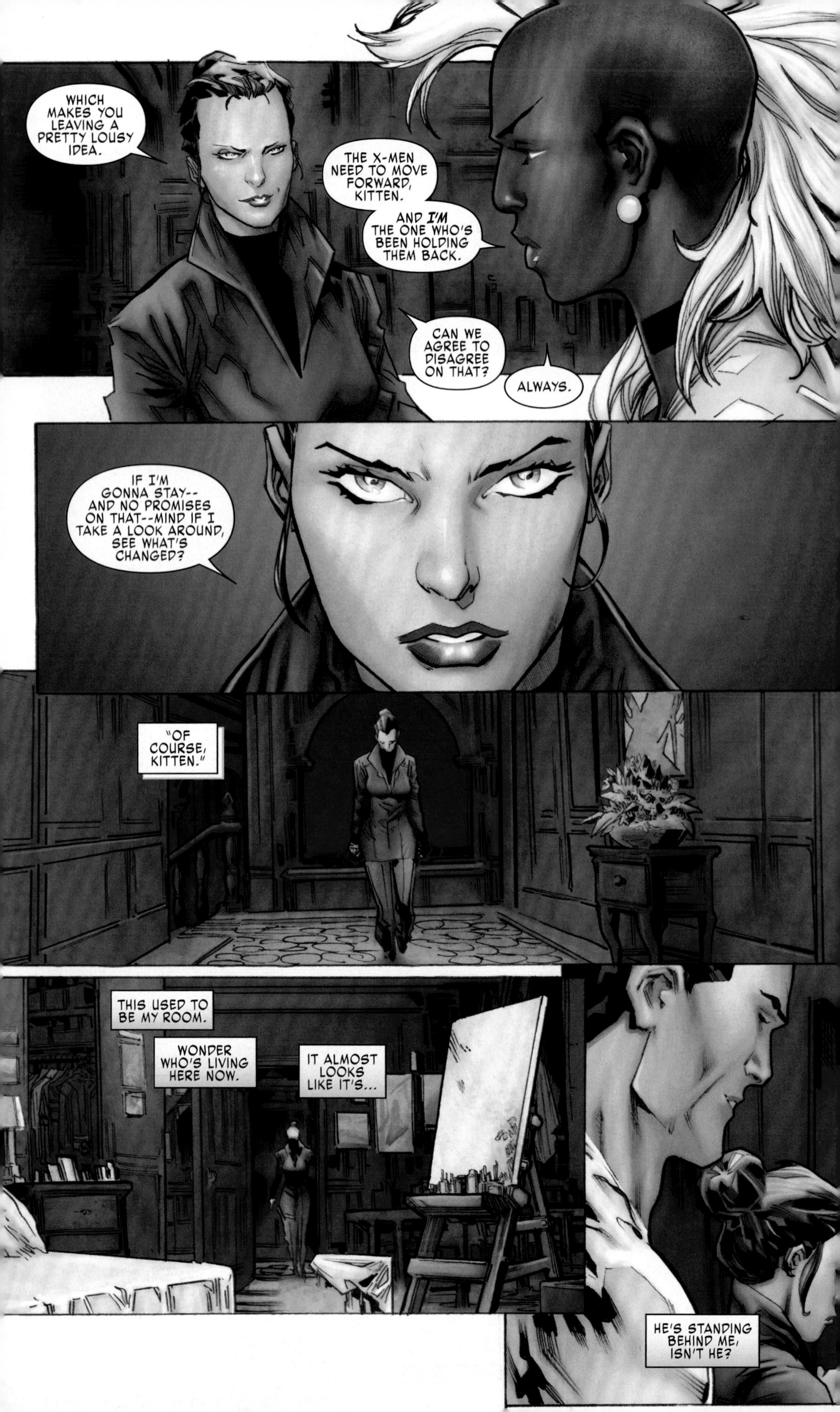
WHICH MAKES YOU LEAVING A PRETTY LOUSY IDEA.
THE X-MEN NEED TO MOVE FORWARD, KITTEN.
AND *I'M* THE ONE WHO'S BEEN HOLDING THEM BACK.
CAN WE AGREE TO DISAGREE ON THAT?
ALWAYS.
IF I'M GONNA STAY-- AND NO PROMISES ON THAT--MIND IF I TAKE A LOOK AROUND, SEE WHAT'S CHANGED?
"OF COURSE, KITTEN."
THIS USED TO BE MY ROOM.
WONDER WHO'S LIVING HERE NOW.
IT ALMOST LOOKS LIKE IT'S...
HE'S STANDING BEHIND ME, ISN'T HE?

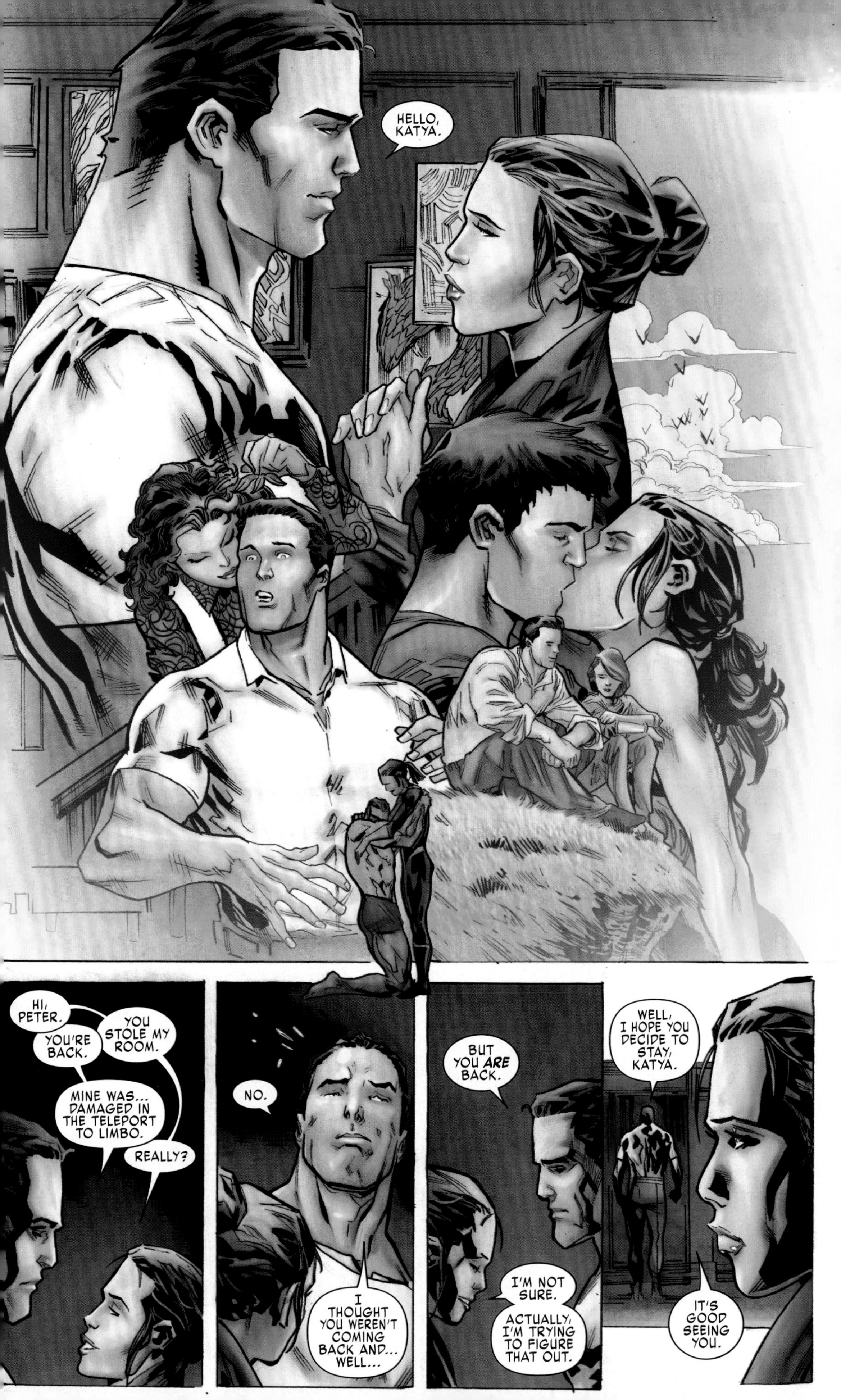

HELLO, KATYA.
HI, PETER.
YOU'RE BACK.
YOU STOLE MY ROOM.
MINE WAS... DAMAGED IN THE TELEPORT TO LIMBO.
REALLY?
NO.
I THOUGHT YOU WEREN'T COMING BACK AND... WELL...
BUT YOU *ARE* BACK.
I'M NOT SURE.
ACTUALLY, I'M TRYING TO FIGURE THAT OUT.
WELL, I HOPE YOU DECIDE TO STAY, KATYA.
IT'S GOOD SEEING YOU.

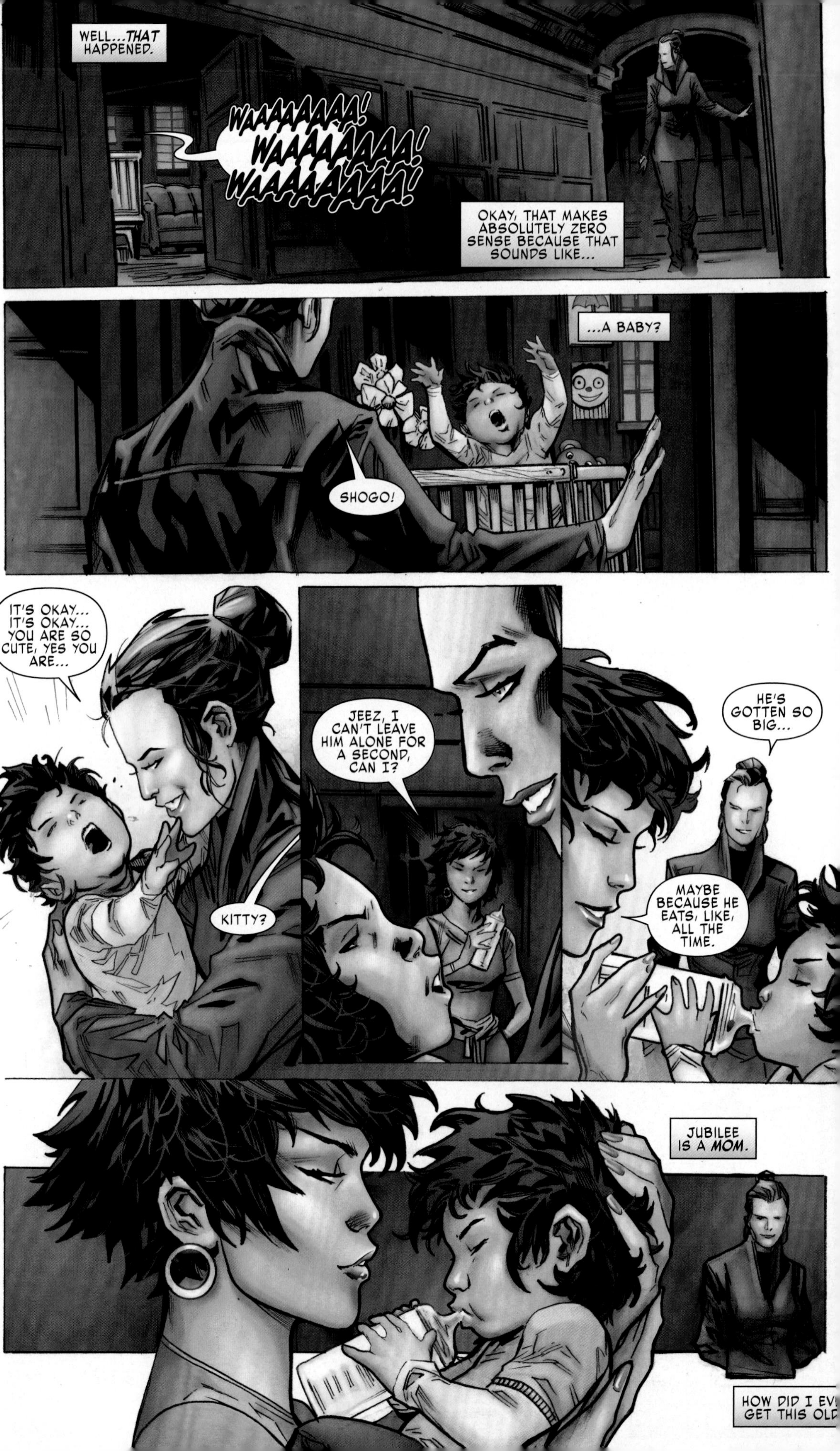

WELL...THAT HAPPENED.
WAAAAAAAA! WAAAAAAAA! WAAAAAAAA!
OKAY, THAT MAKES ABSOLUTELY ZERO SENSE BECAUSE THAT SOUNDS LIKE...
...A BABY?
SHOGO!
IT'S OKAY... IT'S OKAY... YOU ARE SO CUTE, YES YOU ARE...
KITTY?
JEEZ, I CAN'T LEAVE HIM ALONE FOR A SECOND, CAN I?
HE'S GOTTEN SO BIG...
MAYBE BECAUSE HE EATS, LIKE, ALL THE TIME.
JUBILEE IS A MOM.
HOW DID I EV
GET THIS OLD

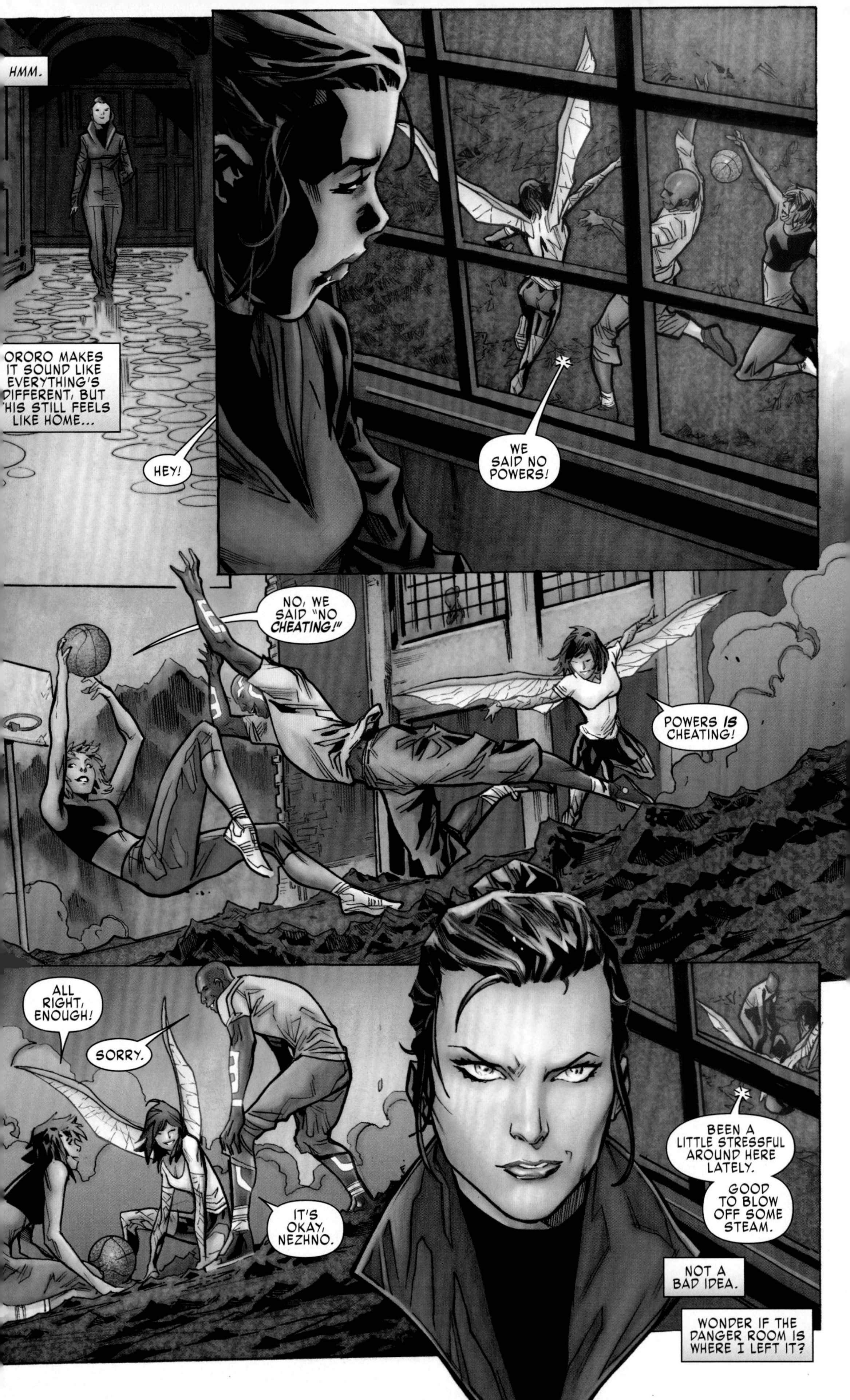
HMM.
ORORO MAKES IT SOUND LIKE EVERYTHING'S DIFFERENT, BUT THIS STILL FEELS LIKE HOME...
HEY!
WE SAID NO POWERS!
NO, WE SAID "NO CHEATING!"
POWERS IS CHEATING!
ALL RIGHT, ENOUGH!
SORRY.
IT'S OKAY, NEZHNO.
BEEN A LITTLE STRESSFUL AROUND HERE LATELY.
GOOD TO BLOW OFF SOME STEAM.
NOT A BAD IDEA.
WONDER IF THE DANGER ROOM IS WHERE I LEFT IT?

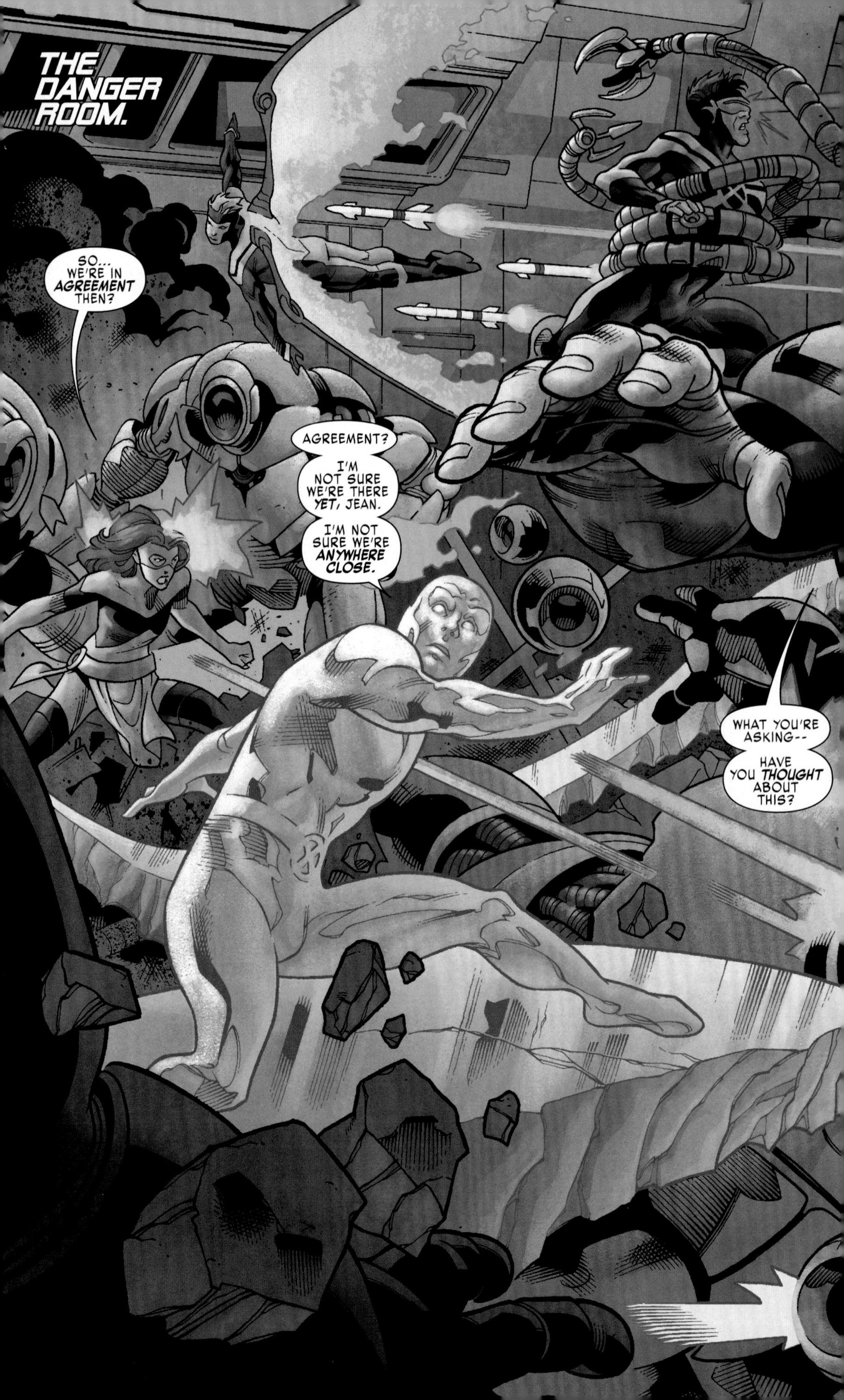
THE DANGER ROOM.
SO... WE'RE IN AGREEMENT THEN?
AGREEMENT?
I'M NOT SURE WE'RE THERE YET, JEAN.
I'M NOT SURE WE'RE ANYWHERE CLOSE.
WHAT YOU'RE ASKING--
HAVE YOU THOUGHT ABOUT THIS?

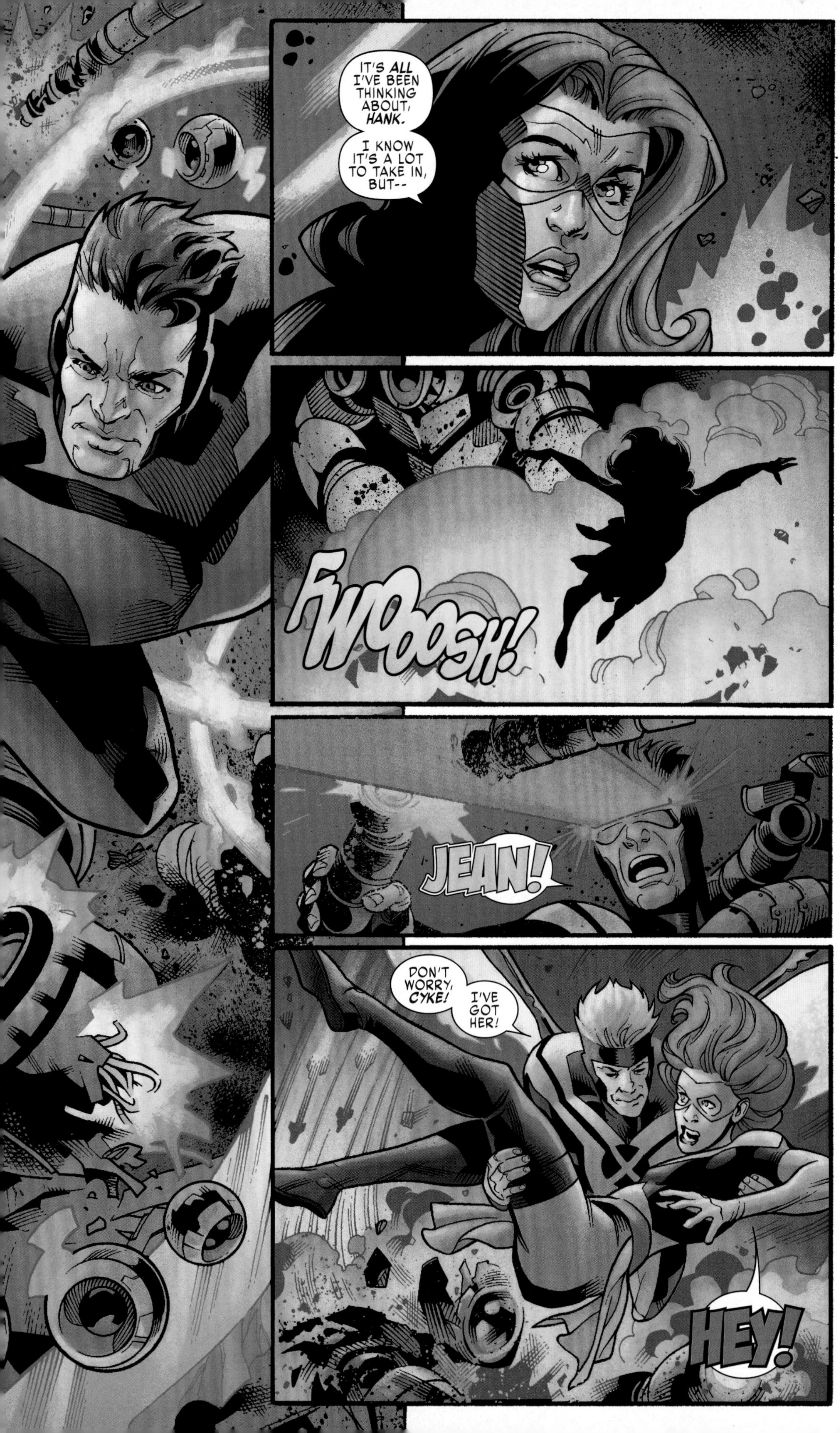

IT'S ALL I'VE BEEN THINKING ABOUT, HANK.
I KNOW IT'S A LOT TO TAKE IN, BUT--
FWOOOSH!
JEAN!
DON'T WORRY, CYKE!
I'VE GOT HER!
HEY!

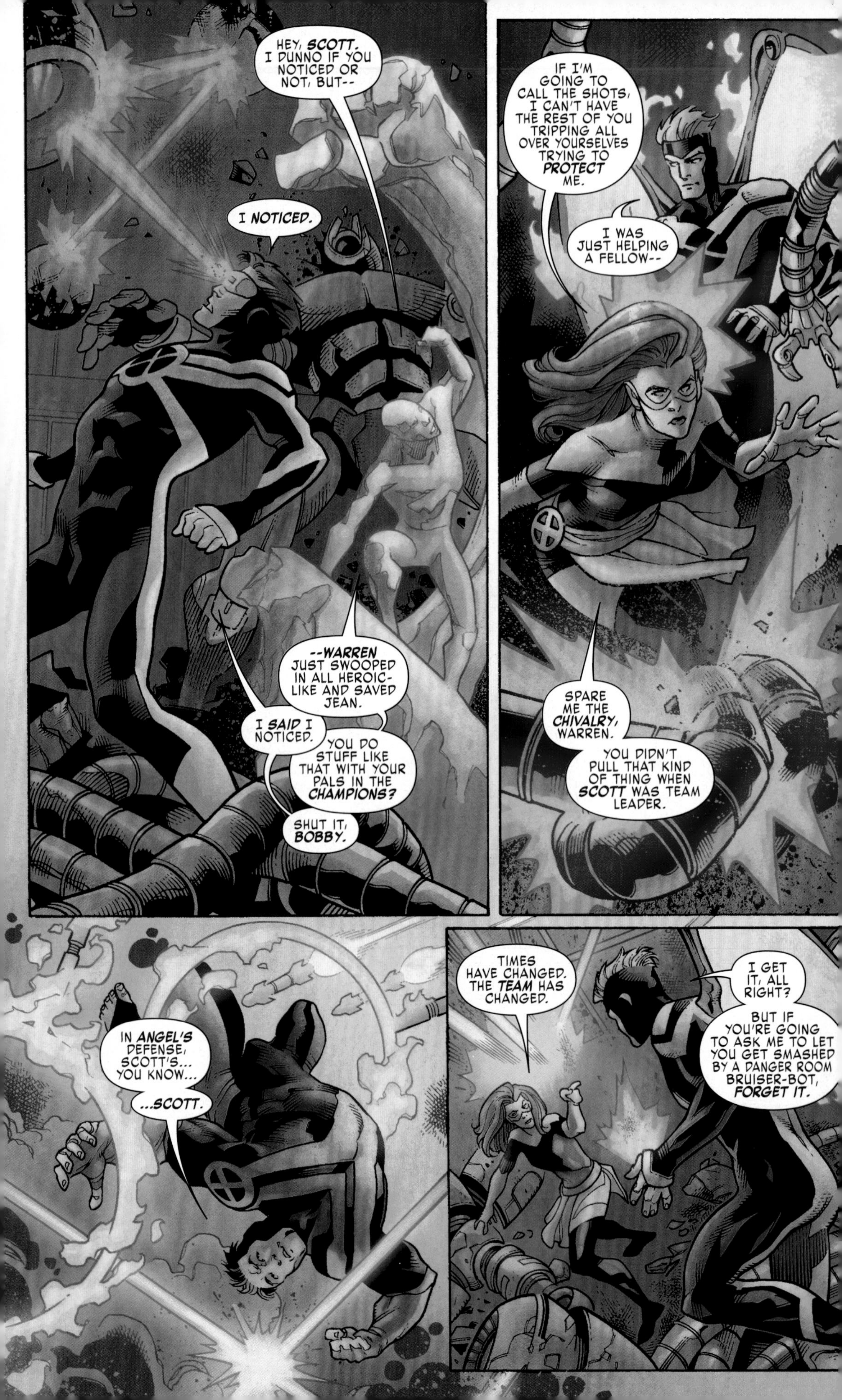
HEY, SCOTT. I DUNNO IF YOU NOTICED OR NOT, BUT--
I NOTICED.
--WARREN JUST SWOOPED IN ALL HEROIC-LIKE AND SAVED JEAN.
I SAID I NOTICED.
YOU DO STUFF LIKE THAT WITH YOUR PALS IN THE CHAMPIONS?
SHUT IT, BOBBY.
IF I'M GOING TO CALL THE SHOTS, I CAN'T HAVE THE REST OF YOU TRIPPING ALL OVER YOURSELVES TRYING TO PROTECT ME.
I WAS JUST HELPING A FELLOW--
SPARE ME THE CHIVALRY, WARREN.
YOU DIDN'T PULL THAT KIND OF THING WHEN SCOTT WAS TEAM LEADER.
IN ANGEL'S DEFENSE, SCOTT'S... YOU KNOW...
...SCOTT.
TIMES HAVE CHANGED. THE TEAM HAS CHANGED.
I GET IT, ALL RIGHT?
BUT IF YOU'RE GOING TO ASK ME TO LET YOU GET SMASHED BY A DANGER ROOM BRUISER-BOT, FORGET IT.

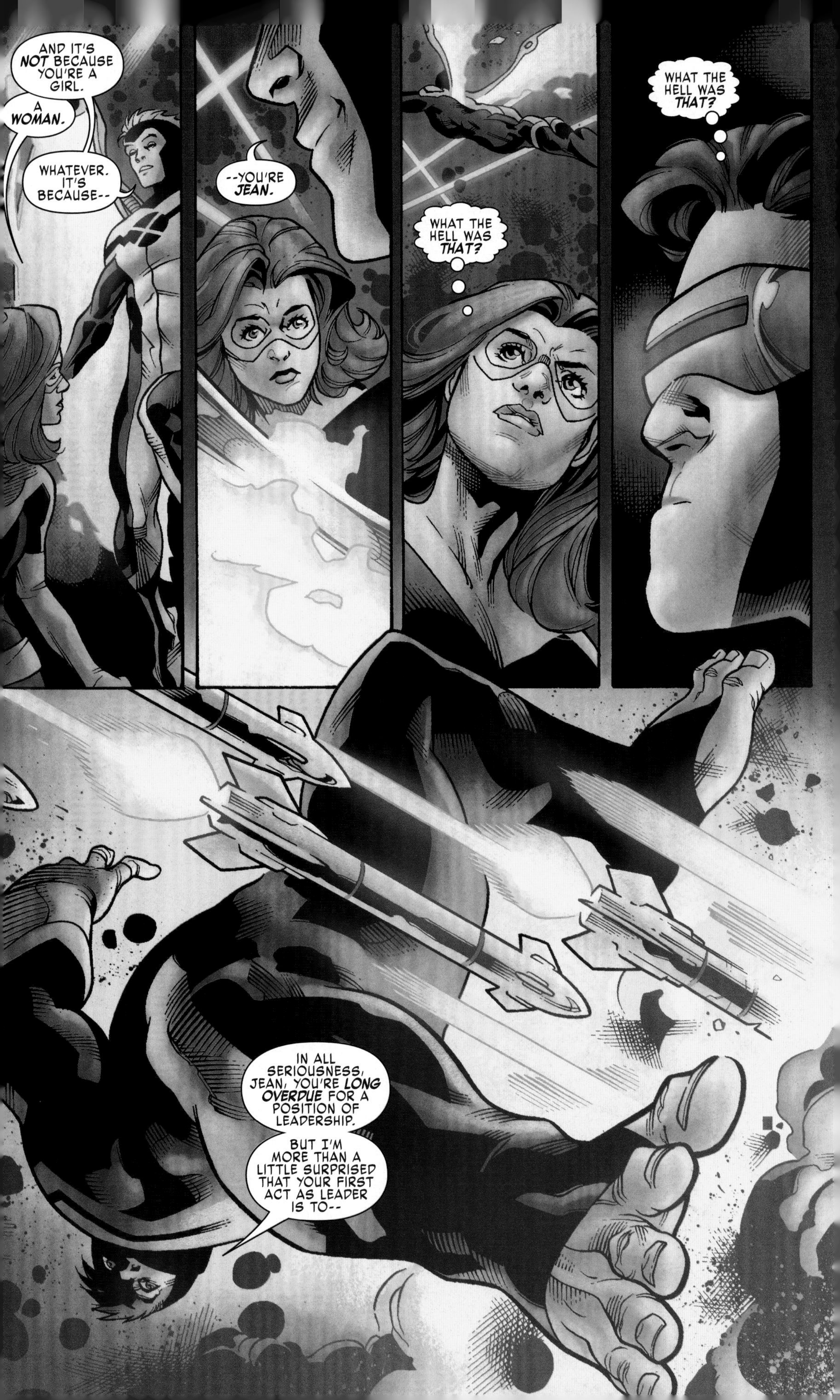
AND IT'S NOT BECAUSE YOU'RE A GIRL.
A WOMAN.
WHATEVER. IT'S BECAUSE--
--YOU'RE JEAN.
WHAT THE HELL WAS THAT?
WHAT THE HELL WAS THAT?
IN ALL SERIOUSNESS, JEAN, YOU'RE LONG OVERDUE FOR A POSITION OF LEADERSHIP.
BUT I'M MORE THAN A LITTLE SURPRISED THAT YOUR FIRST ACT AS LEADER IS TO--

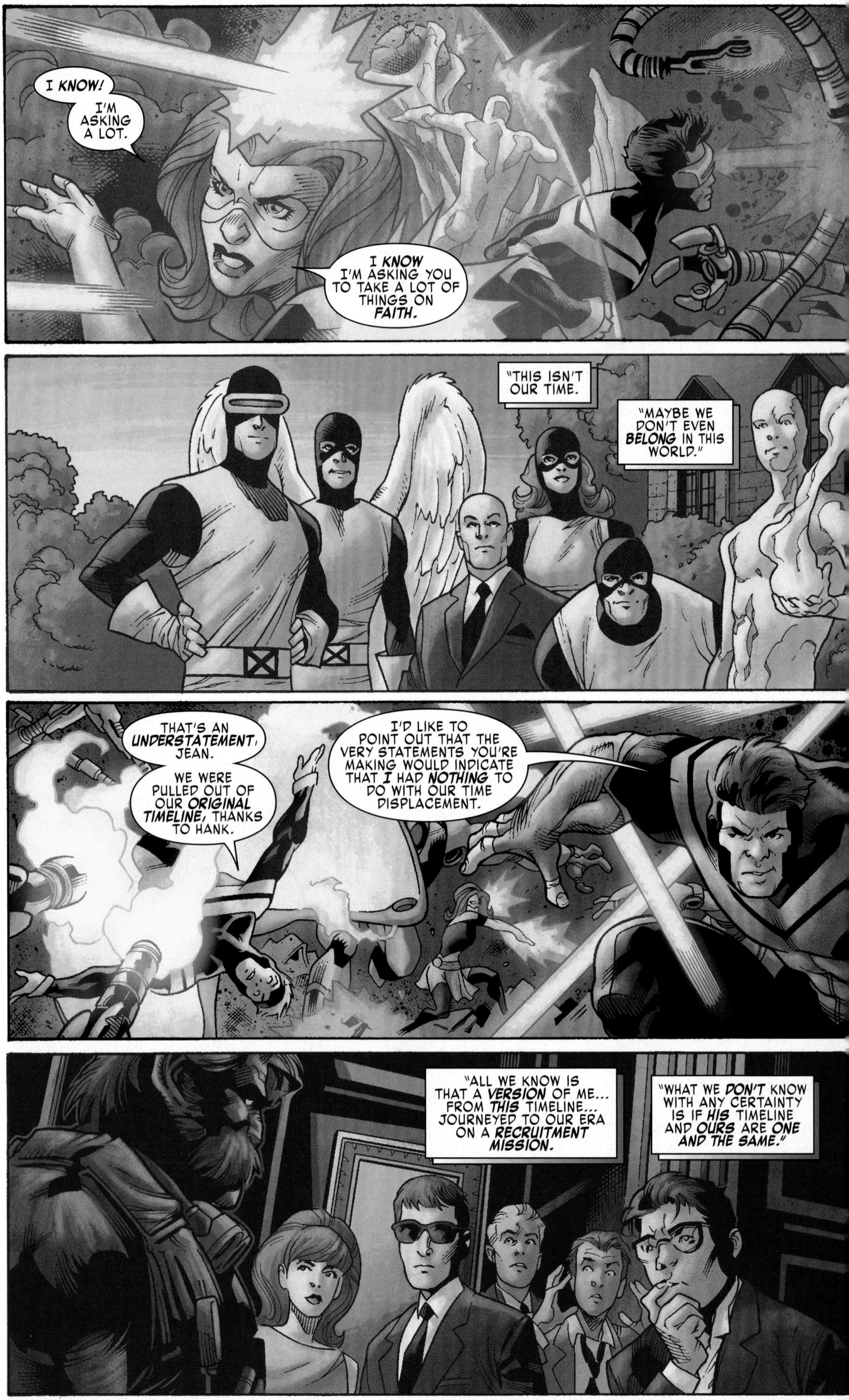
I KNOW!
I'M ASKING A LOT.
I KNOW I'M ASKING YOU TO TAKE A LOT OF THINGS ON FAITH.
"THIS ISN'T OUR TIME.
"MAYBE WE DON'T EVEN BELONG IN THIS WORLD."
THAT'S AN UNDERSTATEMENT, JEAN.
WE WERE PULLED OUT OF OUR ORIGINAL TIMELINE, THANKS TO HANK.
I'D LIKE TO POINT OUT THAT THE VERY STATEMENTS YOU'RE MAKING WOULD INDICATE THAT I HAD NOTHING TO DO WITH OUR TIME DISPLACEMENT.
"ALL WE KNOW IS THAT A VERSION OF ME... FROM THIS TIMELINE... JOURNEYED TO OUR ERA ON A RECRUITMENT MISSION.
"WHAT WE DON'T KNOW WITH ANY CERTAINTY IS IF HIS TIMELINE AND OURS ARE ONE AND THE SAME."

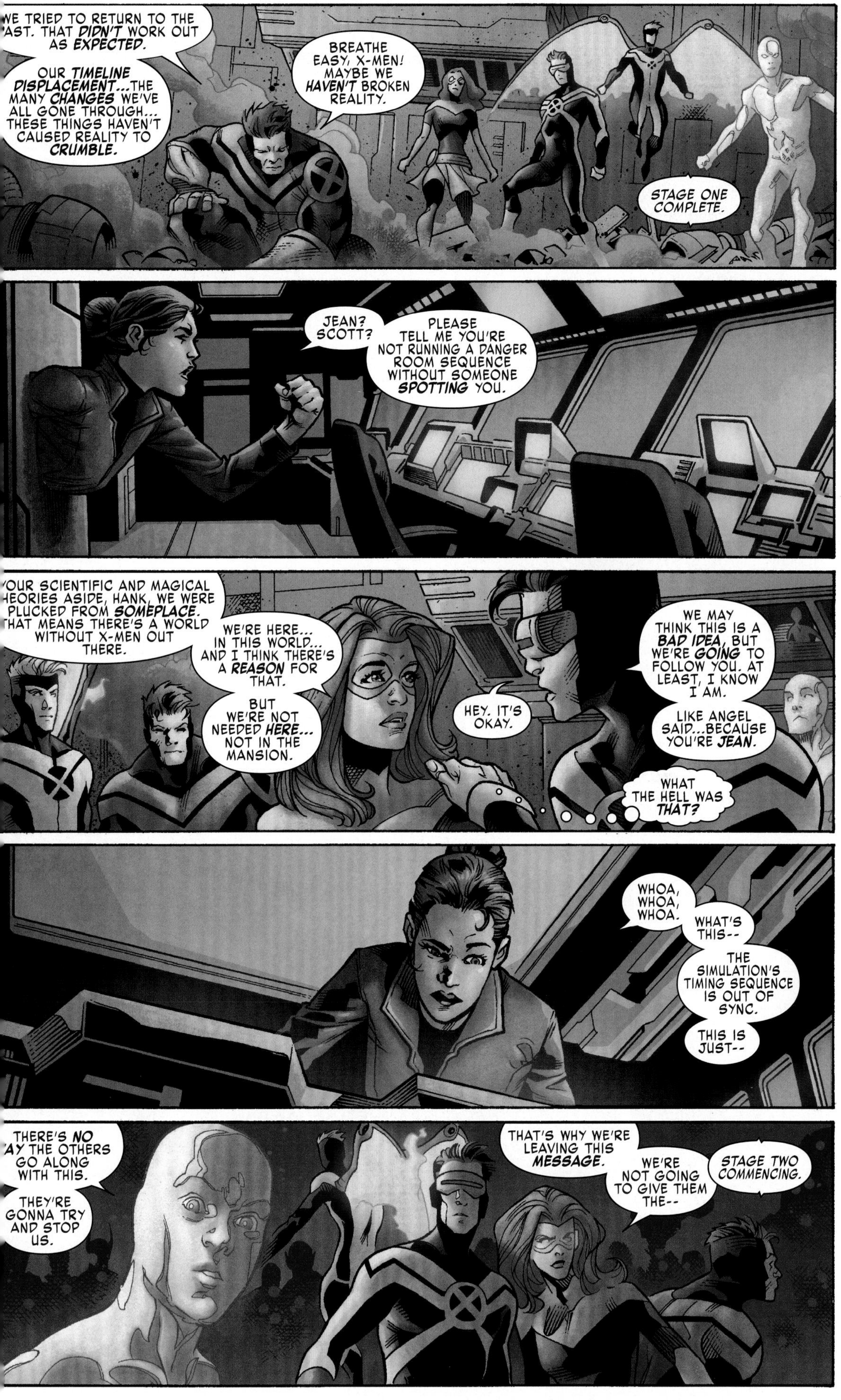
WE TRIED TO RETURN TO THE PAST. THAT DIDN'T WORK OUT AS EXPECTED.
OUR TIMELINE DISPLACEMENT...THE MANY CHANGES WE'VE ALL GONE THROUGH... THESE THINGS HAVEN'T CAUSED REALITY TO CRUMBLE.
BREATHE EASY, X-MEN! MAYBE WE HAVEN'T BROKEN REALITY.
STAGE ONE COMPLETE.
JEAN? SCOTT?
PLEASE TELL ME YOU'RE NOT RUNNING A DANGER ROOM SEQUENCE WITHOUT SOMEONE SPOTTING YOU.
YOUR SCIENTIFIC AND MAGICAL THEORIES ASIDE, HANK, WE WERE PLUCKED FROM SOMEPLACE. THAT MEANS THERE'S A WORLD WITHOUT X-MEN OUT THERE.
WE'RE HERE... IN THIS WORLD... AND I THINK THERE'S A REASON FOR THAT.
BUT WE'RE NOT NEEDED HERE... NOT IN THE MANSION.
HEY. IT'S OKAY.
WE MAY THINK THIS IS A BAD IDEA, BUT WE'RE GOING TO FOLLOW YOU. AT LEAST, I KNOW I AM.
LIKE ANGEL SAID...BECAUSE YOU'RE JEAN.
WHAT THE HELL WAS THAT?
WHOA, WHOA, WHOA.
WHAT'S THIS--
THE SIMULATION'S TIMING SEQUENCE IS OUT OF SYNC.
THIS IS JUST--
THERE'S NO WAY THE OTHERS GO ALONG WITH THIS.
THEY'RE GONNA TRY AND STOP US.
THAT'S WHY WE'RE LEAVING THIS MESSAGE.
WE'RE NOT GOING TO GIVE THEM THE--
STAGE TWO COMMENCING.

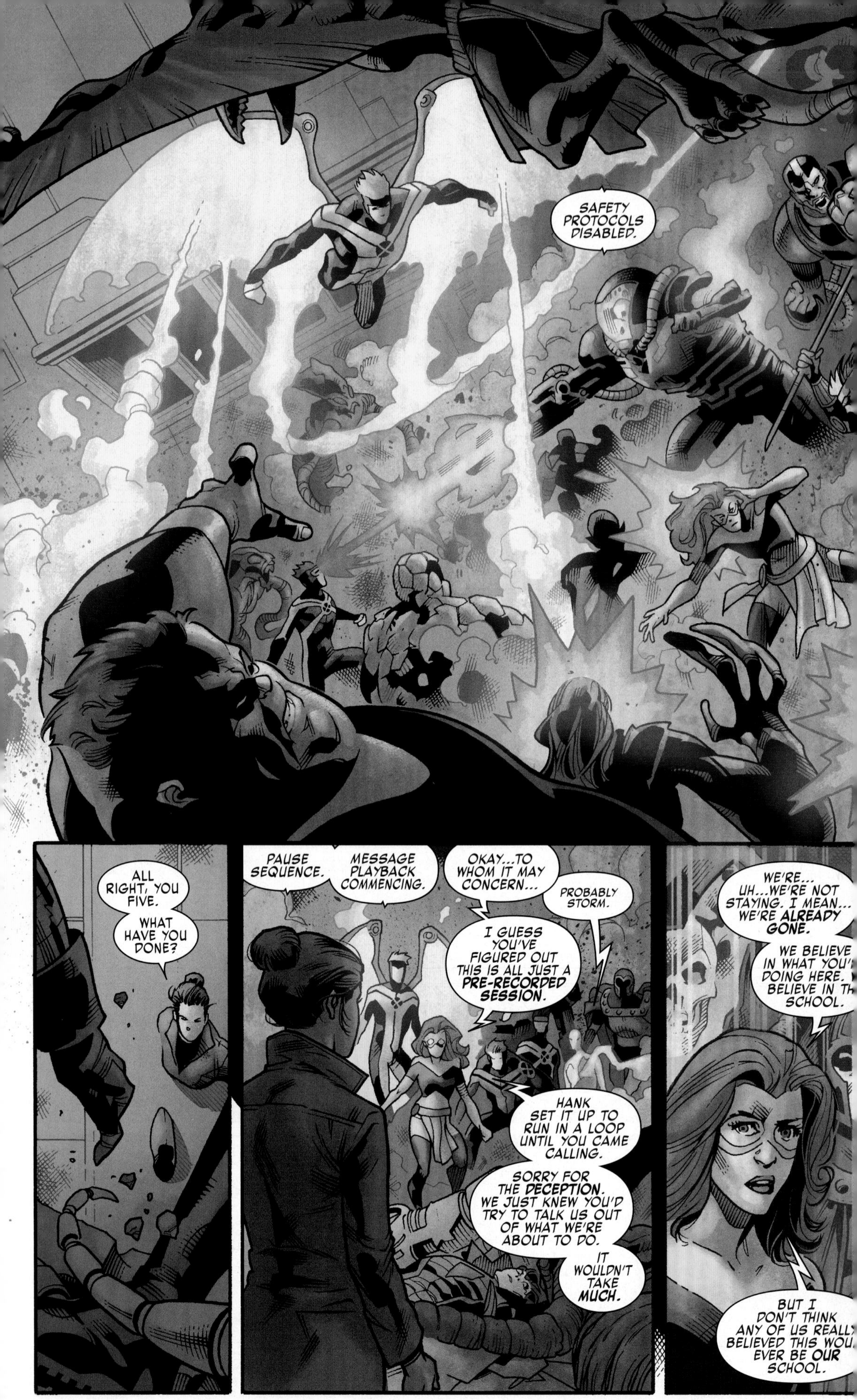
SAFETY PROTOCOLS DISABLED.
ALL RIGHT, YOU FIVE.
WHAT HAVE YOU DONE?
PAUSE SEQUENCE.
MESSAGE PLAYBACK COMMENCING.
OKAY...TO WHOM IT MAY CONCERN...
PROBABLY STORM.
I GUESS YOU'VE FIGURED OUT THIS IS ALL JUST A **PRE-RECORDED SESSION**.
HANK SET IT UP TO RUN IN A LOOP UNTIL YOU CAME CALLING.
SORRY FOR THE **DECEPTION**. WE JUST KNEW YOU'D TRY TO TALK US OUT OF WHAT WE'RE ABOUT TO DO.
IT WOULDN'T TAKE **MUCH**.
WE'RE... UH...WE'RE NOT STAYING. I MEAN... WE'RE **ALREADY GONE**.
WE BELIEVE IN WHAT YOU' DOING HERE. BELIEVE IN TH SCHOOL.
BUT I DON'T THINK ANY OF US REALL BELIEVED THIS WOU EVER BE **OUR** SCHOOL.

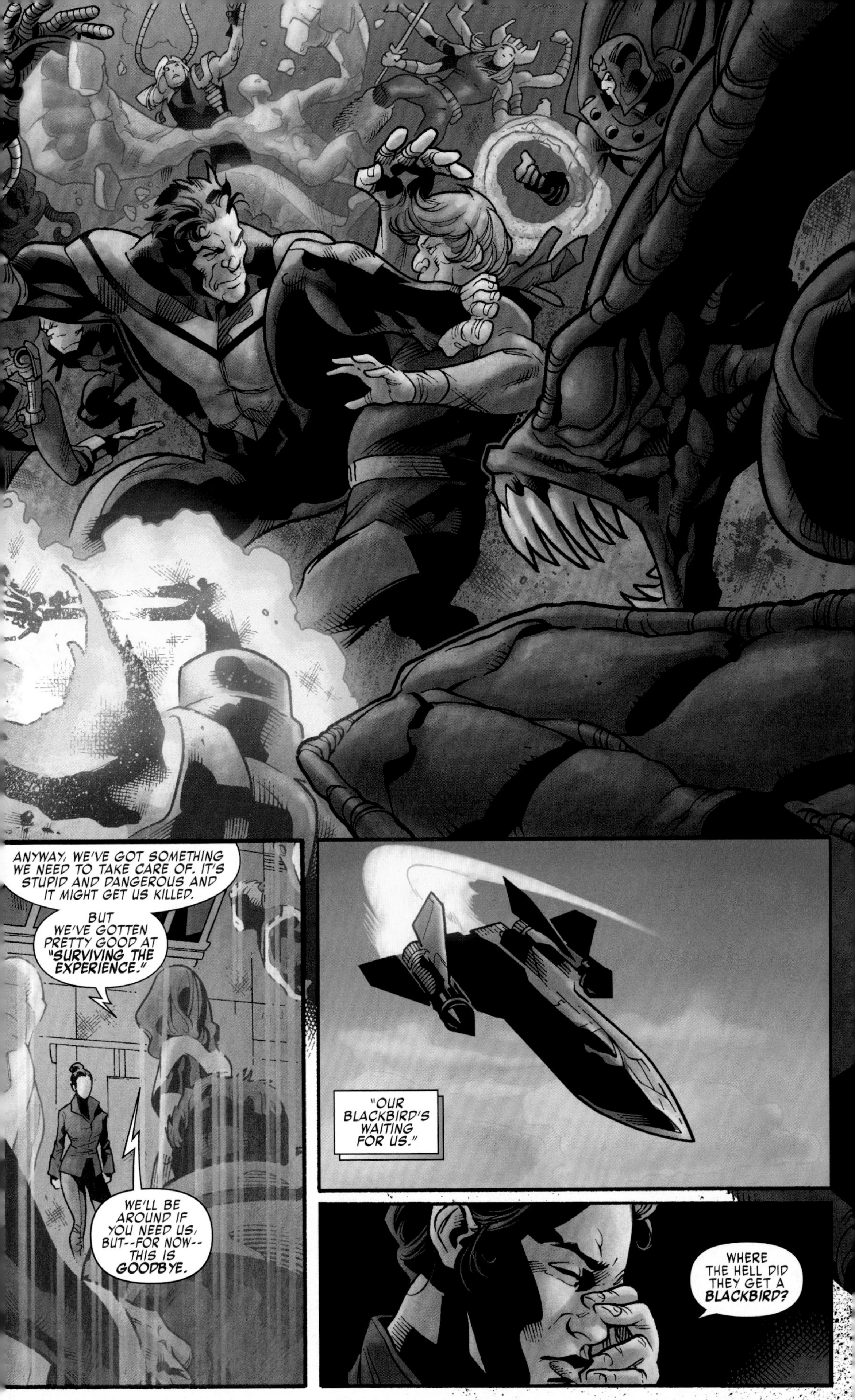
ANYWAY, WE'VE GOT SOMETHING WE NEED TO TAKE CARE OF. IT'S STUPID AND DANGEROUS AND IT MIGHT GET US KILLED.
BUT WE'VE GOTTEN PRETTY GOOD AT "SURVIVING THE EXPERIENCE."
WE'LL BE AROUND IF YOU NEED US, BUT--FOR NOW--THIS IS GOODBYE.
"OUR BLACKBIRD'S WAITING FOR US."
WHERE THE HELL DID THEY GET A BLACKBIRD?

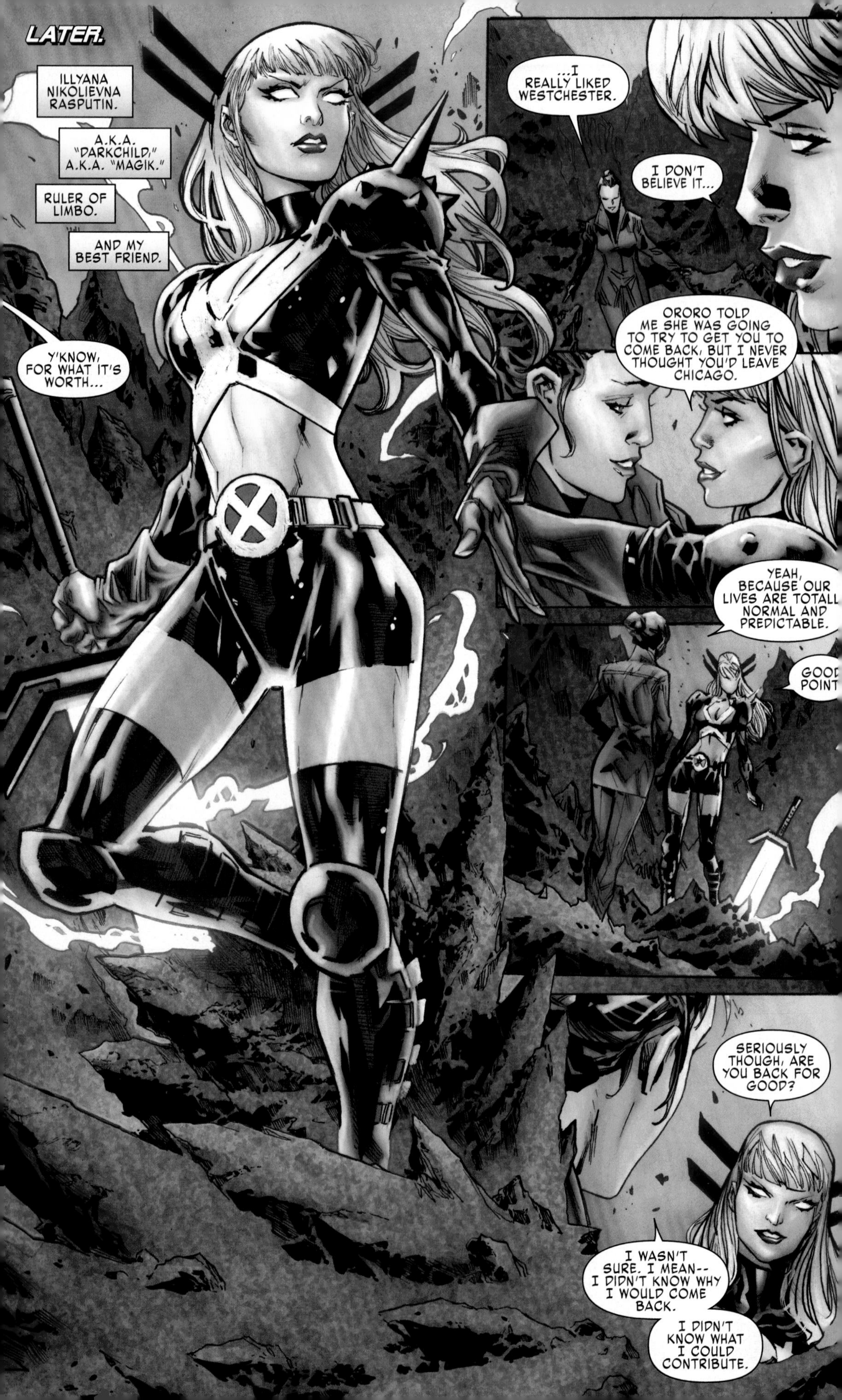
LATER.
ILLYANA NIKOLIEVNA RASPUTIN.
A.K.A. "DARKCHILD," A.K.A. "MAGIK."
RULER OF LIMBO.
AND MY BEST FRIEND.
Y'KNOW, FOR WHAT IT'S WORTH...
...I REALLY LIKED WESTCHESTER.
I DON'T BELIEVE IT...
ORORO TOLD ME SHE WAS GOING TO TRY TO GET YOU TO COME BACK, BUT I NEVER THOUGHT YOU'D LEAVE CHICAGO.
YEAH, BECAUSE OUR LIVES ARE TOTALL NORMAL AND PREDICTABLE.
GOOD POINT
SERIOUSLY THOUGH, ARE YOU BACK FOR GOOD?
I WASN'T SURE. I MEAN-- I DIDN'T KNOW WHY I WOULD COME BACK.
I DIDN'T KNOW WHAT I COULD CONTRIBUTE.

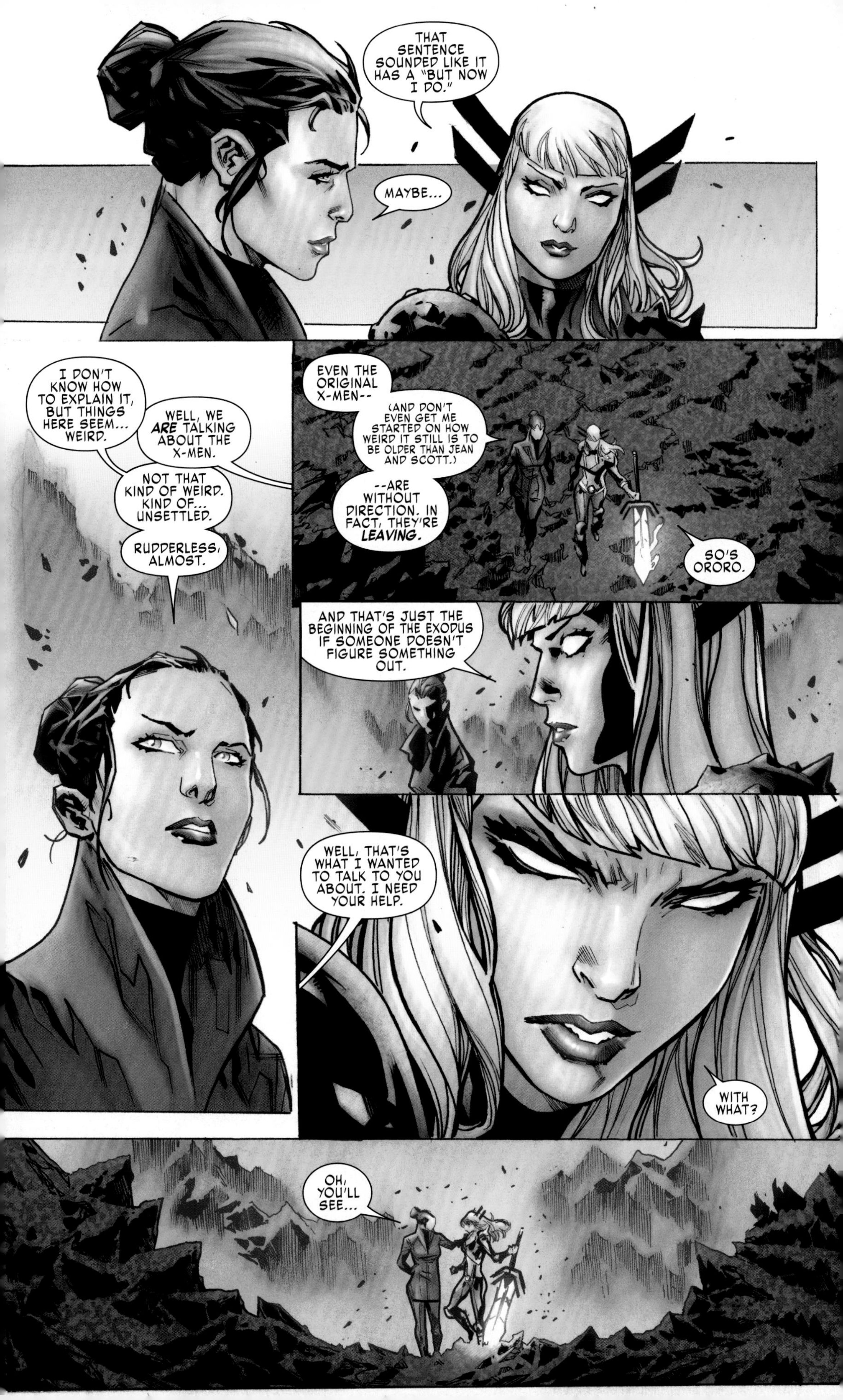
THAT SENTENCE SOUNDED LIKE IT HAS A "BUT NOW I DO."
MAYBE...
I DON'T KNOW HOW TO EXPLAIN IT, BUT THINGS HERE SEEM... WEIRD.
WELL, WE ARE TALKING ABOUT THE X-MEN.
NOT THAT KIND OF WEIRD. KIND OF... UNSETTLED.
RUDDERLESS, ALMOST.
EVEN THE ORIGINAL X-MEN--
(AND DON'T EVEN GET ME STARTED ON HOW WEIRD IT STILL IS TO BE OLDER THAN JEAN AND SCOTT.)
--ARE WITHOUT DIRECTION. IN FACT, THEY'RE LEAVING.
SO'S ORORO.
AND THAT'S JUST THE BEGINNING OF THE EXODUS IF SOMEONE DOESN'T FIGURE SOMETHING OUT.
WELL, THAT'S WHAT I WANTED TO TALK TO YOU ABOUT. I NEED YOUR HELP.
WITH WHAT?
OH, YOU'LL SEE...

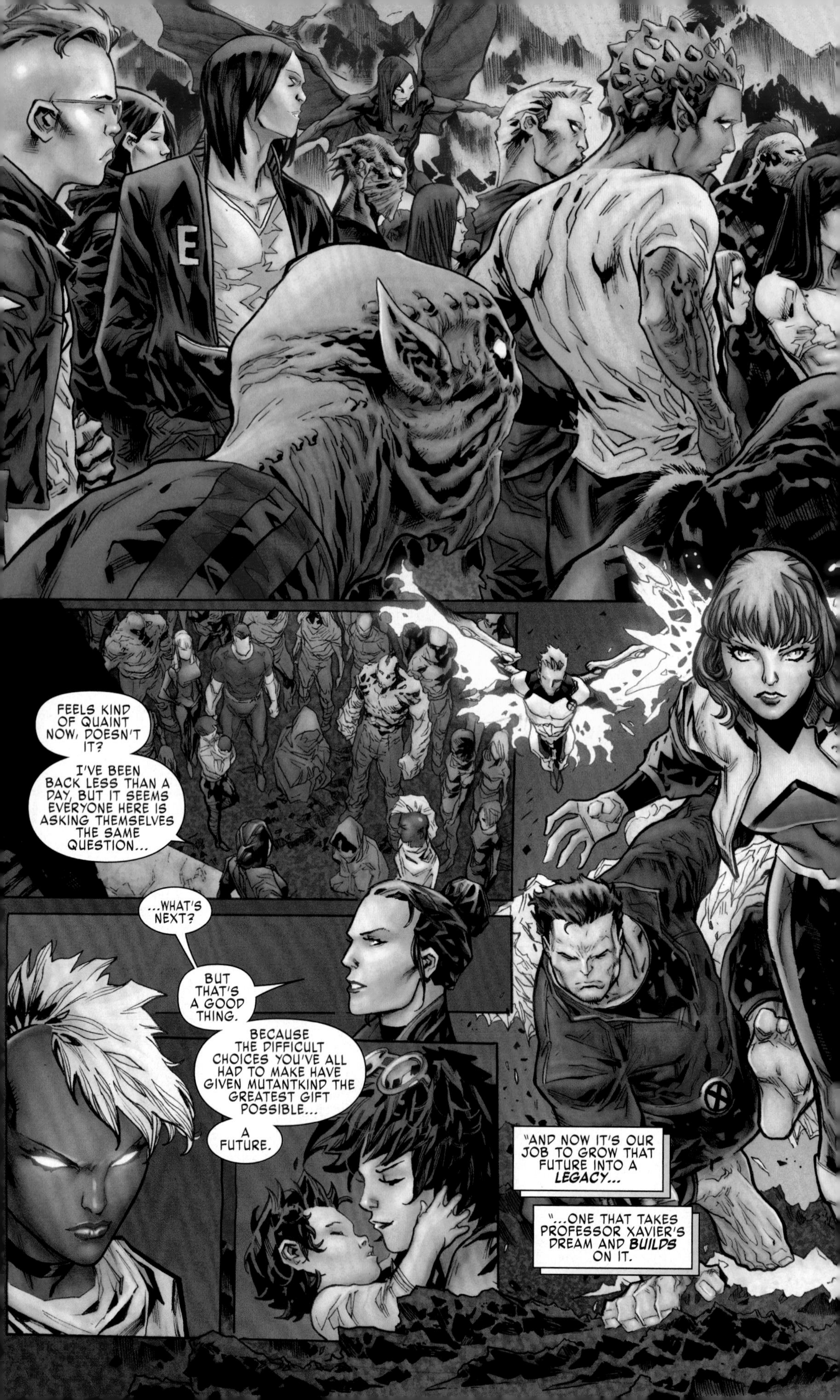
FEELS KIND OF QUAINT NOW, DOESN'T IT?
I'VE BEEN BACK LESS THAN A DAY, BUT IT SEEMS EVERYONE HERE IS ASKING THEMSELVES THE SAME QUESTION...
...WHAT'S NEXT?
BUT THAT'S A GOOD THING.
BECAUSE THE DIFFICULT CHOICES YOU'VE ALL HAD TO MAKE HAVE GIVEN MUTANTKIND THE GREATEST GIFT POSSIBLE...
A FUTURE.
"AND NOW IT'S OUR JOB TO GROW THAT FUTURE INTO A *LEGACY*...
"...ONE THAT TAKES PROFESSOR XAVIER'S DREAM AND *BUILDS* ON IT.

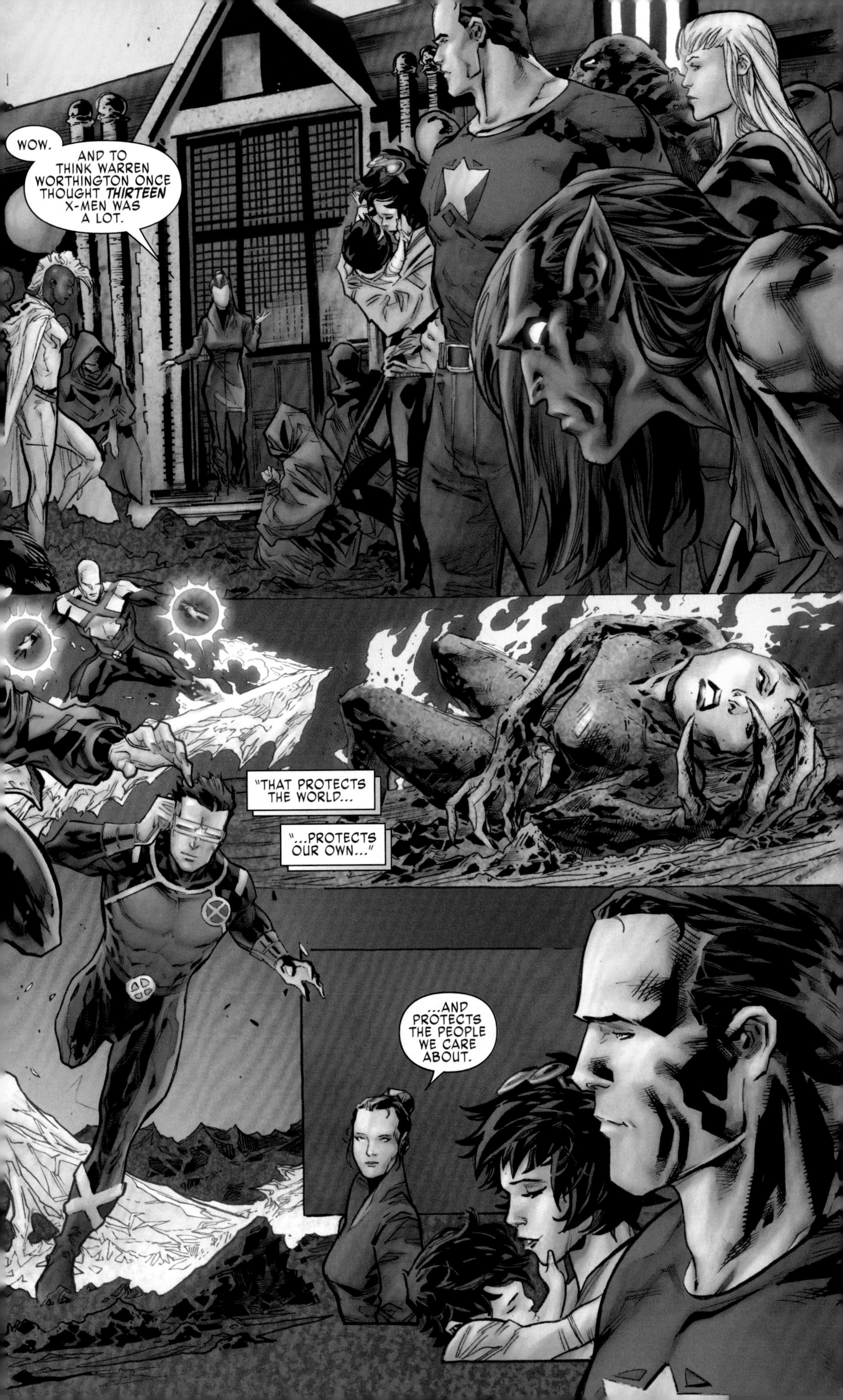
WOW.
AND TO THINK WARREN WORTHINGTON ONCE THOUGHT THIRTEEN X-MEN WAS A LOT.
"THAT PROTECTS THE WORLD...
"...PROTECTS OUR OWN..."
...AND PROTECTS THE PEOPLE WE CARE ABOUT.

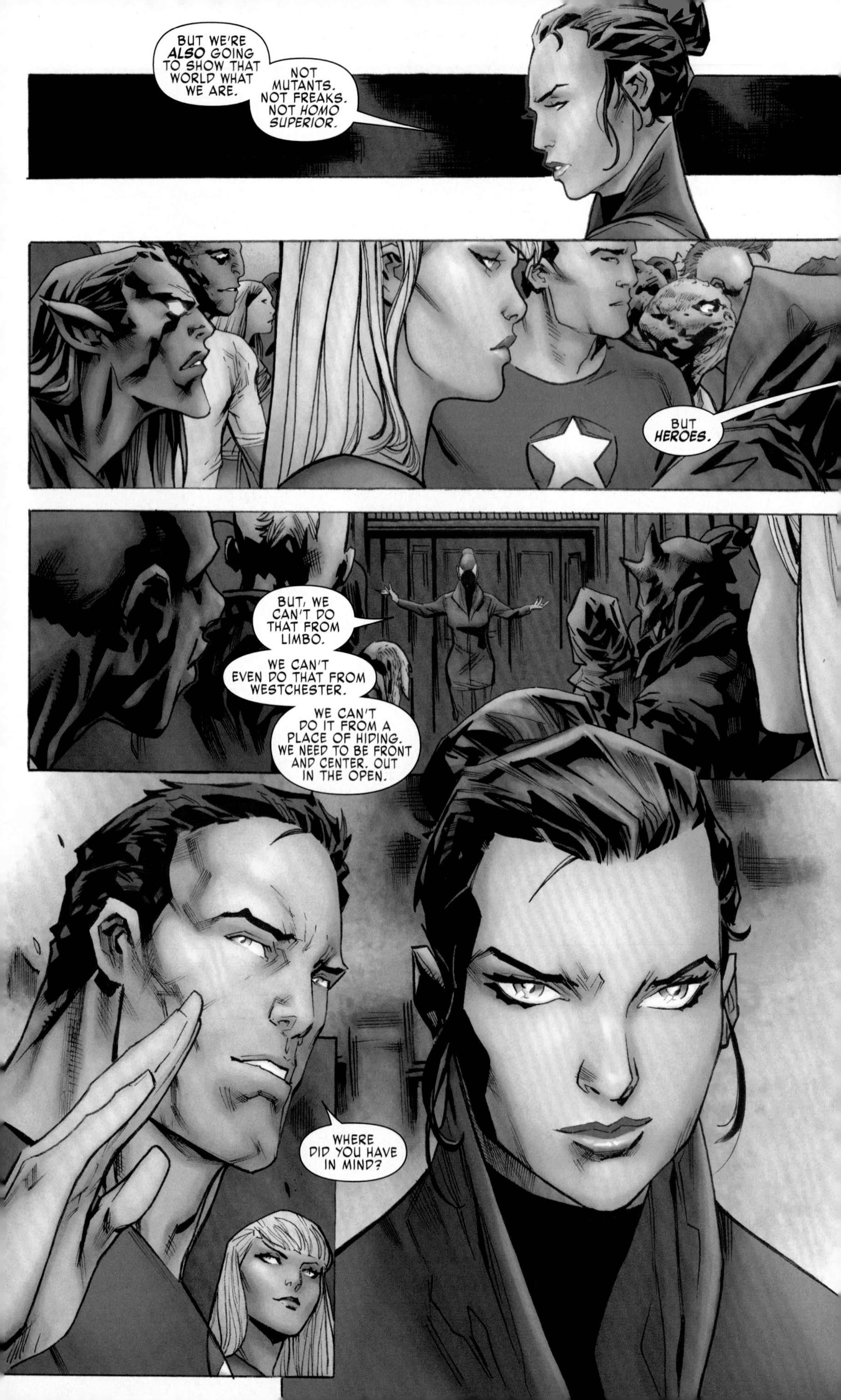

BUT WE'RE *ALSO* GOING TO SHOW THAT WORLD WHAT WE ARE.
NOT MUTANTS. NOT FREAKS. NOT *HOMO SUPERIOR*.
BUT *HEROES*.
BUT, WE CAN'T DO THAT FROM LIMBO.
WE CAN'T EVEN DO THAT FROM WESTCHESTER.
WE CAN'T DO IT FROM A PLACE OF HIDING. WE NEED TO BE FRONT AND CENTER. OUT IN THE OPEN.
WHERE DID YOU HAVE IN MIND?

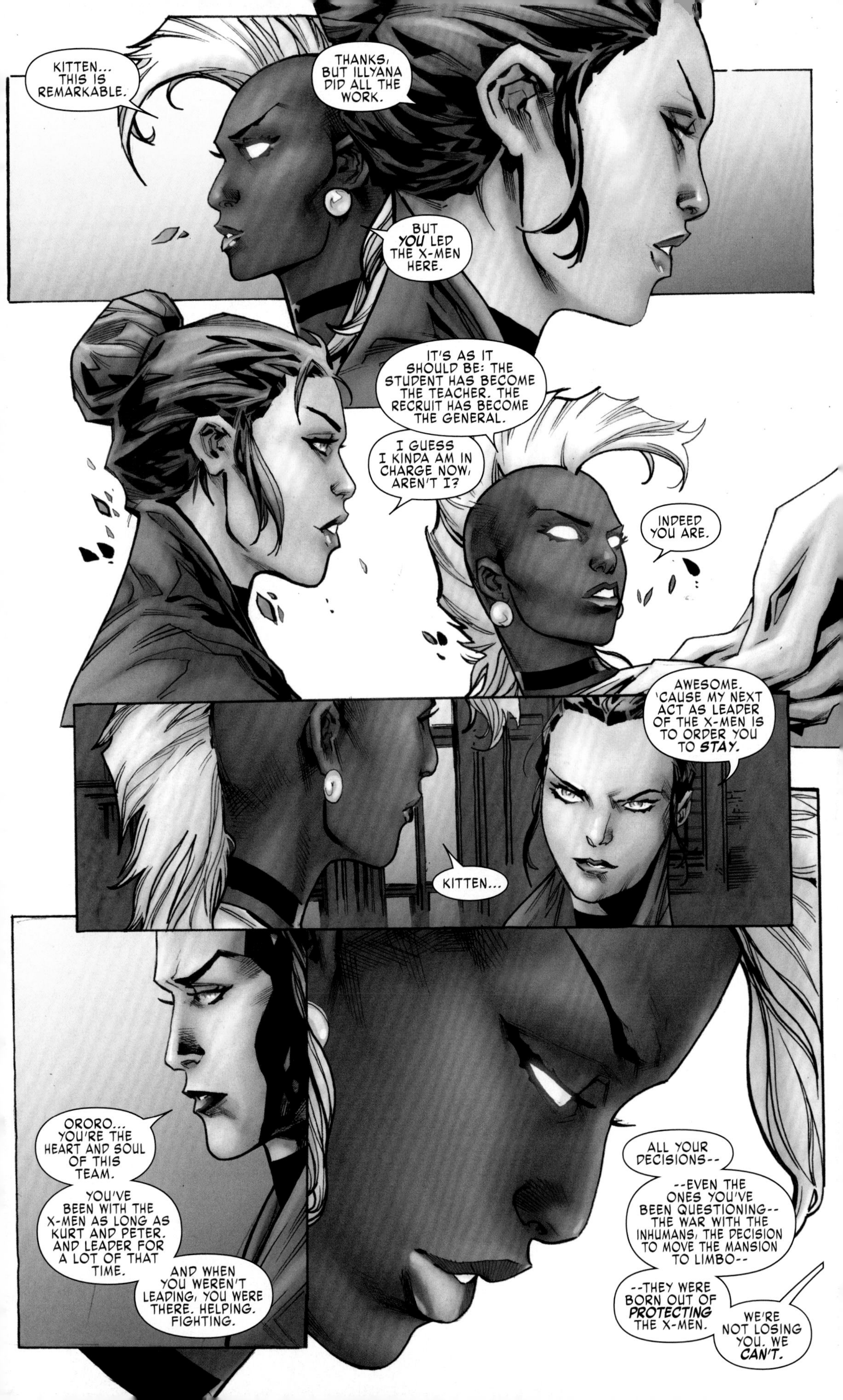
KITTEN... THIS IS REMARKABLE.
THANKS, BUT ILLYANA DID ALL THE WORK.
BUT YOU LED THE X-MEN HERE.
IT'S AS IT SHOULD BE: THE STUDENT HAS BECOME THE TEACHER. THE RECRUIT HAS BECOME THE GENERAL.
I GUESS I KINDA AM IN CHARGE NOW, AREN'T I?
INDEED YOU ARE.
AWESOME. 'CAUSE MY NEXT ACT AS LEADER OF THE X-MEN IS TO ORDER YOU TO STAY.
KITTEN...
ORORO... YOU'RE THE HEART AND SOUL OF THIS TEAM.
YOU'VE BEEN WITH THE X-MEN AS LONG AS KURT AND PETER. AND LEADER FOR A LOT OF THAT TIME.
AND WHEN YOU WEREN'T LEADING, YOU WERE THERE. HELPING. FIGHTING.
ALL YOUR DECISIONS--
--EVEN THE ONES YOU'VE BEEN QUESTIONING-- THE WAR WITH THE INHUMANS, THE DECISION TO MOVE THE MANSION TO LIMBO--
--THEY WERE BORN OUT OF PROTECTING THE X-MEN.
WE'RE NOT LOSING YOU. WE CAN'T.

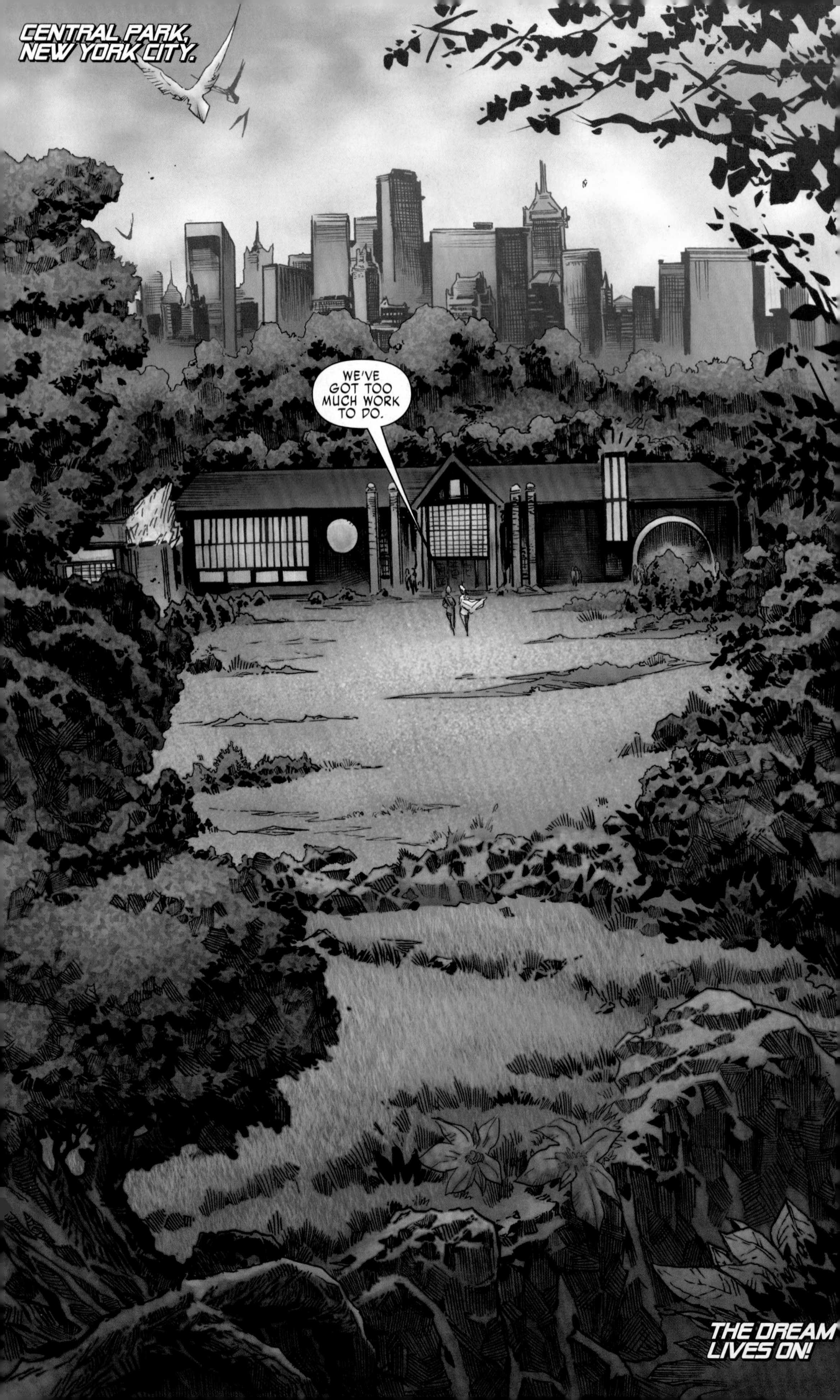
CENTRAL PARK, NEW YORK CITY.
WE'VE GOT TOO MUCH WORK TO DO.
THE DREAM LIVES ON!

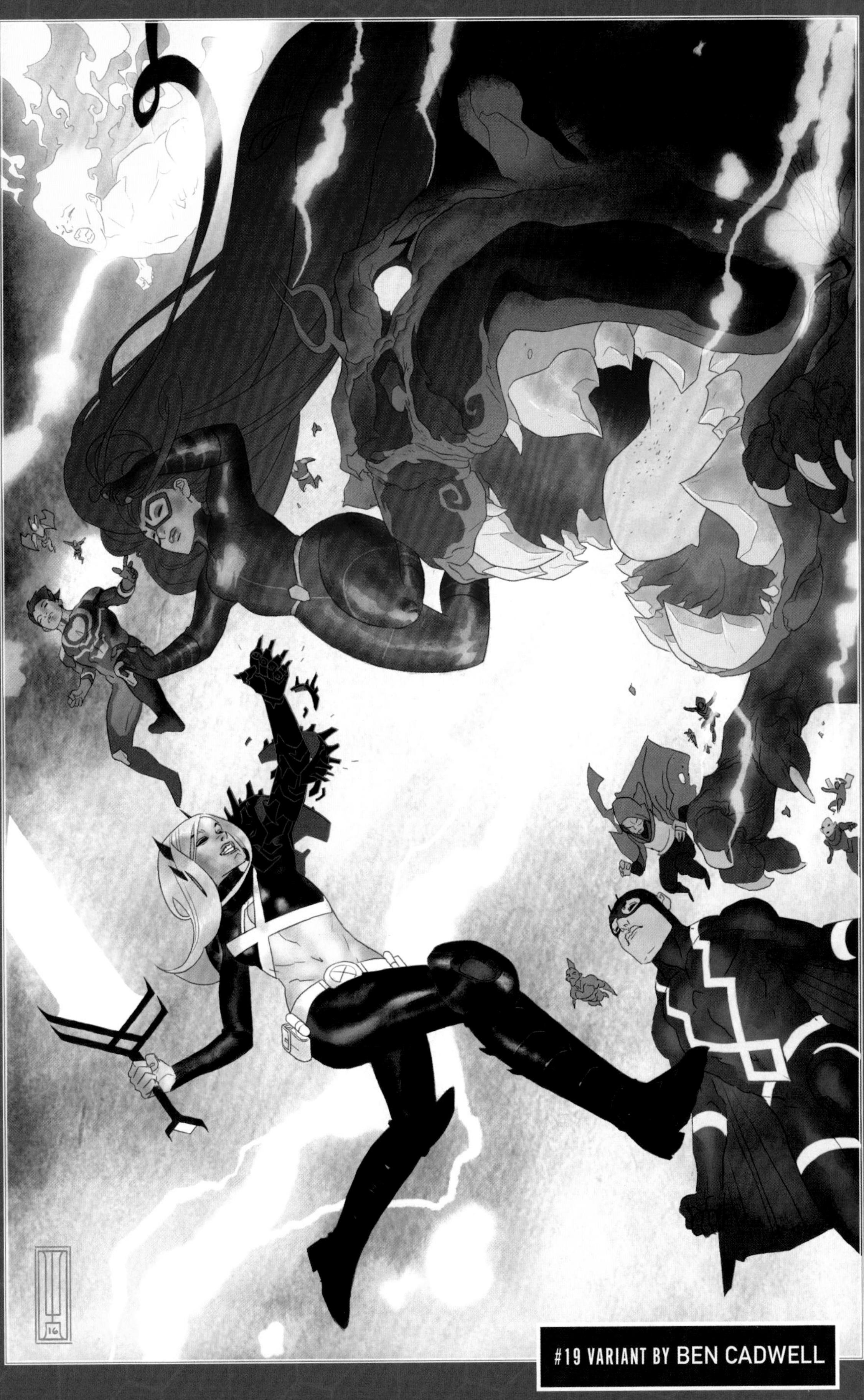

#19 VARIANT BY BEN CADWELL

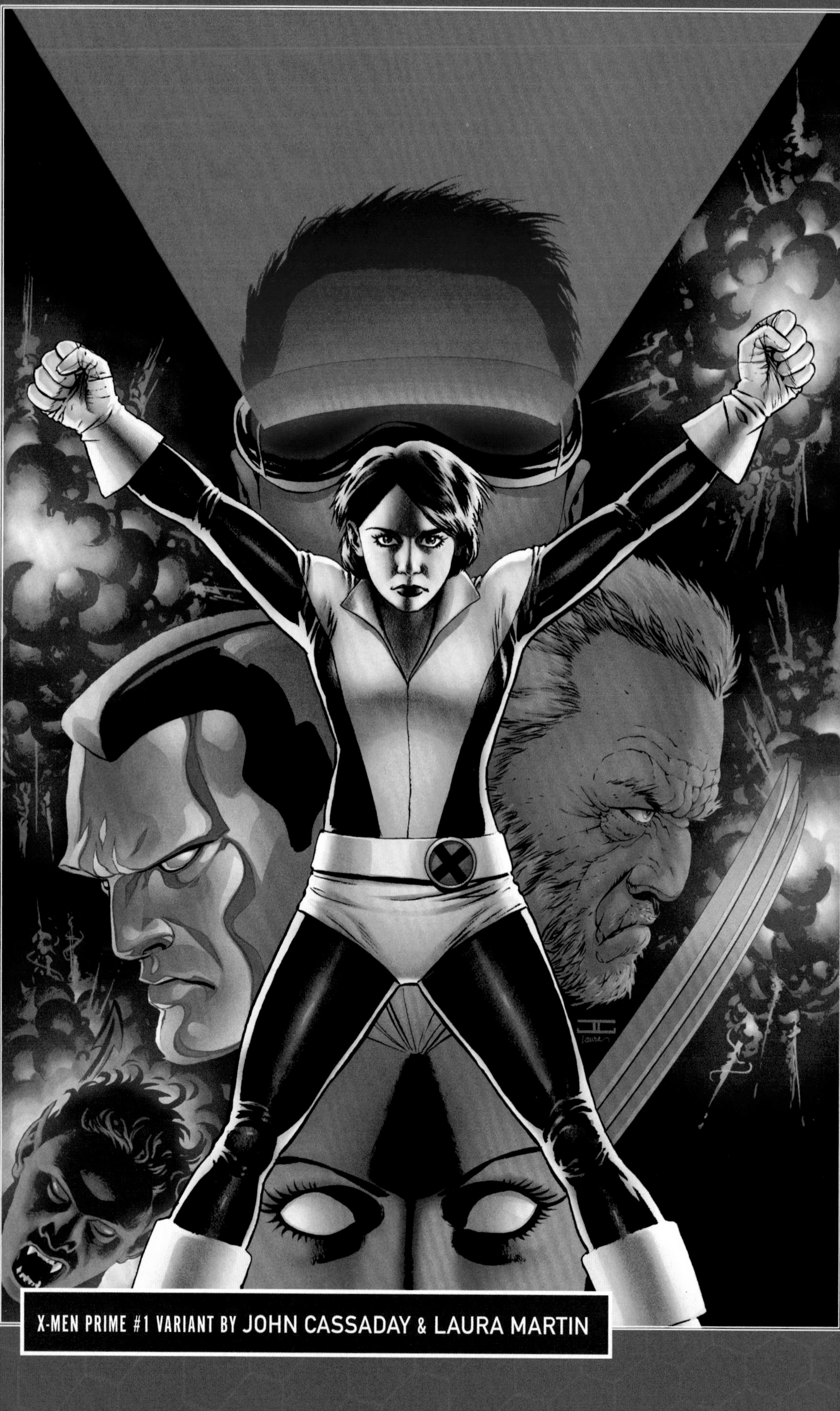

X-MEN PRIME #1 VARIANT BY JOHN CASSADAY & LAURA MARTIN

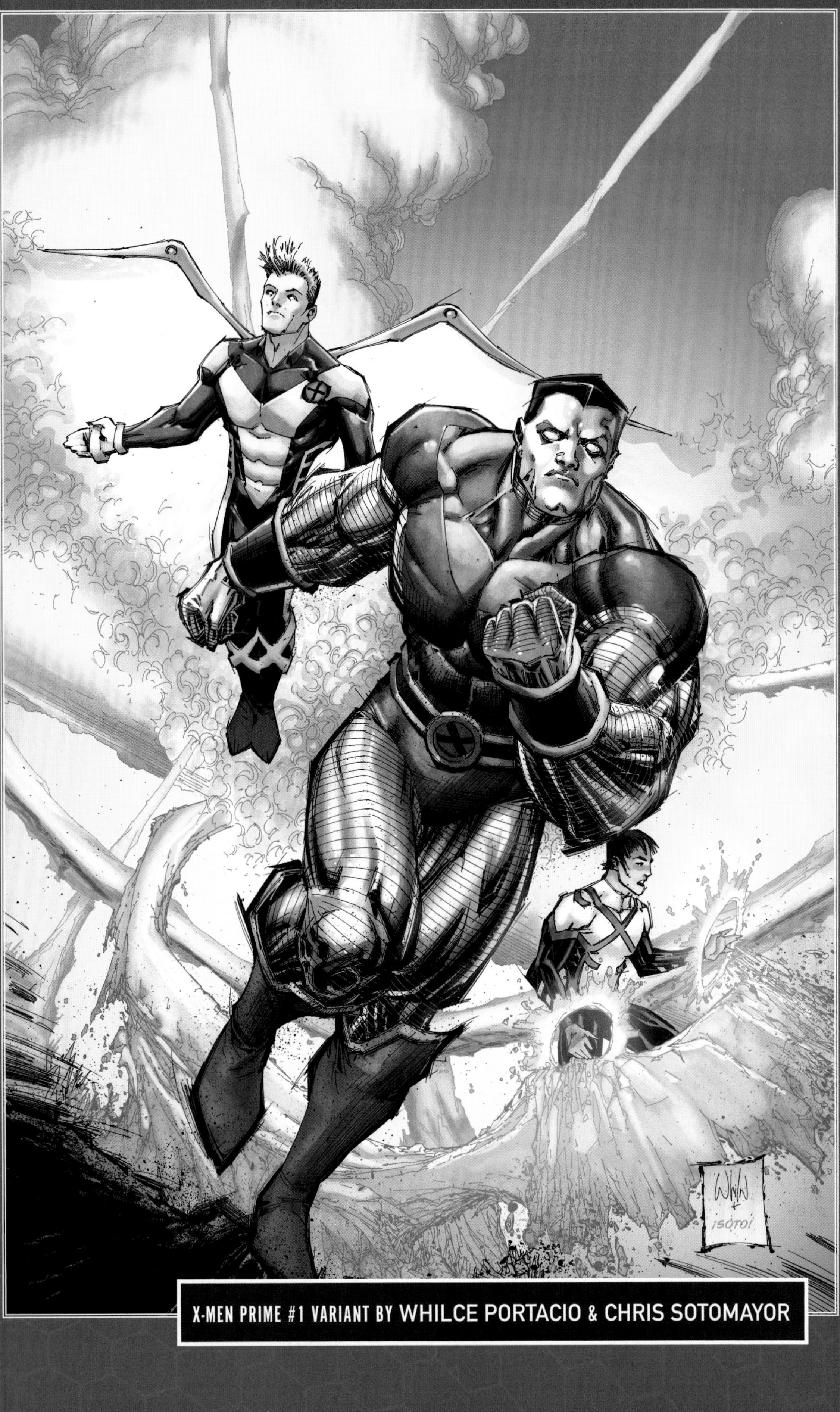

X-MEN PRIME #1 VARIANT BY WHILCE PORTACIO & CHRIS SOTOMAYOR

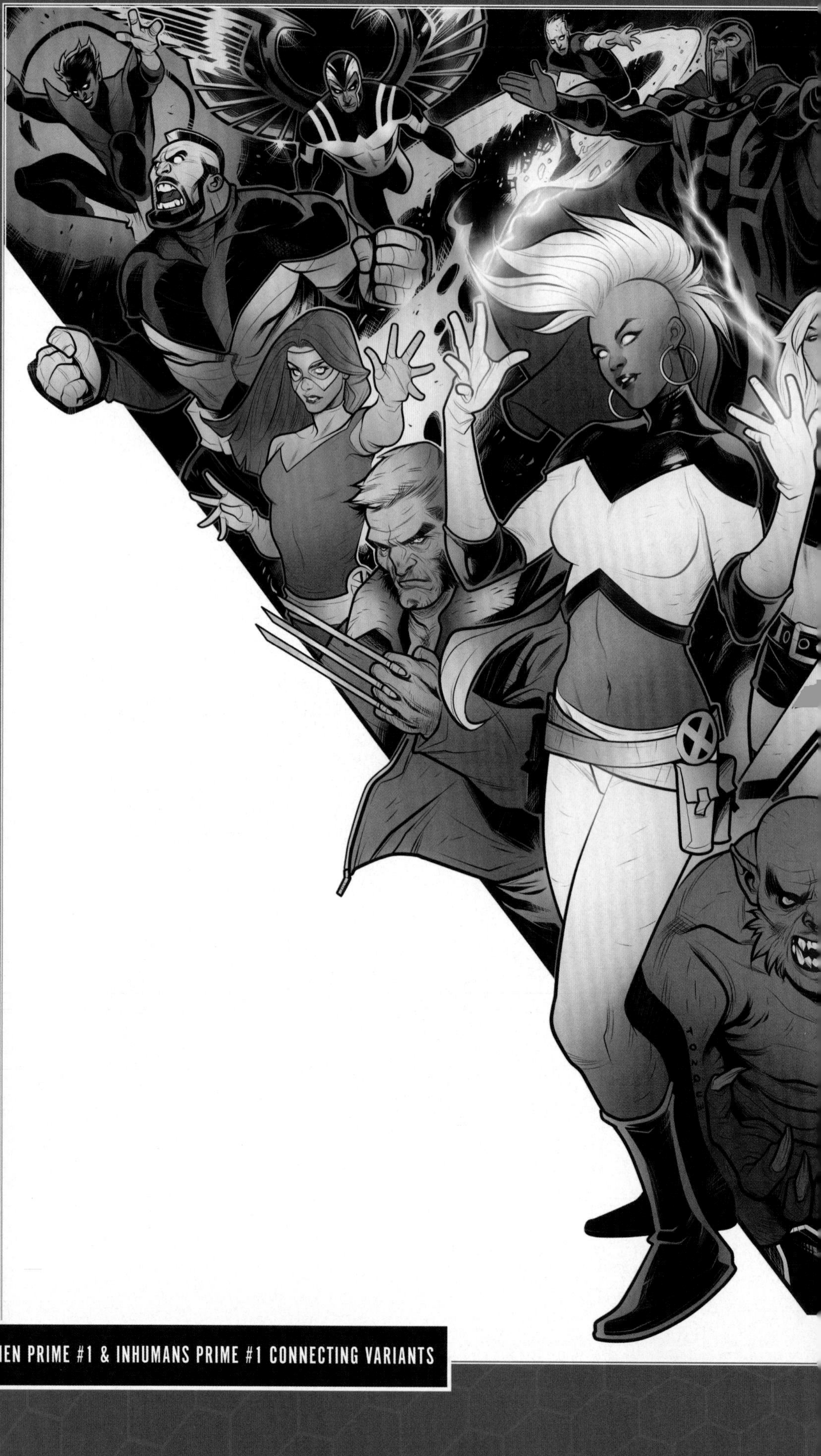

X-MEN PRIME #1 & INHUMANS PRIME #1 CONNECTING VARIANTS

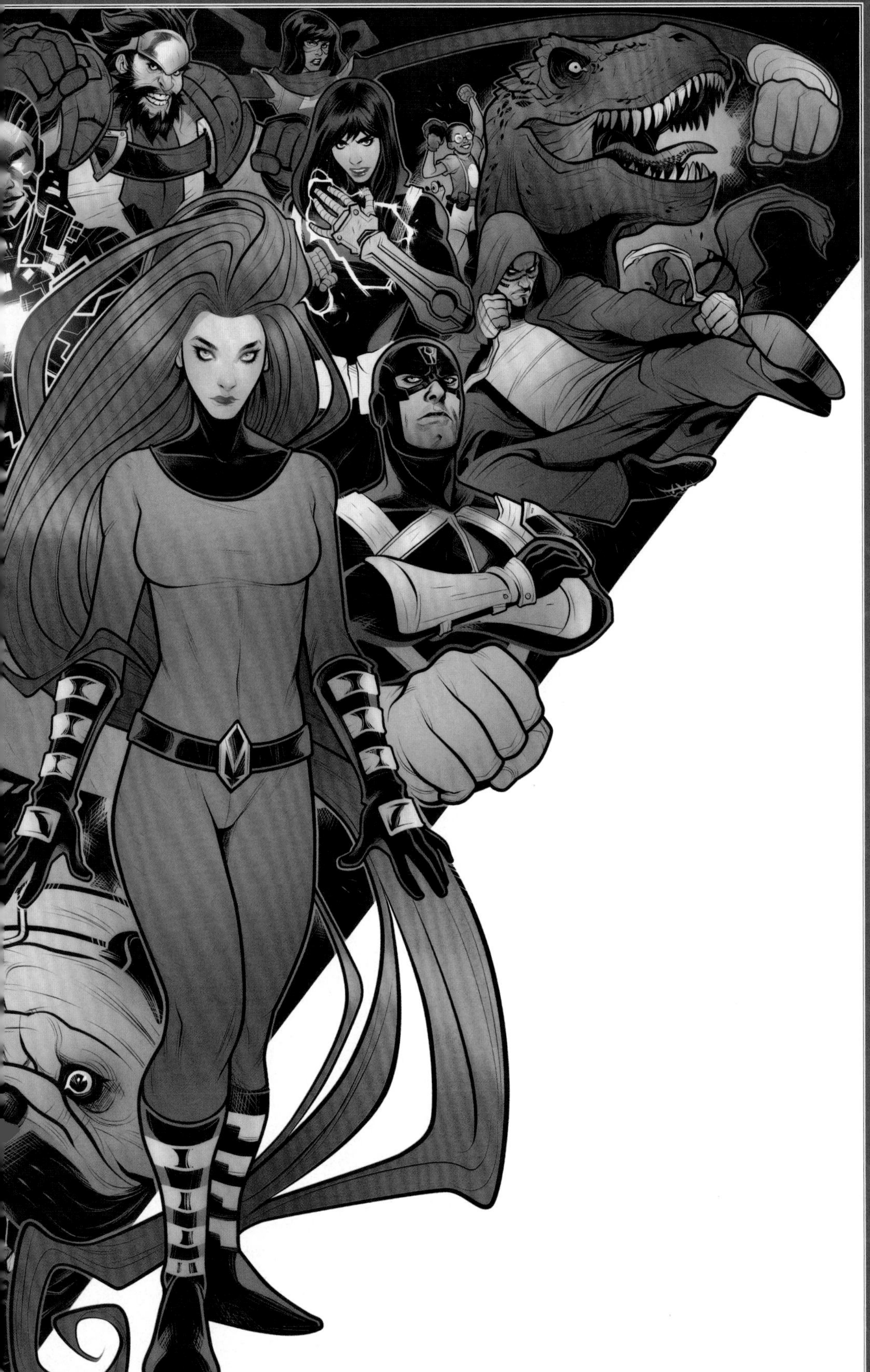

BY ELIZABETH TORQUE

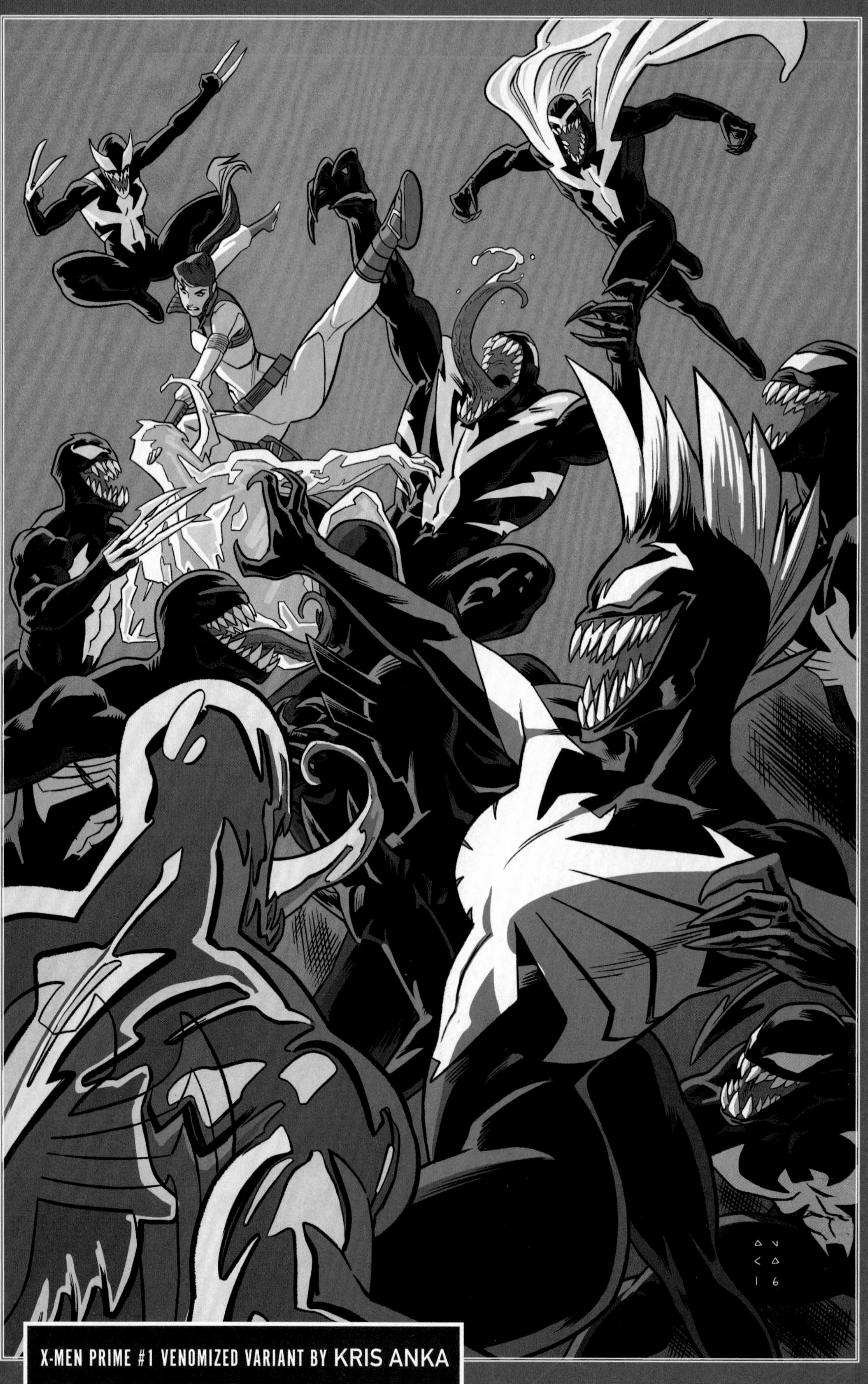

X-MEN PRIME #1 VENOMIZED VARIANT BY KRIS ANKA